A Comparative Vocabulary Study Guide

Spanish to English

Una Guía de Estudios Comparativa del Vocabulario Español e Inglés

Highlighting over 7,500 selected Spanish words that have either the same spelling and meaning as their English language counterparts or contain easily recognizable English meanings.

Destacando más de 7,500 palabras seleccionadas en Español que tienen, ya sea la misma ortografía y significado que su contraparte en Inglés, o contienen significados en Inglés fácilmente reconocibles.

Robert D. O'Brian

Buenos Aires, Argentina

Winter-Spring 2010

For Joseph, Rosie, Grace, Carlos and Mark
with special thanks to Mechel and Maria Cristina

FIRST EDITION

ISBN: 978-1-936989-67-6

Library of Congress Control Number: 2012953143

Published by
NewBookPublishing.com, a division of Reliance Media, Inc.
515 Cooper Commerce Drive, #140, Apopka, FL 32703
NewBookPublishing.com

Printed in the United States of America

Reliance Media

Introduction

This guide is alphabetical, A through Z, with each letter comprising a separate listing, further divided into three sections: words that are interchangeable between Spanish and English (same spelling and meaning); Spanish nouns, adjectives and adverbs containing easily recognizable English language meanings; and, Spanish verbs with easily recognizable English language meanings.

All Spanish words appearing in this guide are given the general meanings used in Argentina. Word pronunciations vary between spoken Spanish and English, including almost all of the interchangeable words. All listings in this guide are the compiler's personal selections and are not intended to be all-inclusive and, English definitions often include all relevant meanings.

An appendix, appearing on page 242, illustrates how to expand the use of this guide. For example, there are over 375 Spanish "ación" ending nouns, which have been converted into verbs of the preterite (past) tense.

The guide also is useful in expanding Spanish verb infinitives into the present progressive tense – what is happening now. There are over 1,100 easily recognizable verbs appearing in the guide that can be expanded into the present progressive. As in English, there are two parts to this tense: the auxiliary "to be" and the present participle (the "ing" verbal ending). The Spanish auxiliary is "estar". The present participles of regular verbs are formed by dropping the "ar" from the "ar" ending verbs and adding "ando" to the stem; for "ir" and "er" ending verbs add "iendo" to the stem. Examples:

Estoy aceptando	I am accepting
Estás activando	You are activating
Ellos están admitiendo	They are admitting

Verbal expansions also are formed by adding a Spanish verb infinitive to the verbs for "want" or "need", for example.

Necesito pasar, abolir	I need to pass, abolish
Quiero acusar, aceptar	I want to accuse, accept

Also note:

No pasar = no admittance (do not pass, no passing)
No aceptar = (we) I do not accept
No entrar = no entrance, admittance

Not all possible or conceivable words that could fit the guide's objective have been listed. Only the most obvious and useful words are shown and the user is given space to augment the listings according to his or her preferences.

The signs and symbols appearing in this guide are identified as follows:

(A) = the feminine ending
(f) = feminine
(m) = masculine
(n) = noun
(adj) = adjective
(adv) = adverb

ó = or
ú = or
sthg = something
sb = somebody
s = plural

(AERO) = aeronautics
(AGRIC) = agriculture
(ANAT) = anatomical
(ARCHIT) = architecture
(ARTE) = art, artistic
(ASTROL) = astrology
(ASTRON) = astronomy
(AUTO) = automotive
(BIOL) = biology
(BOT) = botany
(CINE) = cinema
(COM) = commercial
(DER) = legal
(ECON) = economics
(ELECTR) = electrical
(FIS) = physics
(FOTO) = photography
(GEN) = general meaning

(GEOG) = geography
(GEOL) = geology
(GRAM) = grammar
(INFORM) = inf. technology
(LITER) = literature
(MAT) = mathematics
(MECAN) = mechanical
(MED) = medical
(METEO) = meteorological
(MIL) = military
(MUS) = music
(NAUT) = nautical
(POL) = politics
(FIN) = financial
(QUIM) = chemistry
(RELIG) = religion
(TECNOL) = technology
(ZOOL) = zoology

Pronunciation Guide

Spanish Pronunciation Guide for English speakers

Below is a guide to the pronunciation of the letters of the Spanish alphabet:

A: as the **a** in *father*

B,v: when found at the beginning of a word or following a consonant, these are pronounced as a **b**. Otherwise, they have a sound which falls somewhere between the English **b** and **v** sounds.

C: before a consonant or **a**, **o**, or **u**, as the **c** in *cat*; before **e** or **i** as an **s**

CH: as the **ch** in ***church***

D: as the English **d** except between vowels and following **l** or **n** where it is pronounced as the **th** in ***this***

E: for a syllable ending in a vowel, as the **e** in *they*; for a syllable ending in a consonant, as the **e** in *get*

F: as the **f** in *for*

G: before **e** or **i**, as the Spanish **j**; otherwise as the **g** in *get*

H: silent

I: as **i** in *machine*

J: as an **h** but stronger; silent when at the end of a word

K: as the **k** in *kilo*

L: as an **l in** *lee*

LL: as the **y** in *you*. However, in Argentina it is pronounced as **sh** in ***shoe***

M: as an **m** in ***mother***

N: as an **n**; except where it appears before a **v**, as an **m**

Ñ: as the **n** in *onion*

O: for a syllable ending in a vowel, as the **o** in *vote*; for a syllable ending in a consonant, as the **o** in *pot*

P: as a **p** in *pot*

Q: as a **k**; always followed by a silent **u**

R: pronounced with a strong trill at the beginning of a word and following an **l**, **n**, or **s**; very little trill when at the end of a word; and medium trill in other positions

RR: strongly trilled

S: before consonants **b**, **d**, **g**, **l**, **m**, **n**, as a **z**; otherwise as an **s**

T: as a **t**

U: as the **u** in *rule*; silent after **q** and in the groups **gue** and **gui**

V: see **b, v**

W: usually pronounced as a **v**

X: when between vowels, as the **x** in *box*; before a consonant, as an **s**

Y: when used as a vowel, such as in the words **y** and **voy**, it is pronounced as the Spanish **i**. As a consonant it is pronounced as **Y** in *yes*

Z: as an **s**

Notes:

If the word has an accent mark, only that syllable is stressed; for words ending in a vowel, or n or s, the next to last syllable is stressed; for words ending in a consonant other than n or s the stress falls on the last syllable.

The vowels a, e, and o are “strong” vowels, i and u are “weak”. Two vowels fall together the following applies:

If the word has an accent mark, then that syllable is stressed (cóncavo, enfermería); a weak + strong combination belongs to one syllable with the stress falling on the strong vowel (cauto, caliente); a weak + weak combination belongs to one syllable with the stress falling on the second vowel (construir, cuidado); and, a strong + strong combination is divided into two syllables.(aca-rre- ar, co-rre-a)

English Pronunciation Guide for Spanish speakers

Algunas letras en Inglés tienen varias formas de pronunciación. Los sonidos proporcionados en Español son sólo una aproximación.

Letra en Inglés	Sonido aproximado	Ejemplo
A	**a** como en ***arco***	car
	e como ***eco***	many
(antes de consonante + **e** final)	**ei** como en ***peine***	fate
(entre consonantes)	**ai** como **ei** en ***peine***	rain
	au similar a la **a** de *bata*	cause
B	como en ***bomba***	boy
C (antes de **a, o, u**)	como en ***cama***	cat
(antes de **e, i**)	como en ***cena***	cereal
	ch como en ***cheque***	check
D	como en ***doble***	David
	dge como en **ya**	knowle**dge**
E	entre **"a"** y **"e"**	thanks
	e como en ***estar***	let
	i como en *cinco*	he, be
(final de monosílabo)	**iu** como en ***diurno***	new, few
(final de la palabra)	(muda)	fine, live
(antes de **t, d**)	**ea** como **i** en *rival*	read, eat
	ea como **ei** en ***rey***	great
	ea como **e** en ***error***	sweater

(después de consonante)	**ee** como **i** en *kilo*	**bee**, **see**
	ei como **i** en *nido*	n**ei**ther
	ei como **ei** en *peine*	**ei**ght
F	como en *fallo*	**f**ace
G (antes de **a, o, u**)	como en ***gato***	**g**ame
(antes de **e, i**)	entre "**ch**" y "**y**"	George
(al final de palabra)	**gh** se pronuncia **f** como en *faro*	lau**gh**
	gh (es muda)	**gh**ost
H (como en ***j*** suave)	***g**ente, **j**aula*	**h**ome
I	**i** (pero más relajada)	s**i**ster
(final de la sílaba)	**ai** como en ***vai**na*	h**i**
	i como en *n**i**ño*	mar**i**ne
	ie como **i** en *n**i**do*	f**ie**ld
	ie como en **ai** en ***vai**na*	p**ie**
J	como en ***y**a* (entre "**ch**" y "**y**")	**j**aguar
K (antes de **n**)	como en ***c**ama*	**k**eep
	(es muda)	**k**nown
L	como en ***l**imón*	**l**imb
	ll como "**l**" en *catálogo*	vi**ll**a
M	como en ***m**adre*	**m**ail
N	como en ***n**ada*	**n**ever
O (entre consonantes)	**a** como en ***ha**bla*	**n**o**t**
(después de **d, t**)	**u** como en ***u**so*	**to**, **do**
	au como en ***Lau**ra*	h**o**w

(final de la palabra)	**o** alargada "**ou**"	hell**o**
(entre consonante y **t** final)	**oa** como **o** (pero más alargada)	**coa**t
	oo como en **u** en *pulso*	f**oo**d
	oo como en **u** en *pulso* (pero más relajada)	g**oo**d
	ou como en **u** en *pulso*	y**ou**
	ou como **au** en *Laura*	r**ou**nd
	ou como en **a** (pero más relajada)	t**ou**gh
P	como en *pobre*	sto**p**
	ph como **f** en *foca*	tele**ph**one
Q	**qu** como en *cual*	**qu**ack
R	como en *raro*	**r**ace
S (principio o final de sílaba)	como en *siempre*	**s**ame
(entre vocales)	como en *zumbido*	ro**s**e
(antes de **ure**)	*¡shhh!*	**s**ure
	sh como en *¡shhh!*	**sh**oes
T (principio o final de sílaba)	como en *tarea*	**t**op, correc**t**
(antes de ***ion***)	*¡shhh!*	condi**t**ion
(antes de ***ure***)	como en *mucho*	na**t**ure
(en verbos, sustantivos, etc.)	**th** como **z** en *zapato*	**th**anks
(en artículos como la, pronombres, etc.)	**th** como **d** en lado	**th**e
U (antes de consonante + ***e*** final)	**iu** como en *diurno*	exc**u**se
	u como en *pulso* (más relajada)	p**u**t
	u como en *pulso*	attit**u**de
	a (más relajada)	**u**nder

V	como en *vino*	valet
W	como en ***hu**evo*	**w**eapon
(antes de **o**)	**wh** como **j** en *jugo*	**wh**o
(antes de **a, i, e**)	**wh** como **w** en ***w**hiskey*	**wh**ite, **wh**ere
X (al principio de palabra)	**z** como en *zinc*	**x**ylophone
(cuando va entre vocales)	se pronuncia **gs**	e**x**empt
(en los demás casos)	como en e*x**acto***	bo**x**
Y (final de palabra después de consonante)	**ai** como en *v**ai**na*	m**y**, b**y**
(principio de la palabra)	como en *ya* (muy suave)	**y**ellow
Z	como en *zumbido*	**z**oo

A

Interchangeable Words *(Mismo Significado)*

ABDOMEN

ABDOMINAL

ABOMINABLE

ABRASIÓN

ACCIDENTAL

ACNÉ

ACRE; *also can mean caustic, bitter, pungent, acrid*

ACTOR, *film, movie*

ACTUAL, *current, present*

ADAGIO

AD HOC

ADAPTABLE

ADHESIÓN

ADMIRABLE

ADOBE

ADONIS

ADORABLE

ADVERBIAL

AEROSOL

AFRO

AGENDA; *work schedule; diary, directory*

AIRBAG

ALBINO (A)

ÁLBUM, *stamps, photos*

ALBUMEN (m); ALBÚMINA (f)

ALCOHOL

ALFALFA

ALGA, *alga, seaweed*

ÁLGEBRA

ALIAS; *nickname*

ALMA MATER

ALOE ó ALÓE

ALTAR

ALTER EGO

AMATEUR

AMBROSIA

AMEBA ó AMOEBA

AMEN

AMNESIA

AMORAL

ANACONDA

ANAL

ANALGESIA

ANCESTRAL

ANDANTE (MUS)

ANEMIA

ÁNGEL

ANGELICAL, *angelic*

ÁNGELUS

ANGINA

ANGORA

ANIMAL

ANON

ANOREXIA

ANTENATAL, *prenatal*

ANTERIOR

ANTICLERICAL

ANTICLÍMAX

ANTISOCIAL

AORTA

APACHE, *Apache Indian*

APARTHEID

ARDOR; *heartburn* (MED)

ÁREA

ARGOT

ARIA

ARMADILLO

AROMA

ARSENAL; *a shipyard*

ART DECO

ARTERIAL*; a principal road*

ARTIFICIAL

ASEXUAL

ASOCIAL

ASTRAL

ATLAS

ATONAL

AU PAIR

AUDIBLE

AUDIO

AUDIOVISUAL

AUDITOR (A)

AURA (f), HALO (m)

AUTO

AUTOCLAVE (MED)

AVERSIÓN

AXIAL

AZALEA

Note:

All interchangeable words appear in their Spanish spellings.

Easily Recognizable Nouns, Adjectives and Adverbs

(Nombres o Sustantivos, Adjetivos y Adverbios Fácilmente Reconocibles)

ÁBACO, *abacus*

ABANDONADO (A), *abandoned, deserted; derelict*

ABANDONO, *abandon, leave, desert; neglect*

ABATIDO (A), *depressed*

ABATIMIENTO, *depression*

ABDICACIÓN, *abdication*

ABERRACIÓN, *aberration; departure, lapse*

ABERRANTE, *aberrant*

ABISMAL, *vast, enormous; irreconcilable*

ABISMO, *abyss, chasm*

ABLATIVO, *ablative*

ABLUCIÓN, *ablution*

ABNEGACIÓN, *abnegation, self-denial*

ABNEGADO (A), *self-denying, self-sacrificing*

ABOLICIÓN, *abolition, elimination, termination*

ABOMINACIÓN, *abomination*

ABORTO, *abortion; miscarriage*

ABRASIVO (A), *abrasive; grinding; harsh, hurtful*

ABRIL, *April*

ABSCESO, *abscess*

ABSENTISMO, *absenteeism*

ABSOLUTAMENTE, *absolutely*

ABSOLUTO (A), *absolute, perfect, unqualified*

ABSORBENCIA, *absorbency*

ABSORBENTE, *absorbent; interesting, absorbing*

ABSORCIÓN, *absorption; takeover*

ABSORTO (A), *absorbed, engrossed, involved, immersed*

ABSTEMIO (A), *teetotaler*

ABSTENCIÓN, *abstention*

ABSTINENCIA, *abstinence, self-denial, temperance*

ABSTRACCIÓN, *abstraction*

ABSTRACTO (A), *abstract*

ABSTRUSO (A), *abstruse, obscure, profound*

ABSURDO (A), *absurd, ridiculous, nonsense*

ABUNDANCIA, *abundance, plenty; affluent*

ABUNDANTE, *abundant, plentiful, rich*

ABUSIVO (A), *exorbitant, outrageous, improper; very bad, appalling, unfair*

ABUSO, *abuse, overuse, misuse*

ABYECTO (A), *vile, wretched, abject*

ACADEMIA, *academy, school*

ACCESIBLE, *accessible; approachable; affordable*

ACCESO, *access; entrance, entry; admittance*

ACCESORIO (A), *accessory, incidental, extra*

ACCIDENTADO (A), *rough, uneven; troubled*

ACCIDENTALMENTE, *accidentally, unintentionally*

ACCIDENTE, *accident, chance; collision, accident*

ACCIÓN, *action, act; movement*

ACELERACIÓN, *acceleration*

ACELERADO (A), *rapid, quick, accelerated*

ACELERADOR, *accelerator, gas pedal*

ACENTO, *accent, stress, emphasis*

ACENTUACIÓN, *accentuation; emphasis, force*

ACEPTABLE, *acceptable, passable*

ACEPTACIÓN, *acceptance, approval; popularity*

ACERBO, *bitter, sour; harsh*

ACETATO, *acetate*

ACETONA, *acetone*

ACIDEZ, *acidity; sourness*

ÁCIDO (A), *acid, sharp, sour; acid* (QUIM)

ACLAMACIÓN, *acclamation, applause*

ACOMODADIZO (A), *accommodating, obliging; pliable*

ACORDE, *in accord/agreement with; compliance*

ACOTACIÓN, *marginal note*

ACORDEÓN, *accordion*

ACRÓBATA, *acrobat*

ACROBÁTICO (A), *acrobatic*

ACTITUD, *attitude, position, feeling, view*

ACTIVIDAD, *activity*

ACTIVISTA, *activist*

ACTIVO (A), *active, hardworking, lively, energetic*

ACTO, *act, action*

ACTRIZ, *actress*

ACTUACIÓN; *performance*

ACTUALIDAD, *nowadays; currently, presently*

ACTUALIZACIÓN, *updating*

ACTUALMENTE (adv), *currently, at present, presently*

ACUÁRIUM, *aquarium*

ACUÁTICO (A), *aquatic*

ACUMULACIÓN, *accumulation, accretion*

ACUMULANDO, *accumulating, increasing, adding*

ACUMULATIVO (A), *cumulative; progressive*

ACUPUNTURA, *acupuncture*

ACUSACIÓN, *charge, accusation, indictment*

ACUSADO (A), *accused; marked, pronounced*

ACUSATORIO (A), *accusatory, accusing*

ACÚSTICA, *acoustics*

ACÚSTICO (A), *acoustic*

ADAGIO, *adage, proverb; adagio* (MUS)

ADAPTABILIDAD, *adaptability, versatility*

ADAPTACIÓN, *adjustment, adaptation*

ADHERENCIA, *adherence*

ADHERENTE, *adhesive, sticky*

ADHESIVO (A), *adhesive, adherent*

ADICCIÓN, *addiction to drugs, food*

ADICIÓN, *addition* (MAT)

ADICIONAL, *additional, extra*

ADICTIVO (A), *addictive, compulsive, obsessive*

ADICTO (A), *addict, abuser; enthusiast*

ADITIVO, *additive*

ADJETIVO, *adjective*

ADMINISTRACIÓN, *administration, management*

ADMINISTRADOR (A), *administrator, manager*

ADMINISTRATIVO (A), *administrative, managerial*

ADMIRACIÓN, *admiration*

ADMIRADOR (A), *admirer*

ADMISIBLE, *admissible, acceptable*

ADMISIÓN, *admission, acceptance*

ADMONICIÓN, *warning, reprimand, reprove*

ADOLESCENCIA, *adolescence*

ADOLESCENTE (adj), *adolescent*

ADOPCIÓN, *adoption, acceptance, assumption*

ADORACIÓN, *adoration, worship*

ADORNO, *adornment, ornament, ornamentation*

ADQUISICIÓN, *acquisition, purchase*

ADRENALINA, *adrenaline*

ADULACIÓN, *adulation, flattery*

ADULTERACIÓN, *adulteration*

ADULTERIO, *adultery*

ADÚLTERO (A), *adulterer, adulteress*

ADULTO (A), *adult, grown-up*

ADVERBIO, *adverb*

ADVERSARIO (A), *adversary, opponent*

ADVERSIDAD, *adversity, setback, mishap*

ADVERSO (A), *adverse*

ADVERTENCIA, *warning, word of advice*

AERONÁUTICO (A), *aeronautical*

AEROPUERTO, *airport*

AFABLE, *affable, genial*

AFAMADO (A), *famous, noted*

AFECCIÓN (MED), *complaint, disease*

AFECTACIÓN, *affectation*

AFECTADO (A), *affected, moved, touched; afflicted*

AFECTO, *affection, fondness; inclined*

AFECTUOSO (A), *affectionate, loving, attached*

AFICIONADO (A), *keen, enthusiastic, fan* (DEP)

AFILIACIÓN, *affiliation, membership*

AFÍN, *similar, related*

AFINIDAD, *affinity, similarity*

AFIRMACIÓN, *affirmation, assertion, confirmation*

AFIRMATIVO (A), *affirmative, positive*

AFLAUTADO (A), *high, fluty*

AFLICCIÓN, *suffering, sorrow, affliction*

AFORTUNADAMENTE, *fortunately, luckily*

AFORTUNADO (A), *lucky, fortunate*

AGENCIA, *agency, office, bureau*

AGENTE, *agent*

ÁGIL, *agile, quick, swift; dexterous; lively*

AGILIDAD, *agility, nimbleness*

ÁGILMENTE, *nimbly, quickly, swiftly*

AGITACIÓN, *shaking, stirring, bustle*

AGITADO (A), *choppy, rough, turbulent, bumpy, agitated*

AGITADOR (A), *political activist*

AGNÓSTICO (A), *agnostic*

AGONÍA, *death throes, dying moments*

AGONÍAS (adj), *moaner, whiner*

AGONIZANTE, *dying*

AGORAFOBIA, *agoraphobia*

AGOSTO, *August*

AGRADABLE, *pleasant, nice, agreeable*

AGRAVAMIENTO, *aggravation; worsening* (MED)

AGRAVANTE, *aggravating circumstance/factor*

AGRAVIO, *offense, insult, grievance*

AGRESIÓN, *attack, aggression, assault*

AGRESIVIDAD, *aggressiveness*

AGRESIVO (A), *aggressive, combative, antagonistic*

AGRESOR (A), *aggressor, attacker, assailant*

AGRESTE, *wild, rough; uncouth person*

AGRÍCOLA, *agricultural, farming*

AGRICULTOR (A), *farmer*

AGRICULTURA, *agriculture, farming*

AGRONOMÍA, *agronomy*

AGRÓNOMO (A), *agronomist*

AGRUPACIÓN, *group, association, grouping*

AGRUPAMIENTO, *grouping*

AGUA, *water*

AGUADO (A), *watery, thin; watered down, weak*

AGUAMARINA, *aquamarine*

AIRE, *air*

ALABASTRO, *alabaster*

ALARMA, *alarm*

ALARMANTE, *alarming, frightening, terrifying, shocking*

ALBATROS, *albatross*

ÁLCALI, *alkali*

ALCALINO, *alkaline*

ALCALOIDE, *alkaloid*

ALCOHÓLICO (A), *alcoholic*

ALCOHOLISMO, *alcoholism*

ALEGACIÓN, *declaration, statement*

ALEGORÍA, *allegory; symbol; metaphor*

ALEGÓRICO (A), *allegorical, allegoric; figurative*

ALERGIA, *allergy*

ALÉRGICO (A), *allergic*

ALERTA, *alert, watchful; wary, cautious*

ALFA, *alpha*

ALFABETO, *alphabet*

ALGEBRAICO (A), *algebraic*

ALIENACIÓN, *alienation, distance, antagonize*

ALIENÍGENA, *alien*

ALINEACIÓN, *alignment; lineup* (DEP)

ALITERACIÓN, *alliteration*

ALOCUCIÓN, *address, speech, allocution*

ALPINO (A), *Alpine*

ALTAMENTE (adv), *highly*

ALTERACIÓN, *alteration, change; upset, disturbance*

ALTERADO (A), *upset*

ALTERCADO, *altercation, argument*

ALTERNADOR, *alternator*

ALTERNANCIA, *alternation, rotation*

ALTERNATIVA, *alternative, option, choice*

ALTERNATIVAMENTE, *alternatively*

ALTERNATIVO (A), *alternating; alternative*

ALTITUD, *altitude*

ALTIVO (A), *haughty, arrogant*

ALTRUISMO, *altruism, selflessness, unselfish*

ALTRUISTA, *altruistic, altruist*

ALTURA, *height, high, lofty, peak*

ALUCINACIÓN, *hallucination*

ALUMINIO, *aluminum*

ALUMNADO, *student body*

ALUMNO (A), *student, pupil*

ALUSIÓN, *allusion; reference, hint*

ALUSIVO (A), *allusive, passing, covert, indirect*

AMABILIDAD, *kindness, courtesy*

AMABLE, *kind, nice*

AMABLEMENTE, *kindly*

AMALGAMA, *amalgam, mixture, blend*

AMATISTA, *amethyst*

ÁMBAR, *amber*

AMBICIÓN, *ambition, drive, enterprise, initiative*

AMBICIOSO (A), *ambitious, zealous, energetic*

AMBIDEXTRO (A), *ambidextrous*

AMBIENTAL, *background, environmental*

AMBIENTACIÓN, *atmosphere, ambient; setting*

AMBIENTE, *surroundings*

AMBIGUAMENTE, *ambiguously*

AMBIGÜEDAD, *ambiguity*

AMBIGUO (A), *ambiguous, equivocal, vague*

AMBIVALENTE, *ambivalent*

AMBULANCIA, *ambulance*

AMBULANTE, *mobile*

AMENO, *pleasant, nice, agreeable, amenable*

AMIGABLE, *amicable, friendly, sociable*

AMIGO (A), *friend*

AMISTAD, *friendship*

AMISTOSO (A), *friendly, amiable, cordial, genial*

AMNISTÍA, *amnesty, pardon, reprieve, commute*

AMONÍACO, *ammonia*

AMOROSO (A), *amorous, loving, affectionate*

AMORTIZACIÓN, *amortization, redemption*

AMPERIO, *ampere*

AMPLIABLE, *expandable*

AMPLIACIÓN, *expansion, extension, enlargement*

AMPLIFICACIÓN, *amplification*

AMPLITUD, *roominess, spaciousness*

AMPUTACIÓN, *amputation*

AMULETO, *amulet*

ANAGRAMA, *anagram*

ANALGÉSICO, *analgesic*

ANÁLISIS, *analysis*

ANALISTA, *analyst*

ANALÍTICO (A) (adj), *analytical, analytic*

ANALÓGICO (A), *analogical*

ANALOGÍA, *analogy, similarity*

ANÁLOGO (A), *analogous, similar; analogue*

ANATEMA, *anathema; detested, rejected*

ANATOMÍA, *anatomy*

ANATÓMICO (A), *anatomical*

ANCESTRO, *ancestor, predecessor, precursor*

ANCHOA, *anchovy*

ÁNCORA, *anchor*

ANDROIDE, *android*

ANÉCDOTA, *anecdote, short story*

ANECDÓTICO, *anecdotal; trivial, superficial*

ANÉMICO (A), *anemic*

ANEXIÓN, *annexation*

ANEXO (A), *connected, attached, enclosed; enclosure*

ANFIBIO (A), *amphibious, amphibian*

ÁNFORA, *amphora*

ANGLÓFILO (A), *anglophile*

ANGLÓFOBO (A), *anglophobe*

ÁNGULO, *angle* (MAT)

ANGULOSO (A), *angular, sharp*

ANIMACIÓN, *liveliness, activity, animation*

ANIMOSIDAD, *animosity, ill will, antagonism, acrimony*

ANIMOSO (A), *spirited, lively*

ANISETE, *anisette*

ANIVERSARIO, *anniversary*

ÁNODO, *anode*

ANOMALÍA, *anomaly, irregularity, oddity*

ANÓMALO (A), *anomalous, irregular, abnormal*

ANÓNIMO, *anonymous, unknown, undeclared*

ANORMAL, *abnormal; silly, cretinous*

ANORMALIDAD, *abnormality, strange, unnatural*

ANOTACIÓN, *note, entry, annotation*

ANSIOSO (A), *impatient, anxious, worried, eager*

ANTAGÓNICO (A), *antagonistic, hostile, combative, opposing, contrary, averse; inhospitable*

ANTAGONISMO, *antagonism, animosity, enmity, rancor*

ANTAGONISTA, *opponent, antagonist, rival, enemy*

ANTECÁMARA, *antechamber, anteroom*

ANTECEDENTE, *preceding, history, background; antecedent* (MAT); *previous, former, prior*

ANTECESOR (A), *predecessor, ancestor*

ANTEDILUVIANO, *antediluvian*

ANTENA, *antenna*

ANTERIORIDAD, *beforehand, prior, anterior*

ANTERIORMENTE (adv), *previously, before*

ANTES (adj), *before*

ANTIBIÓTICO, *antibiotic*

ANTICIPACIÓN, *to be early, timely*

ANTICIPADAMENTE, *in advance, beforehand*

ANTICIPADO, *early; advance payment*

ANTICIPO, *foretaste, advance*

ANTICOAGULANTE, *anticoagulant*

ANTICONGELANTE, *antifreeze*

ANTICONSTITUCIONAL, *unconstitutional*

ANTICORROSIVO (A), *anticorrosive*

ANTICRISTO, *antichrist*

ANTIDEPRESIVO (A), *antidepressant*

ANTÍDOTO, *antidote*

ANTIESTÉTICO (A), *unsightly, ugly*

ANTÍGENO, *antigen*

ANTIGUO (A), *old, vintage, antique; ancient*

ANTÍLOPE, *antelope*

ANTINATURAL, *unnatural*

ANTIPATÍA, *antipathy, dislike, aversion*

ANTIPÁTICO, *unpleasant, disagreeable*

ANTISÉPTICO (A) (adj), *antiseptic*

ANTÍTESIS, *antithesis, opposite, contrasting, conflicting*

ANTOLOGÍA, *anthology*

ANTÓNIMO (A), *antonym*

ANTORCHA, *torch*

ANTRACITA, *anthracite*

ÁNTRAX, *anthrax*

ANUAL, *annual, yearly*

ANUALMENTE, *annually, yearly*

ANVERSO, *obverse, front side; counterpart*

APARENTE, *apparent, visible*

APARENTEMENTE, *apparently, seemingly*

APARTADO (A), *away from, remote, isolated; unsociable*

APARTAMENTO, *apartment*

APARTAMIENTO, *separation, seclusion, isolation*

APARTE, *apart, separate, away, aside*

APASIONADO (A), *passionate, enthusiastic*

APASIONANTE, *exciting, thrilling*

APATÍA, *apathy, indifference, lassitude, languor*

APÁTICO (A), *apathetic, unfeeling, lethargic, indifferent*

APELATIVO, *term of address, nickname*

APELLIDO, *surname, last name*

APÉNDICE, *appendix, appendage*

APENDICITIS, *appendicitis*

APERITIVO, *aperitif, appetizer; in the beginning*

APERTURA, *opening, start; beginning*

APESTOSO (A), *stinky, stinking, reeking, putrid, awful*

APETITO, *appetite*

APETITOSO (A) (adj), *appetizing, tasty; tempting*

APLAUSO, *applause, clapping*

APLICACIÓN, *application* (INFORM) (MED), *use*

APLICADO (A), *diligent, conscientious, hardworking*

APLICADOR, *applicator*

APLOMO, *composure, assurance; tranquility, confidence*

APOCALIPSIS, *calamity, disaster, tragedy, adversity*

APÓCRIFO (A), *apocryphal, doubtful, unreliable, uncertain*

APOGEO, *apogee, height, peak*

APOSICIÓN, *apposition*

APÓSTATA, *apostate*

APÓSTOL, *apostle*

APÓSTROFO, *apostrophe*

APRECIABLE, *appreciable, substantial, considerable*

APRECIACIÓN, *appreciation, evaluation, appraisal*

APRECIADO, *worthy, esteemed*

APRECIATIVO (A), *appreciative*

APRENSIÓN, *fear, squeamishness, misgiving; apprehension, perception; intuition, observance*

APRENSIVO (A), *apprehensive, overanxious, worried*

APROBACIÓN, *approval, approbation, endorsement*

APROBADO, *passing grade*

APROBATORIO (adj), *approving*

APROPIACIÓN, *appropriation*

APROPIADO (A), *suitable, appropriate, fitting, right*

APROXIMACIÓN, *approximation; approach*

APROXIMADAMENTE, *approximately*

APROXIMADO (A), *approximate distance, duration*

APROXIMATIVO, *approximate, rough calculation*

APTITUD, *ability, aptitude, fitness, suitability*

APTO, *suitable, fit, apt*

ARBITRARIAMENTE, *arbitrarily*

ARBITRARIEDAD, *arbitrariness*

ARBITRARIO (A), *arbitrary*

ARBITRIO, *free will, discretion, volition, inclination*

ARCADA, *arcade; arch, span*

ARCAICO (A), *archaic*

ARCANO (A), *arcane, recondite, abstruse, obscure*

ARCHIVO, *archive, file; archives, files*

ARDOROSO (A), *ardent, fervent, eager, zealous, avid*

ARDUAMENTE, *arduously, enthusiastically, avidly*

ARDUO (A), *arduous, hard, difficult, tough, onerous*

ARGUMENTACIÓN, *line of argument, reasoning*

ARGUMENTO, *argument, storyline, assertion, contention*

ÁRIDO (A), *dry, arid, parched, barren*

ARISCO (A), *surly, unfriendly, unsociable*

ARISTOCRACIA, *aristocracy*

ARISTÓCRATA, *aristocrat*

ARISTOCRÁTICO (A), *aristocratic*

ARITMÉTICA, *arithmetic*

ARMA, *arm, weapon* (MIL)

ARMADA, *navy*

ARMADO, *armed*

ARMAMENTO, *armament, arms, armaments*

ARMISTICIO, *armistice*

ARMONÍA, *harmony*

ARMÓNICA, *harmonica, mouth organ*

ARMÓNICO, *harmonic*

ARMONIOSO (A), *harmonious*

AROMÁTICO (A), *aromatic, fragrant*

AROMATIZADOR, *air freshener*

ARPA, *harp*

ARPÍA, *harpy, old hag, witch; harridan*

ARPÓN, *harpoon*

ARQUEOLOGÍA, *archeology*

ARQUEÓLOGO (A), *archeologist*

ARQUETIPO, *archetype*

ARQUITECTO (A), *architect*

ARQUITECTÓNICO (A), *architectural*

ARQUITECTURA, *architecture*

ARRESTO, *arrest; detention* (MIL); *confinement*

ARROGANCIA, *arrogance, presumptuous, assertive*

ARROGANTE, *arrogant, haughty, assuming, pompous*

ARROYO, *stream, brook*

ARSÉNICO, *arsenic*

ARTE, *art*

ARTEFACTO, *device, machine, appliance; artifact*

ARTERIA, *artery* (MED); *arterial street*

ÁRTICO (A), *Arctic*

ARTICULACIÓN, *articulation, joint; fluent, coherent*

ARTICULADO (A), *articulated, hinged, joined*

ARTÍCULO, *article, item, thing; news article*

ARTIFICIALMENTE (adv), *artificially*

ARTIFICIO, *device; artifice, trick; cunning, sly*

ARTIFICIOSO (A), *contrived*

ARTILLERÍA, *artillery*

ARTISTA, *artist*

ARTÍSTICO (A), *artistic*

ARTRÍTICO (A), *arthritic*

ARTRITIS, *arthritis*

ASALTANTE, *attacker, assailant, raider*

ASALTO, *assault, robbery, attack*

ASAMBLEA, *assembly, meeting, law body*

ASBESTO, *asbestos*

ASCENDENTE, *ascending, rising, increasing, ascendant*

ASCENSIÓN (f) ó ASCENSO (m), *ascent, rise*

ASCENSOR, *elevator*

ASÉPTICO (A) (adj), *ascetic* (MED); *detached*

ASERCIÓN (f) ó ASERTO (m), *assertion, declaration*

ASEVERACIÓN, *contention, claim, affirmation, assertion*

ASFALTO, *asphalt, blacktop*

ASFIXIA, *suffocation, asphyxiation; asphyxia*

ASFIXIANTE, *stifling, asphyxiating; suffocating*

ASIGNACIÓN, *assignment, allocation, allowance*

ASIMÉTRICO (A), *asymmetrical; asymmetric*

ASIMILACIÓN, *assimilation, absorption*

ASISTENTE, *orderly* (MIL); *assistant, helper*

ASMA, *asthma*

ASMÁTICO (A), *asthmatic*

ASOCIACIÓN, *association, union, organization, society*

ASOCIADO (A), *associated, affiliated, aligned, united*

ASPECTO, *aspect, look; face, bearing; appearance*

ASPIRACIÓN, *inhalation* (MED); *short pause* (MUS)

ASPIRANTE, *aspiring; candidate, applicant*

ASPIRINA, *aspirin*

ASTERISCO, *asterisk*

ASTEROIDE, *asteroid*

ASTIGMATISMO, *astigmatism*

ASTRINGENTE, *astringent*

ASTRO, *star, heavenly body; movie star*

ASTROLOGÍA, *astrology*

ASTRÓLOGO (A), *astrologer, astrologist*

ASTRONAUTA, *astronaut*

ASTRONOMÍA, *astronomy*

ASTRONÓMICO (A), *astronomical*

ASTRÓNOMO (A), *astronomer*

ASTUCIA, *cunning, astuteness, cleverness, guile*

ASTUTO (A), *astute, clever; crafty, sly*

ATÁVICO (A), *atavistic*

ATEMPORAL, *timeless, everlasting, immortal, endless*

ATENCIÓN, *attention; concentration; regard*

ATENTAMENTE, *attentively, intently, carefully*

ATENTO (A), *attentive, watchful, alert, aware*

ATENUANTE, *extenuating, mitigating, tempering*

ATESTADO (A), *affidavit, statement; packed/stuffed with*

ÁTICO, *attic, penthouse*

ATÍPICO (A), *atypical, exceptional*

ATLÁNTICO, *Atlantic (ocean, seaboard)*

ATLÉTICO (A), *athletic*

ATMÓSFERA, *atmosphere*

ATMOSFÉRICO (A), *atmospheric*

ATOLÓN, *atoll*

ATÓMICO (A), *atomic*

ÁTOMO, *atom*

ATONÍA, *lethargy, apathy, indifference*

ÁTONO (A), *atonic, unstressed*

ATRACCIÓN, *attraction, attractiveness, charm*

ATRACTIVO (A), *attractive person, idea, offer; appeal*

ATRIBUCIÓN, *attribution; assignment, connection* (POL)

ATRIBUTIVO (A), *attributive*

ATRIBUTO, *attribute, ascribe, impute, assign*

ATROCIDAD, *atrocity, outrage, crime, offense*

ATROFIA, *atrophy* (MED), *deterioration*

ATROZ, *atrocious; cruel, inhuman*

AUDACIA, *audacity, boldness; imprudence; rashness*

AUDAZ, *bold, audacious, daring, intrepid*

AUDICIÓN, *audition, concert; medical hearing*

AUDIENCIA, *audience*

AUDITORIO, *auditorium, hall*

AUGUSTO (A) (adj), *august, venerable, impressive*

AUMENTO, *increase, rise; magnification*

AURORA, *dawn*

AUSPICIOS, *sponsorship; protection, support*

AUSPICIOSO (A), *promising, encouraging, favorable*

AUSTERIDAD, *austerity*

AUSTERO (A), *austere*

AUTENTICIDAD, *authenticity*

AUTÉNTICO (A), *genuine, real, authentic*

AUTISMO, *autism*

AUTISTA, *autistic*

AUTOADHESIVO (A), *self-adhesive*

AUTOBIOGRAFÍA, *autobiography*

AUTOBIOGRÁFICO (A), *autobiographical*

AUTOBÚS, *bus*

AUTOCOMPASIÓN, *self-pity*

AUTOCONTROL, *self-control*

AUTOCRÍTICA, *self-criticism*

AUTODEFENSA, *self-defense*

AUTODESTRUCCIÓN, *self-destruction*

AUTODIDACTA, *self-taught*

AUTODISCIPLINA, *self-discipline*

AUTOESTIMA, *self-esteem*

AUTÓGRAFO, *autograph*

AUTÓMATA, *automation, robot*

AUTOMÁTICO (A), *automatic; fastener*

AUTOMÓVIL, *automobile, car*

AUTONOMÍA, *autonomy, self-government*

AUTONÓMICO (A), *autonomous, acting independently*

AUTOPSIA, *autopsy, post mortem*

AUTOR (A), *author, writer; originator*

AUTORIDAD, *authority*

AUTORIZACIÓN, *permission, authorization*

AUTORIZADO (A), *authorized, official*

AUTOSUGESTIÓN, *autosuggestion*

AUXILIO, *assistance, help; aid* (MED)

AVALANCHA, *avalanche*

AVANCE, *advance*

AVANZADO (A), *advanced, increased, well-ahead*

AVARICIA, *greed, avarice, cupidity*

AVARICIOSO (A) ó AVARIENTO (A), *avaricious, greedy, rapacity*

AVARO (A), *miserly, mean; miser*

AVENTURA, *adventure, enterprise*

AVIACIÓN, *aviation*

AVIADOR (A), *aviator, pilot, airman*

AVIDEZ, *eagerness*

ÁVIDO (A), *avid, eager, greedy*

AVIÓN, *airplane*

AXIOMA, *axiom*

Easily Recognizable Verbs

Verbos Fácilmente Reconocibles

ABANDONAR, *to abandon*

ABOLIR, *to abolish*

ABOMINAR, *to condemn, abominate*

ABORTAR, *to abort, miscarriage, stop*

ABREVIAR, *to shorten*

ABROGAR, *to abrogate*

ABSOLVER, *to acquit, absolve* (RELIG)

ABSORBER, *to absorb*

ABUNDAR, *to abound*

ABUSAR, *to abuse sthg, take advantage, to go too far*

ACAMPAR, *to camp*

ACCIONAR, *to activate*

ACELERAR, *to accelerate, speed up*

ACEPTAR, *to accept*

ACLAMAR, *to acclaim*

ACOMODAR, *to seat sb, to install, accommodate*

ACOMPAÑAR, *to go with, accompany sb*

ACONDICIONAR, *to condition, convert, upgrade*

ACOSAR, *to harass*

ACREDITAR, *to certify, authorize, credit*

ACTIVAR, *to activate*

ACTUAR, *to act, undertake*

ACUMULAR, *to accumulate*

ACUSAR, *to accuse, charge*

ADAPTAR, *to adjust, adapt*

ADHERIR, *to stick, adhere*

ADJUDICAR, *to award, adjudicate*

ADMINISTRAR, *to manage, run, administer*

ADMIRAR, *to admire*

ADMITIR, *to admit*

ADOCTRINAR, *to instruct, indoctrinate*

ADOPTAR, *to adopt, pass, take*

ADORAR, *to worship, adore,*

ADORNAR, *to decorate, adorn*

ADULAR, *to flatter*

AFECTAR, *to affect; upset, sadden*

AFIRMAR, *to confirm, declare, affirm*

AFRONTAR, *to face up to, confront*

AGITAR, *to shake, stir, agitate, wave*

AGLOMERAR, *to bring together, agglomerate*

AGRANDAR, *to make bigger, enlarge*

AGRAVAR, *to aggravate, increase*

AGRAVIAR, *to offend, insult*

AGRUPAR, *to group together, group, gather*

AJUSTAR, *to adjust, tighten, fit, regulate*

ALARMAR, *to alarm, alert; frighten*

ALERTAR, *to alert, give the alarm*

ALIVIAR, *to smooth, relieve, lighten, ease*

ALTERAR, *to alter, agitate, disrupt*

ALTERNAR, *to alternate; to mix, socialize*

ALUDIR, *to allude, refer to*

AMERITAR, *to merit, deserve*

AMPLIAR, *to expand, extend*

AMPLIFICAR, *to amplify*

AMPUTAR, *to amputate, to cut off*

ANALIZAR, *to analyze*

ANEXAR, *to attach, annex, append*

ANOTAR, *to note, make a note of, record*

ANTECEDER, *to precede*

ANTICIPAR, *to anticipate, foresee*

ANULAR, *to cancel, annul, repeal, rescind*

ANUNCIAR, *to announce, advertise*

APARTAR, *to move away, remove, separate*

APELAR, *to appeal*

APLANAR, *to level, make even, flatten*

APLAUDIR, *to applaud, welcome, approve*

APLICAR, *to apply, give*

APRECIAR, *to appreciate, be fond of, like*

APREHENDER, *to apprehend, to arrest, seize, detain*

APRISIONAR, *to imprison*

APROBAR, *to approve, pass, endorse*

APROPIAR, *to adapt, to appropriate, award, assign*

APROVISIONAR, *to supply, provision*

APROXIMAR, *to move closer, bring nearer*

AQUIETAR, *to calm down, allay*

ARBITRAR, *to referee, umpire, arbitrate*

ARCHIVAR, *to file, keep in mind, store away*

ARGUMENTAR, *to argue*

ARRESTAR, *to arrest, detain*

ARROLLAR, *to roll up, coil, wind; knock down*

ARRUINAR, *to ruin, wreck, destroy*

ARTICULAR, *to articulate, speak coherently*

ASALTAR, *to attack, storm, assault*

ASCENDER, *to go up, climb, promote ascend, rise*

ASENTIR, *to assent, agree*

ASFIXIAR, *to asphyxiate, suffocate*

ASISTIR, *to attend to, assist, accompany*

ASUMIR, *to assume, take over, take on*

ATENDER, *to attend to, deal with, look after*

ATORMENTAR, *to torture, torment*

ATRAPAR, *to catch, trap*

ATRIBUIR, *to attribute to, confer on*

AUDITAR, *to audit*

AUGURAR, *to predict, augur, foresee*

AUMENTAR, *to increase, augment, magnify*

AUTOMATIZAR, *to automate*

AUTORIZAR, *to allow, authorize, empower*

AVANZAR, *to advance, move forward, put forward*

AVISAR, *to advise, warn; catch sight of, notify*

AVIVAR, *to rekindle, revive, brighten, intensify*

STUDY NOTES:

The below and following lined spaces are for other words and phrases of particular interest to the reader.

B

Interchangeable Words

BABEL

BACANAL, *orgy*

BACKGAMMON

BACKSTAGE, *area or crew*

BACKUP (INFORM)

BACTERIA

BÁDMINTON

BAH, *bah!, phooey!*

BALANCE, *balance on a financial statement; a sum*

BALLET

BALSA, *wood*

BANAL, *ordinary*

BANANA

BANANA SPLIT

BANJO

BANNER, *internet*

BAOBAB

BAR, *tavern*

BARMAN, *bartender*

BASE, (MIL)

BASÍLICA

BASTIÓN (MIL)

BAZOOKA ó BAZUCA (MIL)

BEAGLE

BEATNIK

BEGONIA

BEIGE

BENEFACTOR

BERIBERI

BESTIAL, *animal, brutal; tremendous*

BEST-SELLER (s)

BETA

BICAMERAL

BÍCEPS

BIDIMENSIONAL

BIFOCAL

BIG BANG (ASTRON)

BIKINI ó BIQUINI

BILATERAL

BINGO; *bingo hall*

BIODEGRADABLE

BIOFEEDBACK

BIPOLAR

BIRDIE, *golf*

BISEXUAL

BIT, (INFORM)

BITTER ó BITTERS

BLOG, (INFORM)

BOA, *boa constrictor*

BODY

BOLERO (MUS)

BONGO, *drum; a large canoe*

BONITO, *tuna; pretty*

BONSÁI

BOOM, *growth, expansion*

BOOMERANG ó BUMERANG

BOSSA NOVA

BOUQUET ó BUQUÉ

BOURBON

BOUTIQUE

BOY SCOUT

BRAHMÁN

BRAILLE

BRAINSTORMING

BRANDY ó COÑAC

BRIDGE, *the game*

BRIGADIER, *general*

BRUNCH

BRUT

BRUTAL

BUFFER, (INFORM)

BUFFET ó BUFÉ

BUG (INFORM)

BULIMIA

BULLDOG ó BULDOG

BULLDOZER ó BULDOZER

BUNGALOW

BUNGEE, *bungee jumping*

BUNKER ó BÚNQUER (MIL), *golf,* (DEP)

BUS, (INFORM) (AUTO)

BYTE, (INFORM)

Easily Recognizable Nouns, Adjectives and Adverbs

BACANAL, *orgy, bacchanal*

BAGATELA, *trifle, bagatelle*

BALADA, *ballad*

BALAUSTRADA, *balustrade*

BALCÓN, *balcony, vantage point*

BALÍSTICO (A), *ballistic*

BALOTA, *ballot*

BALSÁMICO, *balmy; soothing*

BÁLSAMO, *balsam, balm, ointment*

BAMBÚ, *bamboo*

BANANAL, *banana plantation*

BANCO, *bank; bench, pew*

BANDA, *gang, band*

BANDIDO (A), *bandit, outlaw*

BANDO, *edict; bands* (RELIG); *proclamation*

BANQUETE, *banquet, feast*

BARBERÍA, *barber shop*

BARBERO (A), *barber*

BARÍTONO, *baritone*

BARÓMETRO, *barometer*

BARÓN, *baron; political bigwig*

BARONESA, *baroness*

BARRICADA, *barricade*

BARRIL, *barrel (wine, beer, oil)*

BARRIO, *area, district, neighborhood*

BARROCO (A), *baroque; elaborate, gaudy*

BASA, *base* (ARCHIT)

BASALTO, *basalt*

BASAMENTO, *base*

BÁSICO (A), *basic*

BASTARDO (A), *bastard; mean, base*

BASTEDAD, *coarseness, vulgarity*

BASTO (A), *coarse, rude, vulgar, boorish, crude*

BASURA, *garbage; rubbish, litter*

BATALLA, *battle*

BATALLÓN, *battalion*

BATE, *bat* (DEP), *baseball bat*

BATERÍA, *battery* (ELECTR) (MIL)

BAUTISMAL, *baptismal*

BAUTISMO, *baptism, christening*

BAYO, a *bay horse*

BAYONETA, *bayonet*

BAZAR, *bazaar, large retail store*

BEATIFICACIÓN, *beatification*

BEBE (A), *baby*

BEBERCIO, *booze*

BEICON ó TOCINO, *bacon*

BÉISBOL, *baseball*

BÉLICO (A), *war, warlike, bellicose*

BELICOSO (A), *bellicose, aggressive*

BELIGERANTE, *belligerent, militant, hawkish; contentious, argumentative, controversial*

BENEFICIARIO (A), *beneficiary*

BENÉFICO (A), *favorable, beneficial*

BENEFICIOSO (A), *beneficial, useful, profitable*

BESTIA, *thickheaded, stupid person, brute*

BESTIALISMO, *bestiality*

BIANUAL, *biannual*

BIBLIA, *the Bible*

BÍBLICO (A), *biblical*

BICARBONATO, *bicarbonate*

BICENTENARIO, *bicentenary*

BICICLETA, *bicycle, bike*

BIDIRECCIONAL, *bidirectional*

BIFURCACIÓN, *fork, as in the road; junction*

BIGAMIA, *bigamy*

BILINGÜE, *bilingual*

BILIOSO (A), *bilious; bad-tempered, peevish, irritable*

BILLETE, *monetary, note, bill; ticket*

BINARIO, *binary*

BINOCULARES, *binoculars*

BINOMIO, *binomial* (MAT); *partnership*

BIOACTIVO, *bioactive*

BIOAGRICULTURA, *organic farming*

BIOCARBURANTE, *biofuel*

BIOGRAFÍA, *biography*

BIOGRÁFICO (A), *biographical*

BIÓGRAFO (A), *biographer*

BIOLOGÍA, *biology*

BIOLÓGICO (A), *biological; organic*

BIÓLOGO (A), *biologist*

BIOMASA, *biomass*

BIOPSIA, *biopsy*

BIOSFERA, *biosphere*

BÍPEDO (A), *biped*

BIPLANO, *biplane*

BIRRA, *beer*

BISONTE, *bison*

BLOF, *bluff, deceive, dupe*

BOICOT, *boycott, embargo, ban*

BOL ó BOLS, *bowl, bowls*

BOLETÍN, *bulletin; journal, review*

BOLSA, *bag*

BOLSO, *purse, handbag*

BOMBA, *bomb*

BOMBAZO, *explosion; bombshell, smash hit*

BÓRICO, *boric, boric acid*

BOTA, *boot*

BOTÁNICA, *botany*

BOTÁNICO (A), *botanical (adj), botanist (n)*

BOTE, *boat, skiff; bounce, container*

BOTELLA, *bottle*

BOTÓN, *button, knob; key* (MUS)

BOTULISMO, *botulism*

BOXEO, *boxing*

BOYA, *buoy, float*

BOYANTE, *buoyant; prosperous*

BRAVÍO, *fierceness*

BRAVÍO (A), *wild, untamed animal; impetuous person*

BRAVO (A) (adj), *brave, wild; stormy*

BRAVO (n), *well done*

BREVE, *brief, short*

BREVEDAD, *shortness, brevity*

BREVEMENTE, *briefly, concisely, succinctly*

BRIGADA, *brigade* (MIL)

BRILLANTE, *bright, brilliant*

BRILLANTEZ, *brightness, brilliance, splendor*

BRILLOSO (A), *shiny*

BROCADO, *brocade*

BROCHE, *clasp, fastener*

BRÓCOLI ó BRÉCOL, *broccoli*

BRONCE, *bronze, brass*

BRONCO (A), *rough, rugged, harsh; hoarse, coarse; unbroken*

BRONQUIAL, *bronchial*

BRONQUITIS, *bronchitis*

BRUSCO (A), *sudden, brusque, curt*

BRUSQUEDAD, *brusqueness, suddenness*

BRUTALIDAD, *brutality*

BRUTO (A), *brutish, rude, uncouth; stupid, ignorant*

BRUTO, *uncut; crude*

BUCANERO, *buccaneer, pirate*

BUCÓLICO (A), *bucolic, pastoral; rural*

BUENAMENTE, *easily, without difficulty, willingly*

BUENAMOZA, *good looking, pretty*

BUENAZO (A), *kindly, good natured*

BUENAVENTURA, *good luck, good fortune*

BUENMOZO, *good looking, handsome*

BUENO (A), *good, fine*

BÚFALO, *buffalo*

BUFO (adj), *comic, farcical, absurd, risible*

BUFÓN, *buffoon, clown, jester, mocker; fool*

BULA, *bull* (RELIG)

BULBO, *bulb*

BULBOSO, *bulbous; fat, bulging; protuberant*

BULLICIO, *din, hubbub; activity, bustle*

BULLICIOSO (A), *noisy, boisterous*

BUMERANG, *boomerang*

BUROCRACIA, *bureaucracy*

BURÓCRATA, *bureaucrat*

BUROCRÁTICO (A), *bureaucratic*

BURRO (A), *donkey; also a stupid/ obstinate person*

BUSTO, *bust, chest*

BUTANO, *butane*

Easily Recognizable Verbs

BENEFICIAR, *to benefit*

BLASFEMAR, *to blaspheme*

BLOCAR, *to tackle; stop, trap* (DEP)

BLOQUEAR, *to block off, to blockade; to freeze* (FIN)

BOXEAR, *to box*

BRILLAR, *to shine*

BURLAR, *to evade, flout, deceive, trick, outwit*

STUDY NOTES:

C

Interchangeable Words

CABAÑA

CABARET ó CABARÉ

CABLE

CABLEVISIÓN, *cable television*

CACTUS ó CACTO

CADÁVER

CADDIE ó CADI, *golf*

CAFETERÍA, *café*

CAIMÁN

CALIPSO ó CALYPSO

CAMPUS

CANAL, *also T.V. channel*

CANAPÉ; *also a couch, sofa*

CANASTA, *the game; a basket*

CANCÁN

CÁNCER

CANDOR

CANNABIS ó CANABIS

CANON, *as rule, ideal, standard*

CANTATA (MUS)

CANTÓN

CAPITAL, *capital city, money; essential*

CAPO, *mafia capo, drug baron*

CAPÓN

CARCINOMA

CARDBOARD, *carton, cardboard box*

CÁRDIGAN

CARDINAL

CARIES

CARNAL

CÁRTEL, *also means a poster or a billboard*

CARTÓN, *carton, cardboard box*

CASINO

CASSETTE ó CASETE

CASTING (CINE)

CÁTCHER (DEP)

CÁTCHUP ó KÉTCHUP ó CÁTSUP

CAUSAL

CAVIAR

CELESTIAL

CELLO (MUS), *also spelled celo, chelo*

CENSOR (POL)

CENSURABLE

CENTRAL

CENTURIÓN

CERCA, *near, close, about*

CEREAL

CEREBRAL

CEREMONIAL

CERVICAL

CHALET

CHAMÁN

CHANCE

CHAPARRAL

CHARLATÁN (A), *con artist*

CHARLESTÓN, *the dance*

CHÁRTER, *charter plane, flight*

CHAT, *chat room*

CHEF

CHIC

CHICANO (A)

CHINA, *porcelain; a pebble*

CHINCHILLA

CHIHUAHUA

CHIP (INFORM)

CHOCOLATE

CHRISTMAS ó CRISMAS

CIBER CAFÉ, *internet café*

CIRCULAR

CIVIL

CLAMOR

CLAN

CLAQUE

CLERICAL

CLÍMAX

CLIP, *paper clip, hair clip, video clip*

CLÍTORIS

CLOSET ó CLÓSET, *cupboard, clothes closet*

CLUB, *as tennis club*

COAXIAL

COBRA

COCA ó COKE, *cocaine, coke*

COCKER, *cocker spaniel*

COCOA ó CACAO

CODA (MUS)

COERCIÓN

COHESIÓN

COLITIS

COLLAGE

COLLIE, *the dog*

COLON

COLONIAL

COLOR

COMA (MED)

COMBUSTIBLE

COMBUSTIÓN

COMESTIBLE

COMIC; *also means a comic book*

COMPACT, *disc*

COMPARABLE (to)

COMPATIBLE

COMPULSIÓN

COÑAC ó COGNAC ó BRANDY

CONCEPTUAL

CONCERTINA

CONCLAVE

CONCLUSIÓN

CÓNDOR

CONDUCTOR (A)

CONFUSIÓN

CONGESTIÓN

CONSIDERABLE

CONSISTORIAL

CÓNSUL

CONSULAR

CONTINENTAL

CONTRA

CONTRACTUAL

CONTRALTO

CONTROL

CONTUSIÓN

CONVECTOR

CONVENTUAL

CONVERSIÓN

CONVERTIBLE

CONVOY

CONVULSIÓN

COOL, *slang for nice, good*

CORAL, *reef; a choir, choral, chorale*

CORDIAL

CÓRNEA

CÓRNER

CORPORAL, *bodily*

CORPUS

CORRAL, *as yard, pen, farm yard*

CORROSIÓN

CORTICAL

CÓRTEX

COSMOS

COYOTE

CRACK; *crack cocaine, top athlete*

CRÁTER

CRAYÓN, *also means chalk*

CRÉPE ó CREPE, *pancake*

CRESCENDO

CRICKET, *the game*

CRIMINAL

CRISIS

CROCHET ó CROCHÉ,

CROISSANT ó CRUASÁN

CROQUET

CROSS, *cross country, running, race*

CROUPIER ó CRUPIER

CRUCIAL

CRUCIFIXIÓN, *crucifixion*

CRUEL

CULPABLE

CULTIVABLE, *arable*

CULTURAL

CURABLE

CURARE ó CURARI

CURIA

CURRY

CURSOR (INFORM)

Easily Recognizable Nouns, Adjectives and Adverbs

CABAL, *exact, complete, thorough*

CÁBALA, *cabal, intrigue*

CABALÍSTICO, *cabalistic, occult, mysterious*

CABALLERO, *gentleman*

CABINA, *booth, telephone booth*

CABLEGRAMA, *cablegram*

CACOFONÍA, *cacophony*

CADAVÉRICO (A), *cadaverous, deathly pale*

CADENCIA, *rhythm, cadence*

CADETE, *cadet; junior* (DEP)

CADMIO, *cadmium*

CAFÉ, *coffee*

CAFEÍNA, *caffeine*

CALAMIDAD, *calamity, disaster*

CALAMITOSO (A), *calamitous, disastrous*

CALCIFICACIÓN, *calcification*

CALCIO, *calcium*

CALCULADORA, *calculator*

CÁLCULO, *calculation*

CALENDARIO, *calendar*

CALIBRADO, *calibrated*

CALIFICACIÓN, *grade, mark; rating, standing*

CALIFICADO (A), *skilled, qualified*

CALIFICATIVO (A), *qualifying*

CALIPSO, *calypso*

CALLOSO (A), *calloused, rough*

CALMA, *calm, lull; relaxed*

CALMADO (adj), *calm, to be calm*

CALMANTE (adj), *soothing, sedative, painkiller*

CALMOSO (adj), *tranquil, calm; slow, sluggish*

CALOR, *heat, warm; warmth, affection*

CALORÍA, *calorie*

CALUMNIA, *slander, calumny*

CÁMARA, *camera*

CAMARADA, *colleague* (POL); *companion, buddy*

CAMELLO (A), *camel*

CAMELO, *swindle, hoax*

CAMUFLAJE, *camouflage*

CAÑADA, *gorge, ravine, gully*

CANAL, TV *channel; canal* (ANAT); *channel* (GEOL); *artificial waterway*

CANCELACIÓN, *cancellation*

CANCEROSO (A), *cancerous*

CANDELABRO, *candelabra*

CANDIDATO (A), *candidate, applicant*

CANDOROSO (A), *innocent, guileless*

CANÍBAL, *cannibalistic (adj), cannibal (n)*

CANIBALISMO, *cannibalism*

CANOA, *canoe*

CAÑÓN, *gun, cannon; tube*

CANTINA, *cafeteria, snack bar, canteen; saloon*

CAOS, *chaos*

CAÓTICO (A), *chaotic*

CAPA, *cape, cloak*

CAPACIDAD, *capacity*

CAPAZ, *capable, able*

CAPITALISTA, *capitalist*

CAPITALIZACIÓN, *capitalization*

CAPITÁN (MIL), *captain; leader, chief*

CAPITULACIÓN, *capitulation, surrender* (MIL); *pact*

CÁPSULA, *capsule* (MED) (AERO)

CAPTURA, *capture, seizure, catch*

CAQUI ó KAKI ó KHAKI, *khaki*

CARABINA, *carbine, rifle*

CARÁCTER, *character*

CARACTERÍSTICO (A), *characteristic*

CARACTERIZACIÓN, *characterization*

CARAMELO, *sweet, caramel*

CARAVANA, *caravan, trailer, convoy*

CARBÓN, *coal*

CARBONO, *carbon*

CARBONATADO (A), *carbonated*

CARBURADOR, *carburetor*

CARBURANTE, *fuel*

CARDIOGRAMA, *cardiogram*

CARDIOLOGÍA, *cardiology*

CARDIÓLOGO (A), *cardiologist*

CARGAMENTO, *cargo, load*

CARICATURA, *caricature*

CARISMA, *charisma*

CARISMÁTICO (A), *charismatic*

CARMÍN, *carmine; lipstick*

CARNAVAL, *carnival*

CARNÍVORO (A), *carnivorous (adj); carnivore (n)*

CARPA, *carp; tent, big top; awning*

CARPINTERÍA, *carpentry; woodwork*

CARPINTERO (A), *carpenter; also a woodpecker*

CARRUSEL, *carousel; merry-go-round*

CARTA, *letter; also playing card*

CARTEL, *sign, poster*

CASCADA, *cascade, waterfall*

CASTA, *caste, social group; class*

CASTICISMO, *correctness; authenticity, traditional*

CASTIDAD, *chastity, purity*

CASTIGO, *punishment; penalty* (DEP)

CASTO (A), *chaste, pure*

CATAFALCO, *catafalque*

CATALÍTICO (A), *catalytic*

CATALOGABLE (adj), *classifiable*

CATÁLOGO, *catalog*

CATAPULTA, *catapult, slingshot*

CATÁSTROFE, *catastrophe, disaster*

CATASTRÓFICO (A), *catastrophic, disastrous*

CATEDRAL, *cathedral*

CATEGORÍA, *category*

CATEGÓRICO (A), *categorical; express order*

CÁTODO, *cathode*

CAUSA, *cause; lawsuit, case*

CAUSALIDAD, *causality*

CAUSATIVO, *causative*

CÁUSTICO (A), *caustic*

CAVERNA, *cave, cavern*

CAVERNÍCOLA, *cave-dweller; reactionary person*

CAVERNOSO (A), *cavernous, resounding, deep*

CAVIDAD, *cavity; pit, hole, gap, space; crater, hollow; void; empty, vacant*

CEBRA, *zebra*

CELEBRACIÓN, *celebration*

CELEBRANTE, *celebrant*

CÉLEBRE, *famous, noted, celebrated*

CELEBRIDAD, *celebrity, fame*

CELESTE (adj), *heavenly; sky blue*

CELIBATO, *celibacy*

CÉLIBE, *celibate, single; unmarried person*

CELOFÁN, *cellophane*

CELULAR, *cellular, cell; cell phone*

CELULITIS, *cellulite*

CELULOSA, *cellulose*

CEMENTERIO DE COCHES, *scrap yard*

CEMENTERIO, *cemetery, graveyard*

CEMENTO ARMADO, *reinforced concrete*

CEMENTO, *concrete, cement*

CENSO, *census*

CENSURA, *censorship*

CENSURABLE, *reprehensible*

CENTRALIZACIÓN, *centralization*

CÉNTRICO (A), *central*

CENTRÍFUGA, *centrifuge*

CENTRO, *center*

CENTURIA, *century*

CERÁMICA, *ceramics*

CERCADO, *enclosure; fence, wall*

CERCANÍA, *proximity, nearness*

CERCANO (A), *nearby, close*

CERCO, *circle, ring, enclosure; halo; siege*

CEREMONIA, *ceremony*

CEREMONIOSO (A), *formal; ceremonious*

CERO, *zero, nothing*

CERRADO (adj), *closed; clenched; sharp, tight*

CERTIDUMBRE, *certainty, conviction*

CERTIFICACIÓN, *certification*

CERTIFICADO, *certified, registered*

CESACIÓN, *cessation, suspension*

CESANTE, *laid off, suspended; recalled; redundant*

CHACAL, *jackal*

CHAMPÁN ó CHAMPAÑA, *champagne*

CHAMPÚ, *shampoo*

CHARADA, *charade*

CHASIS, *chassis*

CHAUVINISTA, *chauvinistic (adj), chauvinist (n)*

CHEQUE, *check*

CHIMENEA, *chimney, funnel, smokestack, fireplace*

CHIMPANCÉ, *chimpanzee*

CIÁTICA, *sciatica*

CIBERESPACIO, *cyberspace*

CÍCLICO, *cyclical*

CICLO, *cycle; series, season*

CIENTÍFICO (A), *scientific (adj)*

CIENTISTA, *scientist*

CIERTO, *true, accurate, factual, valid, real*

CIGARRILLO, *cigarette*

CIGARRO, *cigar*

CILÍNDRICO (A), *cylindrical*

CILINDRO, *cylinder, roller*

CÍMBALO, *cymbal*

CIMITARRA, *scimitar*

CINC ó ZINC, *zinc*

CINE, *cinema*

CINEMATECA, *film library; archive* (CINE)

CINTURA, *waist* (ANAT)

CIRCO, *circus*

CIRCUITO, *circuit, track*

CIRCULACIÓN, *traffic, money or blood circulation*

CIRCULARIDAD, *circularity*

CIRCULATORIO, *circulatory* (ANAT)

CÍRCULO, *circle*

CÍRCULO VICIOSO, *vicious circle*

CIRCUNCISIÓN, *circumcision*

CIRCUNFERENCIA, *circumference*

CIRCUNSCRIPCIÓN, *circumscription*

CIRCUNSPECCIÓN, *circumspection*

CIRCUNSPECTO (A), *circumspect, prudent*

CIRCUNSTANCIA, *circumstance*

CIRCUNSTANCIAL, *chance, incidental, circumstantial*

CIRROSIS, *cirrhosis*

CISTERNA, *cistern, tank*

CITACIÓN, *citation, summons, quotation, subpoena*

CITADO, *aforementioned*

CÍTRICO, *citric*

CÍVICO (A), *civic-minded, public-spirited*

CIVILIZACIÓN, *civilization*

CIVILIZADO (A), *civilized*

CLAMOROSO (A), *resounding, loud, enormous*

CLANDESTINIDAD, *secrecy*

CLANDESTINO (A), *clandestine, secret*

CLAQUÉ, *tap dancing*

CLARIDAD, *clearness, clarity, light*

CLARIFICACIÓN, *clarification*

CLARIFICADOR, *clarifying, explanatory*

CLARINETE, *clarinet*

CLARO, *clear, understandable;* ¡CLARO!, *of course!*

CLASE, *class, lesson; kind, sort; quality*

CLÁSICO (A), *classic; classical music; outstanding*

CLASIFICACIÓN, *classification, sorting, filing*

CLASIFICADO (A), *classified*

CLASIFICADOR (A), *sorter*

CLASIFICADORA, *sorting machine*

CLAUSTROFOBIA, *claustrophobia*

CLÁUSULA, *closure, closing; cloister*

CLAVÍCULA, *collarbone, clavicle*

CLAXON, *horn, honk*

CLEMENCIA, *mercy, clemency*

CLEMENTE, *merciful, lenient*

CLEPTOMANÍA, *kleptomania*

CLEPTÓMANO (A), *kleptomaniac*

CLERO, *clergy*

CLIC, *click*

CLIMA, *climate*

CLIMÁTICO (A), *climatic*

CLIMATIZADO (A), *air conditioned*

CLÍNICA, *clinic*

CLÍNICO (A), *clinical*

CLIPER, *clipper*

CLON, *clone, duplicate, copy, replicate*

CLOROFORMO, *chloroform*

COAGULACIÓN, *clotting, coagulation*

COAGULANTE, *coagulant*

COÁGULO, *clot, coagulum*

COALICIÓN, *coalition*

COBALTO, *cobalt*

CÓCCIX, *coccyx*

COCHE, *car, automobile*

COCODRILO, *crocodile*

CÓCTEL, *cocktail*

CODEÍNA, *codeine*

CODIFICACIÓN, *codification, encoding*

COEFICIENTE, *coefficient* (MAT); *degree* (MED)

COEXISTENCIA, *coexistence*

COEXISTENTE, *coexistent*

COHABITACIÓN, *cohabitation*

COHERENCIA, *coherence, consistency, cohesion*

COHERENTE, *coherent, consistent, in tune with*

COHIBIDO (A), *shy, timid, self-conscious; awkward*

COHORTE, *cohort*

COINCIDENCIA, *coincidence*

COINCIDENTE, *coincident*

COLABORACIÓN, *collaboration*

COLABORADOR (A), *collaborator, co-worker, contributor*

COLADOR, *colander, strainer*

COLÁGENO, *collagen*

COLAPSO, *collapse, breakdown* (MED)

COLATERAL, *collateral; collateral for loan*

COLECCIÓN, *collection*

COLECCIONABLE, *collectible, worth collecting*

COLECTA, *collection* (RELIG)

CÓLERA *anger, rage; cholera* (MED)

COLÉRICO (A), *bad tempered, angry; irritable*

COLESTEROL, *cholesterol*

CÓLICO, *colic*

COLIFLOR, *cauliflower*

COLLAR, *necklace; dog collar; chain of office*

COLISIÓN, *collision, crash*

COLONIA, *colony*

COLONIZACIÓN, *colonization*

COLONO (A), *colonist, tenant farmer*

COLOQUIAL, *colloquial*

COLOQUIO, *discussion, conversation*

COLORACIÓN, *coloring, coloration*

COLOSAL, *colossal, amazing, fantastic*

COLOSO*, colossus*

COLUMNA, *column*

COLUMNISTA, *columnist*

COMA, *comma; coma* (MED)

COMANDO, *commando, unit, group; command* (MIL)

COMATOSO (A), *comatose*

COMBATE, *fight, battle, combat*

COMBATIENTE, *combatant, fighter*

COMBATIVO (A), *aggressive, combative, spirited*

COMBI, *fridge-freezer, van*

COMBINACIÓN, *combination*

COMEDIA, *comedy*

COMENTARIO, *comment, remark; essay, commentary*

COMENTARISTA, *commentator*

COMERCIAL, *commercial, business; shopping center, shopping*

COMETA, *comet; kite*

COMISIÓN*, to work on a commission basis* (COM); *task*

COMITÉ, *committee*

COMPADRE, *godfather; buddy, mate*

COMPACTO (A), *compact, dense*

COMPAÑERO (A), *companion*

COMPAÑERO DE CLASE (A), *classmate*

COMPAÑERO DE PISO (A), *flatmate*

COMPAÑERO SENTIMENTAL (A), *partner, colleague*

COMPARACIÓN, *comparison*

COMPÁS, *compass*

COMPASIÓN, *compassion, pity*

COMPASIVO (A), *compassionate*

COMPATIBILIDAD, *compatibility*

COMPENDIO, *compendium*

COMPENSACIÓN, *compensation*

COMPETENTE, *competent, suitable*

COMPETICIÓN, *competition*

COMPETIDOR (A), *competing (adj); rival (n)*

COMPETITIVIDAD, *competitiveness*

COMPETITIVO (A), *competitive*

COMPILACIÓN, *compilation*

COMPLACIDO, *pleased, satisfied*

COMPLEJIDAD, *complexity*

COMPLEJO (A), *complex*

COMPLEMENTARIO (A), *complementary*

COMPLEMENTO, *complement* (MAT); *complement*

COMPLETAMENTE, *completely, totally*

COMPLETO (A), *complete, balanced; full, total*

COMPLICACIÓN, *complication*

COMPLICADO (A), *complicated*

CÓMPLICE, *accomplice*

COMPLICIDAD, *complicity, involvement in*

COMPONENTE, *component, constituent*

COMPOSICIÓN, *composition*

COMPOTA, *compote, stewed fruit, preserve*

COMPRENSIBLE, *comprehensible*

COMPRENSIÓN, *comprehension*

COMPRENSIVO (A), *understanding, awareness, insight*

COMPRESIÓN, *compression*

COMPRESOR, *compressor*

COMPROMISO, *commitment, agreement, compromise*

COMPULSIVO (A), *compulsive*

COMPUTADOR, *computer*

COMPUTACIÓN, *computation, calculation; computing*

COMPUTO, *count, answer, estimation*

COMUNAL, *communal*

COMUNICACIÓN, *communication*

COMUNICADO, *announcement, press release; connected, connections, accessible*

COMUNICADO DE PRENSA, *press release*

COMUNICADO OFICIAL, *communiqué*

COMUNIDAD, *community*

COMUNIÓN, *communion*

CÓNCAVO (A), *concave; hollow, cavity*

CONCENTRACIÓN, *concentration, centralized*

CONCENTRADO (A), *concentrated; extract, concentrate*

CONCÉNTRICO (A), *concentric*

CONCEPCIÓN, *conception*

CONCEPTO, *concept, notion; view, judgment*

CONCESIÓN, *concession, granting*

CONCESIVO (A), *concessive*

CONCIENCIA, *conscience*

CONCILIACIÓN, *conciliation, reconciliation* (DER)

CONCILIADOR (A), *conciliatory (adj); conciliator (n)*

CONCILIATORIO (A), *conciliatory*

CONCISIÓN, *conciseness, brevity*

CONCISO (A), *concise, brief, succinct; curt, terse*

CONCOMITANTE, *concomitant*

CONCORDANTE, *concordant*

CONCORDIA, *concord, harmony; conformity*

CONCRECIÓN, *precision; realization*

CONCRETAMENTE, *specifically; exactly*

CONCRETO (A), *concrete, specific, real*

CONCUBINA, *concubine*

CONCUPISCENCIA, *lustfulness, concupiscence; greed, avarice, cupidity, rapacity*

CONCUPISCENTE, *lustful, lewd, concupiscent; greedy, avaricious, selfish*

CONCURRENCIA, *concurrence*

CONCURRENTE, *concurrent*

CONCURRIDO (A), *crowded, busy, popular*

CONDENSACIÓN, *condensation*

CONDENSADO, *condensed, concentrated; consolidated*

CONDENSADOR, *condenser*

CONDICIÓN, *condition, stipulation, requirement*

CONDICIONAL, *conditional*

CONDIMENTO, *seasoning, flavoring, dressing*

CONDOLENCIA, *condolence, sympathy*

CONDUCTA, *conduct, behavior*

CONDUCTIBILIDAD, *conductivity*

CONDUCTO, *pipe, conduit; duct* (ANAT)

CONDUCTOR (A), *driver; having physical conducting properties (adj)*

CONECTOR, *connector*

CONEXIÓN, *connection*

CONFABULACIÓN, *plot, conspiracy; intrigue*

CONFEDERACIÓN, *confederation*

CONFEDERADO (A), *confederate; allied*

CONFERENCIA, *conference, meeting*

CONFESIÓN, *confession*

CONFESOR, *confessor*

CONFETI, *confetti*

CONFIADO (A), *confident, trusting; vain*

CONFIANZA, *trust, reliance, confidence*

CONFIDENCIA, *secret, private*

CONFIDENCIAL, *confidential*

CONFIDENCIALIDAD, *confidentiality*

CONFIDENTE, *confidant, intimate friend; informer*

CONFIGURACIÓN, *configuration, outline, layout*

CONFINAMIENTO, *confinement*

CONFIRMACIÓN, *confirmation*

CONFISCACIÓN, *confiscation*

CONFLAGRACIÓN, *conflagration; outbreak*

CONFLICTIVO (A), *controversial, troubled*

CONFLICTO, *conflict, problem*

CONFLUENCIA, *confluence*

CONFORME, *in accordance/ agreement with; similar*

CONFORMIDAD, *approval, agreement*

CONFORMISMO, *conformism*

CONFORMISTA, *conformist*

CONFORT, *comfort*

CONFORTABLE, *comfortable*

CONFRONTACIÓN, *confrontation*

CONFUSO (A) (adj), *confused, hazy, blurred*

CONGÉNITO (A), *congenital*

CONGREGACIÓN, *congregation, gathering, assembly; guild, association*

CONGRUENTE, *congruent* (MAT); *congruous, suitable*

CONÍFERA, *conifer*

CONÍFERO, *coniferous*

CONJETURA, *conjecture, surmise*

CONJUGACIÓN, *conjugation*

CONJUNCIÓN, *conjunction* (GRAM)

CONJUNTIVITIS, *conjunctivitis*

CONJUNTO (A), *joint, combined*

CONMEMORACIÓN, *commemoration*

CONMEMORATIVO (A), *commemorative*

CONMISERACIÓN, *pity, commiseration*

CONMOCIÓN, *shock, tremor* (GEOL); *concussion* (MED)

CONMUTACIÓN, *commutation; switching* (INFORM)

CONNOTACIÓN, *connotation*

CONO, *cone*

CONQUISTA, *conquest; goal*

CONQUISTADOR (A) *conquering (adj), conqueror (n)*

CONSCRIPCIÓN, *conscription, draft*

CONSCRIPTO, *conscript, draftee*

CONSECUENCIA, *consequence*

CONSECUENTE, *consistent with, consequent*

CONSECUTIVO (A), *consecutive*

CONSENSO, *consensus, consent*

CONSENSUAL, *agreed*

CONSENTIMIENTO, *consent to, agreement*

CONSERVACIÓN, *conservation*

CONSIDERACIÓN, *consideration*

CONSIDERADO (A), *considerate, thoughtful; considered*

CONSISTENCIA, *consistence, consistency*

CONSISTENTE, *solid, firm, tough; sound, valid*

CONSOLACIÓN, *consolation*

CONSOLIDACIÓN, *consolidation*

CONSOMÉ, *consommé*

CONSONANTE, *consonant*

CONSORCIO, *consortium, syndicate*

CONSORTE, *spouse, consort*

CONSPICUO (A), *conspicuous, famous, eminent*

CONSPIRACIÓN, *conspiracy*

CONSTANTE, *persistent, steadfast, constant*

CONSTANCIA, *perseverance*

CONSTELACIÓN, *constellation*

CONSTERNACIÓN, *consternation, dismay*

CONSTIPADO, *constipated; have a cold* (MED)

CONSTITUCIONAL, *constitutional*

CONSTRUCCIÓN, *construction, building project*

CONSTRUCTIVO (A), *constructive*

CONSULTOR (A), *consultant*

CONSUMADO (A), *consummate, thorough*

CONSUMISMO, *consumerism*

CONSUMO, *consumption*

CONSUSTANCIAL, *consubstantial*

CONTACTO, *contact*

CONTAGIO, *infection* (MED); *contamination*

CONTAGIOSO (A), *infectious, catching, contagious*

CONTAMINACIÓN, *contamination, pollution*

CONTAMINANTE, *pollutant*

CONTEMPLACIÓN, *contemplation*

CONTEMPLATIVO (A), *contemplative*

CONTEMPORÁNEO (A), *contemporary*

CONTENCIOSO (A), *contentious, quarrelsome*

CONTENTO (A), *happy, pleased, contented*

CONTEXTO, *context*

CONTIGUO (A), *contiguous; adjacent*

CONTINENCIA, *continence; self-restraint*

CONTINENTE, *continent* (GEOG)

CONTINGENCIA, *eventuality, unpredictability, contingency, possibility*

CONTINGENTE, *unforeseeable, contingent*

CONTINUACIÓN, *continuation*

CONTINUADO (A), *continual*

CONTINUAMENTE, *constantly*

CONTINUIDAD, *continuity*

CONTINUO (A), *continuous*

CONTORNO, *contour* (GEOG); *outline*

CONTORSIÓN, *contortion; twist, tangle, distort*

CONTRABANDISTA, *smuggler*

CONTRACCIÓN, *contraction*

CONTRADICCIÓN, *contradiction*

CONTRADICTORIO (A), *contradictory*

CONTRAOFENSIVA, *counter-offensive*

CONTRAOFERTA, *counteroffer*

CONTRAORDEN, *countermand, cancel, revoke*

CONTRAPOSICIÓN, *conflict, comparison; contrast, clash*

CONTRAPRODUCENTE, *counterproductive*

CONTRAPUNTO, *counterpoint, contrast*

CONTRARIO (A), *opposite, contrary, opposing*

CONTRARREVOLUCIÓN, *counter-revolution*

CONTRASTE, *contrast* (MED)

CONTRATA (f) ó CONTRATO (m), *contract*

CONTRATIEMPO, *setback, reverse; mishap, accident*

CONTRIBUCIÓN, *contribution*

CONTRICIÓN, *contrition, repentance, compunction*

CONTRITO (A), *contrite*

CONTROVERSIA, *controversy*

CONTUMACIA, *obstinacy, stubbornness, contemptuous*

CONVALECENCIA, *convalescence*

CONVALECIENTE, *convalescent*

CONVECCIÓN, *convection*

CONVENCIÓN, *convention*
CONVENCIONAL, *conventional*
CONVENIENTE, *convenient, advisable, suitable, proper*
CONVENTO, *convent, nunnery*
CONVERGENCIA, *convergence*
CONVERGENTE, *convergent, converging*
CONVERSA, *talk, chat*
CONVERSACIÓN, *conversation, talk*
CONVERSADOR (A), *talkative, conversationalist, chatty*
CONVEXO (A), *convex*
CONVICCIÓN, *conviction, certitude, confidence*
CONVICTO (A), *convicted (adj), convict (n)*
CONVINCENTE, *convincing*
CONVULSIVO (A), *convulsive*
COOPERACIÓN, *cooperation*
COOPERANTE, *voluntary worker*
COOPERATIVO (A), *cooperative*
COORDENADA, *coordinate* (MAT)
COORDINACIÓN, *coordination*
COORDINADO (A), *coordinated; combined* (MIL)
COORDINADOR (A), *coordinator (n); coordinating (adj)*
COPIA, *copy, duplicate*
COPIADORA, *copying-machine, photocopier*
COPIOSO (A), *copious, abundant, heavy*
COPROPIETARIO (A), *joint owner, co-owner*
CORDEL, *cord, line*
CORDIALIDAD, *warmth, cordiality*
CORDIALMENTE, *warmly, cordially*
COROLARIO, *corollary*
CORONA, *crown*
CORONACIÓN, *coronation; end, culmination*
CORONEL (A), *colonel*
CORPORACIÓN, *corporation*
CORPORATIVO (A), *corporate*
CORPULENCIA, *corpulence, burliness, stoutness*
CORPULENTO (A), *corpulent, stout, burly; solid*
CORPÚSCULO, *corpuscle*
CORRECCIÓN, *correction*
CORRECCIONAL, *reformatory*
CORRECTAMENTE, *correctly, accurately*
CORRECTIVO (A), *corrective*
CORRECTO (A), *correct, right*
CORRELACIÓN, *correlation*
CORRESPONDENCIA, *correspondence, mail*
CORRESPONDIENTE, *corresponding, respective, appropriate, suitable, proper*

CORRESPONSABLE, *jointly responsible*

CORROSIÓN, *corrosion, erosion* (GEOL)

CORROSIVO (A), *corrosive*

CORRUPCIÓN, *moral corruption, bribery; rot, decay*

CORRUPTELA, *corrupt practice, abuse*

CORRUPTO (A), *corrupt*

CORTESANA, *courtesan*

CORTISONA, *cortisone*

COSHER, *kosher*

COSMÉTICA, *cosmetics*

COSMÉTICO (A), *cosmetic*

CÓSMICO (A), *cosmic*

COSMONAUTA, *cosmonaut*

COSMOPOLITA, *cosmopolitan*

COSTA, *coast, coastline*

COSTO, *cost, price*

COSTOSO (A), *costly, expensive*

COSTUMBRE, *custom; customs and manners*

COTÓN, *cotton fabric*

CRASO (A), *fat, greasy; crass, gross*

CREACIÓN, *creation*

CREADOR (A), *creative (adj), creator (n); artist, designer, the Creator*

CREATIVIDAD, *creativity*

CREATIVO (A), *creative person*

CREDENCIAL, *accrediting document, pass, ID card*

CREDIBILIDAD, *credibility*

CRÉDITO, *credit, reputation; loan, on credit*

CREDO, *creed, the Creed*

CREDULIDAD, *credulity*

CRÉDULO (A), *credulous, gullible*

CREÍBLE, *credible, believable, plausible*

CREMA, *cream*

CREMACIÓN, *cremation*

CREMOSO (A), *creamy*

CRESPÓN ó CRÉPE, *crepe, crape*

CRESTA, *crest; comb*

CRETINO (A), *cretin (n), cretinous (adj)*

CRIMEN, *crime*

CRIMINALIDAD, *criminality*

CRIMINALISTA, *criminal lawyer, criminologist*

CRIMINOLOGÍA, *criminology*

CRIPTA, *crypt*

CRÍPTICO (A), *cryptic, obscure, inscrutable*

CRIPTOGRAFÍA, *cryptography*

CRIPTOGRAMA, *cryptogram*

CRÍQUET, *cricket*

CRISTAL, *glass, crystal*

CRISTALERÍA, *glassware, glassmaking*

CRISTALIZACIÓN, *crystallization*

CRITERIO, *criterion, standard, principal*

CRÍTICA, *criticism, faultfinding, disapproval*

CRITICABLE, *censurable, open to criticism*

CRÍTICO (A), *critic (n), critical (adj)*

CRITICÓN (A), *nit-picker, hypercritical*

CROMÁTICO (A), *chromatic*

CROMO, *chrome, chromium*

CROMOSOMA, *chromosome*

CRÓNICO (A), *chronic; ingrained; persistent, habitual*

CRONOLOGÍA, *chronology*

CRONOLÓGICO (A), *chronological*

CROQUETA, *croquette*

CROSS, *cross-country running*

CRUDO (A), *raw, crude, uncooked; harsh*

CRUELDAD, *cruelty*

CRUSTÁCEO, *crustacean*

CUALIDAD, *quality*

CUALIFICACIÓN, *qualification*

CUALIFICADO (A), *skilled, qualified*

CUALITATIVO (A), *qualitative*

CUANTÍA, *amount, quantity, extent*

CUANTIFICABLE, *quantifiable*

CUANTIOSO (A), *substantial, considerable*

CUANTITATIVO (A), *quantitative*

CUARK, *quark* (FIS)

CÚBICO (A), *cubic*

CUBÍCULO, *cubicle*

CUBO, *cube* (MAT); *bucket, pail, trash can*

CUESTIÓN, *question, matter*

CUESTIONABLE, *questionable, debatable*

CUESTIONARIO, *questionnaire*

CULINARIO (A), *culinary*

CULMINACIÓN, *culmination*

CULMINANTE, *highest* (GEOG); *topmost, culminating*

CULPA, *fault, blame; guilt* (DER)

CULPABILIDAD, *guilt, culpability*

CULTIVADO (A), *cultivated; cultured person*

CULTURA, *culture*

CUNEIFORME, *cuneiform writing*

CUOTA, *quota, share*

CUPIDO, *lady's man; Cupid*

CUPÓN, *coupon, voucher*

CÚPULA, *dome, cupola*

CURACIÓN, *treatment* (MED); *cure, healing*

CURATIVO (A), *curative*

CURIOSIDAD, *curiosity, inquisitiveness*

CURIOSO (A), *curious, inquisitive; prying*

CURRICULUM, *résumé, biography; abstract*

CURVATURA, *curvature*

CURVA, *bend, curve*

CURVO (A), *curved*

CÚSPIDE, *cusp; summit, peak* (GEOG); *apex*

CUSTODIA, *custody, care, safekeeping*

CUSTODIO (A), *custodian*

CUTÍCULA, *cuticle*

Easily Recognizable Verbs

CALCULAR, *to calculate, work out*

CALIBRAR, *to calibrate, gauge, measure*

CALUMNIAR, *to slander, libel*

CAMUFLAR, *to camouflage*

CANCELAR, *to cancel, pay, settle, pay off*

CAPITALIZAR, *to capitalize, capitalize on*

CAPTURAR, *to capture, seize*

CAPITULAR, *to capitulate, surrender*

CARACTERIZAR, *to characterize*

CATAPULTAR, *to catapult*

CATEGORIZAR, *to categorize*

CASTIGAR, *to punish*

CAUSAR, *to cause, make*

CAUTERIZAR, *to cauterize*

CELEBRAR, *to celebrate*

CENTRAR, *to center*

CENTRALIZAR, *to centralize*

CERTIFICAR, *to certify*

CIRCULAR *(adj and verb), to flow, circulate*

CIRCUNNAVEGAR, *to circumnavigate*

CIRCUNSCRIBIR, *to circumscribe*

CIVILIZAR, *to civilize*

CLAMAR, *to exclaim, clamor for, cry out*

CLARIFICAR, *to clarify*

CLASIFICAR, *to classify, sort*

CLONAR, *to clone*

COAGULAR, *to coagulate, clot, congeal; curdle*

CODIFICAR, *to codify*

COEXISTIR, *to coexist* (POL)

COHABITAR, *to cohabit*

COHESIONAR, *to unite, draw together*

COINCIDIR, *to coincide*

COLABORAR, *to collaborate, contribute*

COLAPSAR, *to collapse, block*

COLECCIONAR, *to collect*

COLISIONAR, *to collide*

COLONIZAR, *to colonize*

COLORAR, *to color*

COMANDAR, *to command*

COMBATIR, *to fight*

COMBINAR, *to combine, match, mix*

COMENTAR, *to comment on, discuss*

COMENZAR, *to start, begin, commence*

COMETER, *to commit, carry out*

COMISIONAR, *to commission*

COMPACTAR, *to compress, compact*

COMPARAR, *to compare*

COMPELER, *to compel*

COMPENDIAR, *to summarize, condense, abridge*

COMPENSAR, *to compensate*

COMPETIR, *to compete with or against*

COMPILAR, *to compile*

COMPLACER, *to please, help, oblige*

COMPLEMENTAR, *to complement*

COMPLETAR, *to complete, finish*

COMPLICAR, *to complicate; involve, implicate*

COMPUTAR, *to compute, calculate*

COMUNICAR, *to convey, inform*

CONCEBIR, *to conceive, create*

CONCENTRAR, *to think, concentrate; assemble*

CONCEPTUALIZAR, *to conceptualize*

CONCERNIR, *to concern*

CONCILIAR, *to reconcile, harmonize*

CONCLUIR, *to conclude, finish, complete*

CONCORDAR, *to reconcile, tally*

CONDENSAR, *to condense*

CONDICIONAR, *to condition, make dependent*

CONDIMENTAR, *to season*

CONDONAR, *to forgive, cancel*

CONECTAR, *to connect*

CONFERIR, *to confer*

CONFESAR, *to confess, admit, acknowledge*

CONFIGURAR, *to shape, form*

CONFINAR, *to confine; banish, exile*

CONFIRMAR, *to confirm*

CONFISCAR, *to confiscate*

CONFORMAR, *to conform, shape*

CONFRONTAR, *to confront, face up to*

CONFUNDIR, *to confuse, confound, perplex*

CONGLOMERAR, *to conglomerate*

CONGRATULAR, *to congratulate*

CONGREGAR, *to assemble, congregate*

CONJETURAR, *to guess, surmise, conjecture*

CONMOVER, *to move, touch; shake* (GEOL)

CONMUTAR, *to commute*

CONNOTAR, *to suggest, have connotations, connote*

CONQUISTAR, *to conquer*

CONSENTIR, *to allow, permit, tolerate*

CONSERVAR, *to preserve, sustain, retain*

CONSIDERAR, *to consider*

CONSIGNAR, *to consign, send*

CONSISTIR, *to consist*

CONSOLAR, *to console, comfort*

CONSOLIDAR, *to consolidate, strengthen*

CONSPIRAR, *to conspire, plot*

CONSTITUIR, *to set up, constitute*

CONSULTAR, *to look up, consult, see*

CONSUMAR, *to complete, consummate*

CONSUMIR, *to consume*

CONTACTAR, *to contact, get in touch with*

CONTAMINAR, *to contaminate, pollute*

CONTEMPLAR, *to contemplate, gaze at*

CONTENDER, *to contend, fight with, compete*

CONTENER, *to contain*

CONTENTAR, *to please, keep happy*

CONTESTAR, *to answer, answer back*

CONTINUAR, *to continue, carry on*

CONTRARIAR, *to go against, upset*

CONTRARRESTAR, *to counteract*

CONTRASTAR, *to contrast, check, verify*

CONTRAVENIR, *to contravene, infringe*

CONTRIBUIR, *to contribute to or towards*

CONTROLAR, *to control*

CONTROVERTIR, *to dispute, question, argue*

CONTUSIONAR, *to bruise*

CONVALIDAR, *to recognize, validate*

CONVERGER, *to converge*

CONVERSAR, *to talk, converse*

CONVERTIR, *to convert,* (RELIG), *transform sb,*

CONVIVIR, *to live together*

CONVOCAR, *to convene, call*

CONVULSIONAR, *to convulse*

COOPERAR, *to cooperate with, collaborate*

COORDINAR, *to coordinate*

COPIAR, *to copy, reproduce; imitate*

CORROBORAR, *to corroborate*

COSTAR, *to cost, be expensive*

CRITICAR, *to review, criticize*

CROMAR, *to chrome (plate)*

CRUCIFICAR, *to crucify*

CUALIFICAR, *to qualify*

CUANTIFICAR, *to quantify, assess*

CUESTIONAR, *to question, argue*

CULMINAR, *to crown with, finish, culminate*

CULPAR, *to blame*

CULTIVAR, *to farm, cultivate*

CULTURIZAR, *to educate, enlighten*

CUSTODIAR, *to guard, watch over, defend*

STUDY NOTES:

D

Interchangeable Words

DAIQUIRI

DANDY ó DANDI, *fop*

DEBACLE

DEBATE

DEBUT ó DÉBUT

DEBUTANTE; *rookie, beginner, novice*

DECIBEL ó DECIBELIO

DECIMAL

DECISIÓN

DEDUCIBLE

DÉFICIT

DELTA, *the letter; also delta* (GEOL)

DEMO

DENTAL

DEPLORABLE; *appalling*

DERBY

DERMATITIS

DETECTIVE

DETECTOR

DETESTABLE

DETRACTOR (A)

DETRITUS, (GEOL); *also means debris*

DIABETES

DIAGNOSIS

DIAGONAL

DIAL

DIALECTAL

DIÁSPORA

DICTATORIAL

DIÉRESIS

DIESEL

DIGESTIÓN

DIGITAL (INFORM)

DIMENSIÓN

DIPLOMA

DIRECTOR

DIRIGIBLE

DISKETTE (INFORM)

DISK JOCKEY

DISPENSABLE

DISPERSIÓN

DISPLAY (INFORM)

DISTENSIÓN

DIVA, *prima donna*

DIVÁN, *couch*

DIVERSIÓN, *entertainment, fun*

DIVISIBLE

DIVISIÓN (MAT) (MIL)

DIVISOR (MAT)

DOBERMAN, *a dog*

DOCTOR (A)

DOCTORAL; *pedantic, pompous*

DOCTRINAL

DOGMA

DOLMEN

DONUT ó DOUGHNUT

DOPING, *with drugs*

DORSAL

DOSSIER

DRAGÓN

DRAMA, *play*

DRIVE (DEP)

DUAL

DUCAL

DÚO

DUODENAL

DÚPLEX

DURABLE

DVD

DVD-ROM

Easily Recognizable Nouns, Adjectives and Adverbs

DALIA, *dahlia*

DATACIÓN, *date, dating*

DÁTIL, *date*

DATIVO, *dative*

DATO, *fact*

DÉBIL, *feeble, weak, faint*

DEBILIDAD, *weakness, feebleness*

DEBILITACIÓN, *weakening*

DÉBILMENTE, *weakly, dimly*

DÉBITO, *debit, debt*

DÉCADA, *decade*

DECADENCIA, *decline, decay, decadence*

DECADENTE, *decadent, declining*

DECÁMETRO, *decameter*

DECELERACIÓN, *deceleration*

DECENCIA, *decency*

DECENTE, *decent, upright, respectable*

DECENTRALIZACIÓN, *decentralization*

DECEPCIÓN, *disappointment*

DECIBELIO, *decibel*

DECÍMETRO, *decimeter*

DECISIVO (A), *decisive*

DECLARACIÓN, *declaration*

DECLARADO (A), *declared, professed*

DECLINACIÓN, *decline, fallen, low; declension*

DECLIVE, *incline, gradient; decline*

DECOLORANTE, *bleaching agent*

DECORACIÓN, *decoration*

DECORADOR (A), *interior designer, decorator*

DECORATIVO (A), *decorative*

DECORO, *decorum, decency, dignity*

DECOROSO (A), *decent; decorous, dignified*

DECRÉPITO (A), *decrepit; declining*

DECRETO, *decree, order*

DEDICACIÓN, *dedication, devotion, commitment*

DEDICATORIA, *inscription, dedication*

DEDUCCIÓN, *deduction*

DEDUCTIVO (A), *deductive*

DEFECCIÓN, *defection*

DEFECTO, *defect, lack, fault, shortcoming*

DEFECTUOSO (A), *defective, faulty*

DEFENSA (n), *defense; defender* (DEP)

DEFENSIVO (A), *defensive, justified, protective; excuse, argument; guard, shield; preservative*

DEFENSOR (A), *defender, champion; defense attorney*

DEFERENCIA, *deference, respect*

DEFICIENCIA, *deficiency, shortcoming, defect*

DEFICIENTE, *deficient, lacking, inadequate*

DEFINIBLE (adj), *definable*

DEFINICIÓN, *definition*

DEFINIDO (A), *defined, definite, clear; clearly defined*

DEFINITIVO (A), *definitive, final, decisive*

DEFLACIÓN, *deflation*

DEFLACIONARIO ó DEFLACIONISTA, *deflationary*

DEFUNCIÓN, *death; decrease*

DEFORESTACIÓN, *deforestation*

DEFORMACIÓN, *deformation, distortion, warping*

DEFORME, *deformed, disfigured*

DEFORMIDAD, *deformity; malformation*

DEGENERACIÓN, *degeneration*

DEGENERADO (A), *degenerate, pervert; reprobate*

DEGRADACIÓN, *degradation; deterioration*

DEGRADANTE, *degrading, demeaning, humiliating*

DELEGACIÓN, *delegation*

DELEGADO (A), *representative, delegate*

DELEITE, *delight, pleasure*

DELIBERACIÓN, *deliberation, consideration, discussion*

DELIBERADO (A), *deliberate, considered; intentional*

DELICADO (A), *delicate, fine; exquisite; dainty*

DELICIA, *delight, gladden; enjoy, relish*

DELICIOSO (A), *delicious; delightful*

DELINEACIÓN, *delineation*

DELIRIO, *delirium, delusion*

DEMAGOGO (A), *demagogue, agitator*

DEMANDA, *demand, request*

DEMARCACIÓN, *demarcation, area, district*

DEMENCIA, *dementia, madness, insanity*

DEMENTE, *mad, demented, lunatic*

DEMOCRACIA, *democracy*

DEMÓCRATA, *democratic (adj), Democrat (n)*

DEMOCRÁTICO (A), *democratic*

DEMOGRAFÍA, *demography*

DEMOGRÁFICO (A), *demographic*

DEMOLICIÓN, *demolition*

DEMONIO, *devil, demon*

DEMOSTRACIÓN, *demonstration*

DEMOSTRATIVO (A), *demonstrative*

DENIGRANTE, *degrading, insulting, denigrating*

DENOMINACIÓN, *naming, denomination*

DENOMINADO, *named, called*

DENOMINADOR, *denominator* (MAT)

DENSIDAD, *density, thickness*

DENSO (A), *dense, heavy, thick*

DENTINA, *dentine*

DENTISTA, *dentist*

DENUNCIA, *accusation, denunciation, condemnation*

DEPARTAMENTAL, *departmental*

DEPARTAMENTO, *department, compartment*

DEPENDENCIA, *dependency*

DEPENDIENTE, *dependent, subordinate, conditional; reliant, trustworthy, dependable; a sales clerk*

DEPILACIÓN ó DEPILADO, *depilation*

DEPILATORIO (A), *hair removing substance*

DEPORTACIÓN, *deportation*

DEPOSICIÓN, *depose, overthrow*

DEPÓSITO, *storage, warehouse, tank*

DEPRAVACIÓN, *depravity*

DEPRAVADO (A), *depraved, corrupt; degenerate*

DEPRECIACIÓN, *depreciation*

DEPREDADOR (A), *predatory (adj), predator (n)*

DEPRESIÓN, *depression*, (MED) (METEO); *recession, downturn, decline, financial slump*

DEPRESIVO (A), *depressive* (PSICOL); *a depressant*

DERIVACIÓN, *derivation* (MAT)

DERIVADO (A), *derived; derivative; by-product*

DERMATOLOGÍA, *dermatology*

DERMATOLÓGICO (A), *dermatological*

DERMATÓLOGO (A), *dermatologist*

DÉRMICO (A), *skin*

DEROGACIÓN, *repeal, rescind, revoke, cancel, annul*

DESACOSTUMBRADO (A), *unaccustomed, unusual*

DESAFORTUNADO (A), *unfortunate, unlucky*

DESAGRACIADO (A), *graceless, unattractive*

DESAGRADABLE, *unpleasant, disagreeable*

DESAGRADECIDO (A), *ungrateful, thankless*

DESAGRADO, *displeasure*

DESAMOR, *coldness, indifference, apathy*

DESANIMADO (A), *downhearted, dejected*

DESAPARICIÓN, *disappearance, extinction*

DESAPASIONADO (A), *impartial, dispassionate*

DESAPROBACIÓN, *disapproval*

DESARME, *disarmament*

DESASTRE, *disaster*

DESASTROSO (A), *disastrous, calamitous*

DESATADO (A), *undone, uncontrolled*

DESATENCIÓN, *discourtesy, inattention*

DESATENTO (A), *heedless, careless, discourteous, inattentive, unobservant, unmindful*

DESBANDADA, *breaking up, scattering, rush*

DESCARTABLE, *disposable*

DESCARTE, *discard*

DESCENDENCIA, *descendants, children, progeny*

DESCENDENTE, *downward, diminishing*

DESCENSO, *descent, drop*

DESCENTRADO (A), *off-center, out of tune; disoriented*

DESCOLORIDO (A), *faded, discolored*

DESCOMPOSICIÓN, *decomposition, decay; separation* (QUIM)

DESCOMPRESIÓN, *decompression*

DESCONCERTADO, *disconcerted*

DESCONCERTANTE, *disconcerting*

DESCONFIADO (A), *distrustful, suspicious, incredulous*

DESCONFIANZA, *distrust, mistrust; doubt, question*

DESCONGESTIÓN, *decongestion, relief, clearing*

DESCONSIDERACIÓN, *thoughtlessness*

DESCONSIDERADO (A), *thoughtless, inconsiderate*

DESCONSOLADO (A), *disconsolate, forlorn*

DESCONTENTO (A), *discontented, unhappy, dissatisfied*

DESCONTROL, *lack of control, chaos*

DESCONTROLADO (A), *uncontrolled*

DESCOORDINACIÓN, *uncoordinated*

DESCRÉDITO, *discredit, disrepute*

DESCRIPCIÓN, *description*

DESCRIPTIVO (A), *descriptive*

DESDÉN, *distain, scorn, contempt; disgust; hatred*

DESDENTADO (A), *toothless*

DESEMBARCO, *disembarkation, landing* (MIL); *unloading; leave, detrain, deplane*

DESENCANTO, *disenchantment*

DESERCIÓN, *desertion* (MIL), *defection* (POL)

DESÉRTICO (A) (adj), *desert-like, barren, deserted*

DESESPERACIÓN, *despair, desperation*

DESESPERADO (A), *desperate, hopeless; furious*

DESESPERANTE, *infuriating, hopeless*

DESESPERO, *despair, desperation*

DESFAVORABLE, *unfavorable*

DESFORESTACIÓN, *deforestation*

DESHABITADO (A), *empty, vacant, uninhabited*

DESHIDRATACIÓN, *dehydration, desiccation*

DESHONESTO (A), *dishonest; indecent*

DESHONOR (m), *disgrace; insult, affront*

DESHONRA (f), *dishonor, disgrace*

DESHONROSO (A), *dishonorable, shameful*

DESHORA, *inopportune, unfavorable*

DESIGNACIÓN, *designation, appointment*

DESIGNIO, *plan, design*

DESIGUAL, *unequal, uneven, different*

DESIGUALDAD, *inequality*

DESILUSIÓN, *disillusion, disappointment*

DESILUSIONADO, *disillusioned, disenchanted*

DESINFECTANTE, *disinfectant*

DESINFORMACIÓN, *misinformation, disinformation*

DESINHIBIDO, *uninhibited*

DESINTEGRACIÓN, *disintegration, breakup*

DESINTERÉS, *disinterest, impersonal*

DESINTERESADO (A), *unselfish, disinterested, indifferent*

DESMANO, *out of reach, out of the way*

DESMEDIDO (A), *excessive; boundless*

DESMEMBRACIÓN, *dismemberment, breakup*

DESMORALIZACIÓN, *demoralization*

DESMORALIZADO (A), *demoralized*

DESMOTIVADO, *unmotivated, uninspired, apathetic*

DESNUTRICIÓN, *malnutrition, undernourishment*

DESOBEDIENCIA, *disobedience*

DESOBEDIENTE, *disobedient*

DESOCUPACIÓN, *unemployment; clearance*

DESOCUPADO (A), *free, unemployed; empty, unoccupied, vacant, unrestricted*

DESODORANTE, *deodorant*

DESOLACIÓN, *desolation, distress, grief*

DESOLADO, *desolate; devastated, shattered*

DESOLADOR (A), *heartbreaking*

DESORBITADO (A), *exorbitant; exaggerated*

DESORBITANTE, *excessive, overwhelming*

DESORDEN, *mess, disorder, chaos*

DESORDENADO (A), *untidy, messy, jumbled*

DESORGANIZACIÓN, *disorganization*

DESORIENTACIÓN, *disorientation, confusion*

DESORIENTADO, *disoriented*

DESPENSA, *larder, pantry, storeroom*

DESPERFECTO, *damage, flaw, imperfection, fault*

DÉSPOTA, *despot*

DESPÓTICO, *despotic*

DESPOTISMO, *despotism*

DESPREOCUPACIÓN, *unconcern, carefree, blithe*

DESPREOCUPADO (A), *unworried, unconcerned*

DESPRESTIGIO, *discredit, loss of prestige*

DESPROPORCIÓN, *disproportion*

DESPROPORCIONADO, *disproportionate*

DESPROTECCIÓN, *vulnerability, defenselessness*

DESTILACIÓN, *distillation*

DESTILERÍA, *distillery*

DESTINO, *destiny, fate; destination*

DESTRUCTIVO (A) (adj), *destructive*

DESTRUCTOR, *destroyer* (NAUT)

DETALLADO (A), *detailed, thorough*

DETALLE, *detail*

DETALLISTA, *meticulous, retailer, retail trader*

DETECCIÓN, *perception, detection*

DETENCIÓN, *holdup, delay; arrest, detention*

DETERGENTE, *detergent*

DETERIORO, *damage, deterioration*

DETERMINACIÓN, *determination, decision*

DETERMINADO (A), *certain, definite, determined*

DETERMINANTE (adj), *determinant; decisive*

DETONACIÓN, *detonation, explosion*

DETONADOR (A), *detonator*

DETONANTE, *explosive (adj); trigger, cause (n)*

DETONANTE (n), *explosive*

DETRIMENTO, *detriment*

DEVALUACIÓN, *devaluation*

DEVASTACIÓN, *devastation*

DEVOCIÓN, *devotion* (RELIG)

DEVOTO (A), *devout, devotional*

DIABÉTICO (A), *diabetic*

DIABLO, *devil*

DIABÓLICO (A), *diabolic*

DIÁFANO (A), *transparent, clear, crystal clear*

DIAGNÓSTICO, *diagnosis*

DIAGRAMA, *diagram*

DIALECTO, *dialect*

DIÁLISIS, *dialysis*

DIÁLOGO, *dialogue* (POL)

DIAMANTE, *diamond*

DIAMETRALMENTE, *diametrically*

DIÁMETRO, *diameter*

DIARIO (A), *daily, everyday*

DIARREA, *diarrhea*

DIATRIBA, *diatribe, tirade, harangue, rant*

DICCIÓN, *diction*

DICCIONARIO, *dictionary*

DICIEMBRE, *December*

DICTADO, *dictation*

DICTADOR (A), *dictator*

DICTADURA, *dictatorship*

DIDÁCTICA, *didactics*

DIDÁCTICO (A), *didactic*

DIETA, *diet*

DIETÉTICO (A), *dietary, dietetic*

DIETISTA, *dietician*

DIFAMACIÓN, *slander, libel, defamation*

DIFAMATORIO (A), *defamatory, slanderous*

DIFERENCIA, *difference*

DIFERENCIAL, *distinguishing; differential* (MAT); *differential gear* (AUTO)

DIFERENDO, *dispute, debate, discuss; impugn*

DIFERENTE, *different, unlike, unique, dissimilar*

DIFÍCIL, *difficult, hard*

DIFICULTAD, *difficulty, complexity; obstacle*

DIFICULTOSO (A), *difficult; arduous*

DIFUSIÓN, *diffusion, dissemination, broadcasting*

DIFUSO (A), *diffuse, widespread; wordy*

DIGESTIVO (A), *digestive*

DIGITAL, *digital; finger*

DÍGITO, *digit*

DIGNATARIO (A), *dignitary*

DIGNIDAD, *dignity, decency*

DIGNO (A), *dignified, praiseworthy*

DIGRESIÓN, *digression, deviation, detour*

DILATACIÓN, *dilation* (MED), *expansion*

DILATADO, *dilated; extensive*

DILEMA, *dilemma, predicament, quandary; impasse*

DILETANTE, *dilettante, amateur, dabbler*

DILIGENCIA, *diligence*

DILIGENTE, *diligent, attentive, careful, scrupulous*

DIMINUTIVO (A), *diminutive, miniature, petite*

DIMINUTO (A), *tiny, minuscule, teeny, little*

DIMISIÓN, *resignation*

DINÁMICO (A), *dynamic, vigorous, lively, spirited*

DINAMITA, *dynamite*

DINAMO, *dynamo; an energetic person*

DINASTÍA, *dynasty*

DINOSAURIO, *dinosaur* (ZOOL)

DINTEL, *lintel*

DIÓCESIS, *diocese*

DIODO, *diode*

DIÓXIDO, *dioxide*

DIOXINA, *dioxin*

DIPLOMACIA, *diplomacy*

DIPTONGO, *diphthong*

DIPUTACIÓN, *deputation, congress*

DIRECCIÓN, *address, domicile; direction*

DIRECCIONAL, *automobile directional, indicator*

DIRECTIVO (A), *managerial, managing*

DIRECTO (A), *direct, straight, straightforward*

DIRECTOR (A), *governing, guiding*

DISCAPACIDAD, *disability*

DISCAPACITADO (A), *disabled, incapacitated*

DISCERNIMIENTO, *discernment*

DISCIPLINA, *discipline*

DISCÍPULO (A), *disciple*

DISCIPLINARIO (A), *disciplinary*

DISCO, *disk* (ANAT) (ASTRON) (GEOM) (INFORM); *record* (MUS)

DISCONFORME (adj), *incompatible, discordant*

DISCONFORMIDAD (n), *disagreement*

DISCONTINUO (A) (adj), *discontinuous, interrupted*

DISCORDANCIA, *discord, disagreement*

DISCORDANTE (adj), *discordant* (MUS)

DISCORDE, *discordant, clashing*

DISCORDIA, *discord, strife, dissension, clash*

DISCOTECA, *discotheque, disco*

DISCRECIÓN, *discretion*

DISCRECIONAL, *optional, discretionary*

DISCREPANCIA, *difference, discrepancy*

DISCREPANTE, *divergent, dissenting*

DISCRETAMENTE, *discreetly, cautiously, prudently*

DISCRETO (A), *discreet, sober; modest*

DISCRIMINACIÓN, *sexual and racial discrimination*

DISCRIMINADO, *unfairly treated*

DISCRIMINATORIO (A), *discriminatory*

DISCULPA, *excuse, apology*

DISCURSIVO (A), *discursive, extensive, rambling*

DISCURSO, *speech*

DISCUSIÓN, *argument, discussion*

DISECCIÓN, *dissection*

DISENSIÓN, *dissension, disagreement*

DISENTERÍA, *dysentery*

DISERTACIÓN, *discourse, dissertation*

DISIDENCIA, *dissent, disagree, differ*

DISIDENTE, *dissident (adj), dissenter (n)*

DISFUNCIÓN, *malfunction*

DISGUSTADO, *upset*

DISGUSTO, *displeasure, repulsion*

DISLEXIA, *dyslexia*

DISLOCACIÓN, *dislocation* (MED)

DISOLUBLE, *rescindable, revocable; voidable*

DISOLUCIÓN, *dissolution; liquidation, dissipation*

DISOLUTO (A), *dissolute, corrupt, degenerate*

DISOLVENTE, *solvent*

DISONANCIA, *dissonance* (MUS); *discord*

DISPARIDAD, *disparity*

DISPENSA, *dispensation* (RELIG)

DISPENSARIO, *dispensary, clinic*

DISPEPSIA, *dyspepsia*

DISPERSO (A), *scattered, dispersed; unfocused*

DISPOSICIÓN, *arrangement, layout, disposition*

DISPUTA, *dispute, argument*

DISPUTADO, *close, hard fought*

DISTANCIA, *distance*

DISTANTE, *distant*

DISTENSIÓN, *relaxed atmosphere; strain* (MED)

DISTINCIÓN, *distinction, difference; honor*

DISTINGO, *distinction, honor, award*

DISTINGUIDO (A), *distinguished, refined person*

DISTINTIVO (A), *distinguishing; badge, emblem*

DISTINTO (A), *different, distinct*

DISTORSIÓN, *sprain, distortion*

DISTRACCIÓN, *distraction, pastime, hobby*

DISTRIBUCIÓN, *distribution, delivery*

DISTRIBUIDOR (A), *wholesaler, distributor; highway exit*

DISTRITO, *district, precinct*

DISTURBIO, *riot, disturbance*

DIVERGENCIA, *divergence; divide, fork, split*

DIVERGENTE, *divergent; deviate, wander, digress*

DIVERSIDAD, *diversity, difference, disparity*

DIVERSIFICACIÓN, *diversification, variegated*

DIVERSO (A), *different, varied, diverse, distinct*

DIVERTIDO (A), *entertaining, enjoyable, amusing*

DIVIDENDO, *dividend*

DIVINIDAD, *divinity, God*

DIVINO, *divine, heavenly*

DIVISORIA, *dividing line*

DIVISORIO (A), *dividing*

DIVO (A), *diva, prima donna*

DIVORCIADO (A), *divorced*

DIVORCIO, *divorce; discrepancy*

DIVULGACIÓN, *revelation, disclosure*

DIVULGATIVO, *informative*

DOBLE, *double, dual, extra strong; doubles* (DEP)

DOBLETE, *double for, stand-in* (TEATRO)

DÓCIL, *docile, obedient*

DOCILIDAD, *obedience, docility*

DOCTO, *learned, erudite*

DOCTRINA, *doctrine, teaching*

DOCUMENTACIÓN, *documentation*

DOCUMENTADO (A), *documented, researched*

DOCUMENTAL, *documentary*

DOCUMENTO, *document*

DOGMÁTICO (A), *dogmatic, arbitrary, imperious*

DOGO, *bulldog*

DÓLAR, *dollar*

DOMÉSTICO (A), *domestic; servant*

DOMICILIO, *home, residence, address*

DOMINACIÓN, *dominion, rule, power*

DOMINANTE, *dominant, prevailing, domineering*

DOMINIO, *control over, domain*

DOMINÓ, *dominoes; the domino theory*

DONACIÓN, *donation, gift*

DONANTE, *donor*

DORADO (A), *golden*

DORMITORIO, *bedroom, dormitory*

DORSO, *back* (ANAT)

DOSIS, *dose*

DRAMÁTICO (A), *dramatic*

DRÁSTICO (A), *drastic*

DROGA, *drug*

DRUIDA, *druid*

DUALIDAD, *duality*

DÚCTIL, *ductile, malleable; easily influenced*

DUDA, *doubt*

DUDOSO (A), *doubtful, uncertain, unreliable*

DUELO, *duel*

DUETO ó DÚO, *duet*

DULCE, *sweet; soothing; dulcet*

DUNA, *dune*

DUPLICADO (A), *duplicate, identical, matching*

DUPLICIDAD, *duplicity, deceitfulness, deceptiveness*

DURABILIDAD, *durability*

DURACIÓN, *length (time), duration*

DURADERO (A), *longlasting, hard-wearing*

DURANTE, *during*

DURO (A), *hard, tough, stiff, firm, stale*

Easily Recognizable Verbs

DANZAR, *to dance*

DATAR, *to date, date back, date from*

DEBATIR, *to debate, discuss*

DEBITAR, *to debit*

DECANTAR, *to decant (wine)*

DECAPITAR, *to decapitate, behead*

DECIDIR, *to decide, settle, resolve*

DECLARAR, *to declare*

DECLINAR, *to decline*

DECORAR, *to decorate*

DEDICAR, *to dedicate*

DEDUCIR, *to deduce, infer, derive*

DEFENDER, *to defend, champion*

DEFINIR, *to define, describe*

DEFORMAR, *to deform, distort*

DEFRAUDAR, *to disappoint, cheat, defraud*

DEGENERAR, *to degenerate*

DELEGAR, *to delegate*

DELIBERAR, *to deliberate, debate, discuss*

DELIMITAR, *to define, set limits, delimit*

DELINEAR, *to outline, delineate*

DEMANDAR, *to sue, demand*

DEMOSTRAR, *to prove, demonstrate, show*

DENOTAR, *to indicate, denote, show*

DENUNCIAR, *to report, expose, denounce*

DEPENDER, *to depend*

DEPILAR, *to pluck, wax, remove hair*

DEPLORAR, *to deplore, regret*

DEPORTAR, *to deport*

DEPOSITAR, *to deposit, place; settle*

DERIVAR, *to derive*

DESACTIVAR, *to defuse, deactivate, neutralize*

DESARMAR, *to dismantle, disarm, take away*

DESAUTORIZAR, *to deny, deprive, discredit*

DESCENDER, *to descend, go down, come down*

DESCENTRALIZAR, *to decentralize*

DESCONCERTAR, *to disconcert, agitate, fluster*

DESCONECTAR, *to disconnect, unplug, switch off*

DESCONTENTAR, *to upset, make unhappy*

DESCRIBIR, *to describe, outline, delineate*

DESEMBALAR, *to unpack*

DESENCANTAR, *to disappoint, disenchant, disillusion*

DESENROLLAR, *to unroll, unwind*

DESENVOLVER, *to unwrap; manage, develop*

DESERTAR, *to desert, give up, leave, abandon*

DESESTABILIZAR, *to destabilize*

DESFIGURAR, *to disfigure, deface, deform, distort*

DESFORESTAR, *to deforest*

DESHABITAR, *to abandon*

DESHONRAR, *to dishonor, disgrace, insult*

DESIGNAR, *to appoint, designate*

DESILUSIONAR, *to disappoint, disillusion*

DESINFECTAR, *to disinfect*

DESINFESTAR, *to decontaminate*

DESINFLAR, *to deflate, let down, go flat*

DESINFORMAR, *to misinform, mislead*

DESINTEGRAR, *to disintegrate*

DESMEMBRAR, *to dismember*

DESMONTAR, *to take apart, strip down; dismount, alight*

DESMORALIZAR, *to demoralize*

DESOCUPAR, *to vacate, clear, clear out*

DESORGANIZAR, *to disorganize*

DESORIENTAR, *to disorient, confuse*

DESPACHAR, *to dispatch, sell, finish off*

DETALLAR, *to detail, itemize*

DETECTAR, *to detect, discover, perceive*

DETENER, *to stop, delay; arrest*

DETERIORAR, *to damage, deteriorate*

DETERMINAR, *to determine, settle, assess*

DETESTAR, *to detest, hate, loathe*

DETONAR, *to detonate, explode*

DEVALUAR, *to devalue, devaluate*

DEVASTAR, *to devastate, destroy, overwhelm*

DEVOLVER, *to give back, return, send back*

DEVORAR, *to devour, wolf down*

DIAGNOSTICAR, *to diagnose, identify*

DICTAR, *to dictate, pronounce, issue*

DIEZMAR, *to decimate*

DIFAMAR, *to slander*

DIFERENCIAR, *to distinguish, differentiate*

DIFICULTAR, *to make difficult, hinder, obstruct*

DILUIR, *to dilute, water down*

DISCIPLINAR, *to discipline*

DISCRIMINAR, *to discriminate*

DISCULPAR, *to excuse, forgive; apologize*

DISEMINAR, *to scatter, disseminate, spread*

DISGUSTAR, *to be disgusted, upset*

DISOLVER, *to dissolve, break up, liquidate*

DISPENSAR, *to excuse, dispense, give, grant*

DISPERSAR, *to scatter, disperse, break up*

DISPUTAR, *to contest, play* (DEP)

DISTINGUIR, *to distinguish; set apart, honor*

DISTORSIONAR, *to distort*

DISTRIBUIR, *to distribute, deliver, allocate*

DIVERGIR, *to diverge, differ, disagree*

DIVERSIFICAR, *to diversify*

DIVIDIR, *to divide, split up*

DIVORCIAR, *to divorce*

DIVULGAR, *to disclose, divulge*

DOCUMENTAR, *to document, check, research*

DOMESTICAR, *to domesticate, tame*

DOMINAR, *to dominate, control*

DONAR, *to donate*

DOPAR, *to dope, drug*

DORMIR, *to sleep*

DRAMATIZAR, *to dramatize*

DUPLICAR, *to copy, duplicate*

STUDY NOTES:

E

Interchangeable Words

ECLIPSE

ECZEMA ó ECCEMA

EDEMA

EDÉN, *garden of paradise, Eden*

EDITOR (A), *publisher; publishing*

EDITORIAL, *editorial, leading article*

EGO

ELECTOR (A), *also means voter, electorate*

ELECTORAL

ELECTRÓN

ELEMENTAL, *basic*

ELIXIR

ÉLITE ó ELITE

EMAIL

EMBARGO

EMIR

EMÚ

EMULSIÓN

ENCLAVE

ENEMA

ENIGMA

ENTENTE (POL); *agreement* (COM)

ENTERITIS

EPIDERMIS

EPISCOPAL

EPITOME, *summary*

EÓN ó EON

ERA *(era glacial = ice age)*

EROSIÓN (GEOL)

ERRATA

ERROR

ESTABLISHMENT

ESTIMABLE; *esteemed, substantial*

ETCÉTERA

EUREKA

EURO, *the euro*

EVASIÓN

EVENTUAL

EX, *former*

EXCISIÓN (MED)

EXCITABLE

EXCLUSIÓN

EXCURSIÓN

EXECRABLE

EXÉGESIS

EXPANSIÓN

EXPERIMENTAL

EXPLICABLE

EXPLOSIÓN

EXPULSIÓN

EXTENSIBLE, *extending*

EXTENSIÓN, *area, length, extent, range*

EXTERIOR

EXTRA, *helper, overtime, bonus; best, top quality*

EXTRAJUDICIAL, *out of court*

EXTRAMARITAL

Easily Recognizable Nouns, Adjectives and Adverbs

ÉBANO, *ebony*

EBRIO, *intoxicated, drunk*

ECO, *echo*

ECOLOGÍA, *ecology*

ECONOMÍA, *economy*

ECONÓMICO (A), *economic*

ECONOMISTA, *economist*

ECUACIÓN, *equation*

ECUADOR, *equator* (GEOG); *midpoint*

ECUALIZADOR, *equalizer*

ECUATORIAL, *equatorial*

ECUMÉNICO, *universal*

EDICIÓN, *edition*

EDICTO, *edict*

EDIFICANTE, *edifying, enlightening, teaching*

EDUCACIÓN, *education, teaching*

EDUCACIONAL, *educational*

EDUCADO (A), *polite, well mannered, cultured*

EDUCADOR (A), *teacher, educator*

EDUCATIVO (A), *educational,*

EFECTIVIDAD, *effectiveness*

EFECTIVO (A), *effective; real; cash*

EFECTO, *effect; result*

EFERVESCENCIA, *effervescence*

EFERVESCENTE, *effervescent*

EFICIENCIA, *efficiency*

EFICIENTE, *efficient*

EFÍMERO (A), *ephemeral*

EFUSIVO (A), *effusive, enthusiastic, exuberant*

EGOCÉNTRICO (A), *egocentric, self-centered*

EGOÍSTA, *egotistic*

EGREGIO (A), *illustrious, eminent, distinguished*

EJECUTIVO (A), *executive*

EJECUTOR (A), *executor, executrix*

EJEMPLAR, *exemplary, model, example*

EJEMPLO, *example*

EJERCICIO, *exercise* (DEP), *practice*

ELASTICIDAD, *elasticity*

ELÁSTICO (A), *elastic, flexible, springy*

ELECCIÓN, *election, choice*

ELECTIVO, *elective*

ELECTO (A) (adj), *elect*

ELECTRICIDAD, *electricity*

ELECTRICISTA, *electrical (adj), electrician (n)*

ELÉCTRICO (A), *electric*

ELECTROCARDIOGRAMA, *electrocardiogram*

ELECTROCUCIÓN, *electrocution*

ELECTRÓNICA, *electronics*

ELECTRÓNICO, *electronic*

ELECTRODO, *electrode*

ELECTRÓLISIS, *electrolysis*

ELECTROSTÁTICO (A), *electrostatic*

ELEFANTE (A), *elephant*

ELEGANCIA, *elegance, gracefulness, tastefulness*

ELEGANTE, *elegant, stylish, smart, fashionable*

ELEMENTO, *element; factor*

ELEVACIÓN, *lifting/raising an object; increase, rise; hill, elevation; promotion; loftiness*

ELEVADO (A), *high, lofty, great; elevated*

ELEVADOR, *elevator, hoist*

ELIMINACIÓN, *elimination*

ELIPSE, *ellipse*

ELIPSIS, *ellipsis*

ELÍPTICO (A), *elliptical (adj), elliptic (n)*

ELITISMO, *elitism*

ELITISTA, *elitist*

ELOCUCIÓN, *elocution*

ELOCUENCIA, *eloquence*

ELOCUENTE, *eloquent, articulate, smooth*

ELUSIVO (A), *evasive, elusive, slippery; indirect*

EMANACIÓN, *emanation, emission*

EMANCIPACIÓN, *emancipation*

EMBARAZOSO (A), *awkward, embarrassing*

EMBELLECIMIENTO, *embellishment, enhancement*

EMBLEMA, *emblem, badge, symbol*

EMBOLIA, *embolism*

EMBRIÓN, *embryo, beginnings of an idea*

EMERGENCIA, *emergency*

EMERGENTE, *emerging, emergent*

EMÉRITO (A) (adj), *emeritus*

EMIGRACIÓN, *emigration; migration of animals, persons*

EMIGRANTE (adj), *emigrant, migrant*

EMINENCIA, *eminent figure, leading light, expert*

EMINENTE, *eminent, high, outstanding*

EMISIÓN, *emission, TV and radio broadcasting*

EMOCIÓN, *emotion, excitement*

EMOCIONADO, *moved, stirred, excited*

EMOCIONAL, *emotional*

EMOCIONANTE, *moving, touching, exciting, thrilling*

EMOTIVO (A), *emotive, moving, emotional*

EMPATÍA, *empathy*

EMPERADOR, *emperor*

EMPÍRICO (A), *empirical, empiric*

EMULACIÓN, *emulation* (INFORM), *imitation*

ENCARNACIÓN, *embodiment, personification, incarnation*

ENCARNADO (A), *incarnate; skin-tone, pink, red*

ENCEFALITIS, *encephalitis*

ENCEFALOGRAMA, *encephalogram*

ENCÍCLICA, *encyclical*

ENCICLOPEDIA, *encyclopedia*

ENCICLOPÉDICO (A), *encyclopedic*

ENDÉMICO (A), *endemic* (MED); *rife, chronic*

ENDIABLADO (A), *wicked person, foul type; fiendishly difficult; devilish, impish*

ENDORFINA, *endorphin* (MED)

ENEMIGO (A), *enemy, hostile*

ENEMISTAD, *enmity, animosity*

ENERGÉTICO (A) (adj), *energy*

ENERGÍA, *energy, drive*

ENÉRGICO (A), *energetic, vigorous*

ENERVANTE, *draining, exasperating, annoying*

ÉNFASIS, *emphasis; insistence*

ENFÁTICO (A), *emphatic; insistent*

ENFERMEDAD, *illness, disease*

ENFERMERÍA, *infirmary, nursing, sick bay*

ENFERMO (A), *ill, sick*

ENFISEMA, *emphysema*

ENIGMÁTICO (A), *enigmatic, mysterious*

ENOLOGÍA, *oenology, study of wine*

ENORME, *enormous, huge*

ENORMIDAD, *enormity, immensity; tremendous, great*

ENSALADA, *salad*

ENSALADERA, *salad bowl*

ENSEÑA, *ensign; standard, insignia*

ENTERAMENTE, *entirely, completely*

ENTERO (A), *whole, entire*

ENTIDAD, *entity; body, organization* (POL); *firm, company* (COM)

ENTOMOLOGÍA, *entomology*

ENTONACIÓN, *intonation*

ENTRADA, *entrance*

ENTUSIASMO, *enthusiasm*

ENTUSIASTA, *enthusiastic (adj), enthusiast (n)*

ENUMERACIÓN, *enumeration, listing*

ENUNCIACIÓN, *formulation, enunciation*

ENUNCIADO, *statement; wording*

ENVIDIABLE, *enviable, desirable, coveted*

ENVIDIOSO (A), *envious, jealous, desirous; resentful*

ENZIMA, *enzyme*

EPICENTRO, *epicenter*

ÉPICA (n), *epic poetry*

ÉPICO (A) (adj), *epic*

EPICÚREO (A), *epicurean*

EPIDEMIA (n), *epidemic*

EPIDÉMICO (adj), *epidemic*

EPIDÉRMICO, *superficial, skin-deep*

EPIGLOTIS, *epiglottis*

EPÍGRAFE, *epigraph*

EPILEPSIA, *epilepsy*

EPILÉPTICO (A), *epileptic*

EPÍLOGO, *epilogue*

EPISÓDICO, *episodic*

EPISODIO, *episode, incident, part, series*

EPÍSTOLA, *epistle, letter*

EPÍTETO, *epithet*

ÉPOCA, *epoch, geological age; eon*

EQUIDAD, *fairness, equity*

EQUIDISTANTE, *equidistant*

EQUILÁTERO (A), *equilateral*

EQUILIBRADO (A), *levelheaded, sensible*

EQUILIBRIO, *balance, equilibrium*

EQUINO (A), *equine*

EQUINOCCIO, *equinox*

EQUIPARABLE, *comparable*

EQUIPO, *team* (DEP); *equipment*

EQUITATIVO (A), *fair, evenhanded, reasonable*

EQUIVALENCIA, *equivalence*

EQUIVALENTE, *equivalent*

EQUIVOCACIÓN, *mistake, error, equivocation*

EQUIVOCADO (A) (adj), *mistaken, wrong; misplaced*

EQUÍVOCO (A), *ambiguous, equivocal; suspicious; misunderstanding*

ERECCIÓN, *erection, raising*

ERECTO (A), *erect, upright*

ERÓGENO (A), *erogenous*

EROSION, *wear and tear; erosion; disappearance*

ERÓTICO (A), *erotic*

EROTISMO, *eroticism*

ERRADICACIÓN, *eradication*

ERRADO (A), *mistaken; wide of the mark*

ERRANTE, *wandering, nomadic*

ERRATA, *misprint, printer's error; erratum*

ERRÁTICO (A), *erratic*

ERRÓNEO (A), *incorrect, wrong, erroneous, untrue, false*

ERUDICIÓN, *erudition, learning, scholarship*

ERUDITO (A), *erudite, learned, scholarly*

ERUPCIÓN, *eruption* (GEOL); *skin rash*

ESCÁNDALO, *scandal, outrage; racket, din*

ESCANDALOSO (A), *scandalous, outrageous; rowdy*

ESCÁNER, *scanner*

ESCAPATORIA, *the way out*

ESCAPE, *gas or liquid leak, exhaust; escape*

ESCAPISMO, *escapism*

ESCARLATA, *scarlet*

ESCARLATINA, *scarlet fever*

ESCARPA, *slope* (GEOL), *escarpment*

ESCARPADO (A), *steep, sheer, craggy*

ESCENA, *scene; stage*

ESCENARIO, *stage effects* (TEATRO); *setting, scene*

ESCÉNICO (A), *scenic*

ESCEPTICISMO, *skepticism*

ESCÉPTICO (A), *skeptic (n); skeptical (adj)*

ESCLEROSIS, *sclerosis*

ESCORPIÓN, *scorpion*

ESCROTO, *scrotum*

ESCRÚPULO, *scruple*

ESCRUTINIO, *scrutiny, examination; count*

ESCUADRILLA, *squadron, wing* (AERO)

ESCUADRÓN, *squad, squadron* (MIL)

ESCULTOR (A), *sculptor, sculptress*

ESCULTURA, *sculpture, carving*

ESCULTURAL, *statuesque, sculptural*

ESENCIA, *essence*

ESENCIAL, *essential*

ESFÉRICO (A), *spherical; ball* (DEP)

ESLIP ó SLIP, *slip, underpants, shorts*

ESLOGAN, *slogan*

ESMERALDA, *emerald*

ESNOB (adj), *snobbish, stuck-up; snob*

ESOTÉRICO (A), *esoteric*

ESPACIO, *space*

ESPACIOSO (A), *spacious, roomy*

ESPAGUETI (s), *spaghetti*

ESPÁRRAGO, *asparagus*

ESPASMO, *spasm*

ESPASMÓDICO (A), *spasmodic*

ESPÁSTICO (A), *spastic, fitful; irregular*

ESPECIA, *spice*

ESPECIADO, *spiced, spicy*

ESPECIAL, *special*

ESPECIALIDAD, *specialty*

ESPECIALISTA, *specialist*

ESPECIALIZADO, *specialized, skilled, trained*

ESPECIALIZACIÓN, *specialization*

ESPECIALMENTE, *especially, particularly; specially*

ESPECIFICACIÓN, *specification*

ESPECÍFICAMENTE, *specifically*

ESPECIFICO (A), *specific, definite, precise, exact*

ESPÉCIMEN, *specimen*

ESPECTACULAR, *spectacular, amazing; lavish*

ESPECTÁCULO, *show, performance, spectacle*

ESPECTADOR (A), *spectator, onlooker, viewer*

ESPECTRAL, *spectral, ghostly*

ESPECTRO, *spectrum, range*

ESPECULACIÓN, *speculation*

ESPECULADOR (A), *speculator*

ESPECULATIVO (A), *speculative*

ESPERMA, *sperm*

ESPINACA, *spinach*

ESPINAL, *spinal*

ESPIONAJE, *espionage, spying*

ESPIRAL, *spiral*

ESPÍRITU, *spirit*

ESPIRITUAL (adj), *spiritual; spiritual song*

ESPLÉNDIDO (A), *splendid, magnificent, lovely*

ESPLENDOR, *splendor, greatness, magnificence*

ESPLENDOROSO (A), *magnificent*

ESPÓNSOR, *sponsor*

ESPONTANEIDAD, *spontaneity*

ESPONTÁNEO (A), *spontaneous, instinctive, automatic*

ESPORA, *spore*

ESPORÁDICO (A), *sporadic, scattered, occasional*

ESPRAY ó SPRAY, *spray*

ESPRINT ó SPRINT, *sprint*

ESPRÍNTER ó SPRÍNTER, *sprinter*

ESPUTO, *spit, spittle; sputum* (MED)

ESTABILIDAD, *stability, firmness*

ESTABILIZACIÓN, *stabilization*

ESTABILIZADOR (A), *stabilizing, stabilizer*

ESTABLE, *stable, permanent, regular, steady*

ESTACIÓN, *station*

ESTADIO, *stadium; stage* (MED); *phase*

ESTADO, *state, condition; state* (POL)

ESTÁTICO (A), *static*

ESTATUA, *statue, figure*

ESTATUS, *status*

ESTATUTARIO, *statutory*

ESTATUTO, *statute, rules, bylaws*

ESTÉNCIL, *stencil*

ESTÉREO, *stereo*

ESTEREOTIPADO (A), *stereotyped*

ESTEREOTIPO, *stereotype*

ESTÉRIL, *sterile, barren; vain, futile*

ESTERILIDAD, *sterility; uselessness*

ESTERILIZACIÓN, *sterilization*

ESTEROIDE, *steroid*

ESTÉTICA, *esthetics*

ESTÉTICO, *esthetic*

ESTIGMA, *mark, scar, stigma; stigmata* (RELIG)

ESTILETE, *stiletto*

ESTILÍSTICO (A), *stylistic*

ESTILO, *style*

ESTILOSO, *stylish*

ESTIMA, *esteem, respect*

ESTIMACIÓN, *valuation, estimate; respect*

ESTIMADO (A), *esteemed, respected*

ESTIMATIVO (A), *approximate, rough*

ESTIMULANTE, *stimulating*

ESTÍMULO, *incentive, stimulus; encouragement*

ESTIPULACIÓN, *stipulation, condition*

ESTOICO (A), *stoical, stoic*

ESTÓMAGO, *stomach*

ESTRATAGEMA, *stratagem; trick, ruse*

ESTRATEGA, *strategist*

ESTRATEGIA, *strategy*

ESTRATÉGICO (A), *strategic*

ESTRATO, *stratum* (GEOL)

ESTRATOSFERA, *stratosphere*

ESTRÉS, *stress, tension, pressure; burden*

ESTRESADO (A), *stressed, stressed out*

ESTRESANTE, *stressful*

ESTRICTO (A), *strict, rigid, precise; tight*

ESTRIDENCIA, *stridency, raucousness*

ESTRIDENTE, *strident, shrill, raucous, noisy*

ESTRUCTURA, *structure, frame, framework*

ESTRUCTURAL, *structural*

ESTUARIO, *estuary*

ESTUCO, *stucco, plaster*

ESTUDIANTE, *student, pupil*

ESTUDIOSO (A), *studious; specialist*

ESTUPEFACCIÓN, *astonishment, amazement*

ESTUPEFACTO (A), *astonished, amazed, shocked*

ESTUPENDO (A), *wonderful, great, stupendous*

ESTUPIDEZ, *stupidity, stupid thing to do*

ESTÚPIDO (A), *stupid, idiot*

ESTUPOR, *dazed, amazed; stupor* (MED)

ÉTER, *ether*

ETÉREO, *ethereal*

ETERNAMENTE, *eternally, everlastingly*

ETERNIDAD, *eternity*

ETERNO (A), *eternal, everlasting*

ÉTICA, *ethics*

ÉTICO, *ethical*

ÉTNICO (A), *ethnic*

EUFEMISMO, *euphemism*

EUFORIA, *euphoria, elation*

EUFÓRICO (A), *exuberant, euphoric*

EUNUCO, *eunuch*

EUROPA, *Europe*

EUTANASIA, *euthanasia*

EVACUACIÓN, *evacuation; bowel movement* (MED)

EVACUADO (A), *evacuee*

EVALUACIÓN, *evaluation*

EVANGÉLICO (A), *evangelical, evangelic*

EVANGELIO, *gospel*

EVANGELISTA, *evangelist*

EVAPORACIÓN, *evaporation*

EVASIÓN, *escape, evasion*

EVASIVA, *excuse, evasive answer*

EVASIVO (A) (adj), *evasive, noncommittal*

EVENTO, *event; contingency*

EVENTUALIDAD, *eventuality, contingency*

EVIDENCIA, *evidence, proof; obviousness*

EVIDENTE, *evident, obvious, clear*

EVOCACIÓN, *evocation, invocation*

EVOLUCIÓN, *evolution, development*

EVOLUTIVO (A), *evolutionary*

EXABRUPTO, *sharp word, cutting remark; broadside*

EXACERBANTE, *irritating, provoking*

EXACTAMENTE, *exactly, precisely*

EXACTITUD, *accuracy, precision*

EXACTO (A), *exact* (DER) (MED) (MAT), *precise, correct*

EXAGERACIÓN, *exaggeration, overstatement*

EXAGERADO (A), *exaggerated, flamboyant, excessive*

EXALTACIÓN, *exaltation, elation*

EXALTADO (A), *overexcited, elated*

EXAMEN, *exam, examination*

EXAMINADOR (A), *examiner*

EXASPERACIÓN, *exasperation*

EXASPERANTE, *exasperating, infuriating*

EXCAVACIÓN, *excavation*

EXCAVADORA, *mechanical digger*

EXCEDENTE, *excess, surplus*

EXCELENCIA, *excellence*

EXCELENTE, *excellent, superb, splendid*

EXCÉNTRICO (A), *eccentric*

EXCEPCIÓN, *exception, oddity, quirk, rarity*

EXCEPCIONAL, *exceptional, special, uncommon, rare*

EXCEPCIONALMENTE, *exceptionally*

EXCEPTO, *except for, apart from, except*

EXCESIVO (A), *excessive*

EXCESO, *excess*

EXCITACIÓN, *agitation, arousal, excitation*

EXCITANTE, *exciting, arousing; stimulating* (MED)

EXCLAMACIÓN, *exclamation*

EXCLAMATIVO (A), *exclamatory*

EXCLUSIVA, *exclusive, sole rights* (COM); *monopoly*

EXCLUSIVIDAD, *exclusiveness; exclusive rights* (COM)

EXCLUSIVO (A), *exclusive, sole*

EXCREMENTO, *excrement, excretion*

EXCUSA, *excuse; apology*

EXFOLIACIÓN, *exfoliation*

EXHALACIÓN, *exhalation*

EXHAUSTIVO (A), *exhaustive, thorough, complete*

EXHAUSTO (A), *exhausted, tired, fatigued, weary*

EXHIBICIÓN, *show, display, exhibition*

EXHIBICIONISMO, *exhibitionism*

EXHIBICIONISTA, *exhibitionist*

EXHORTACIÓN, *exhortation*

EXHUMACIÓN, *exhumation*

EXIGENCIA, *demand, requirement, exigency*

EXIGENTE, *demanding, choosy, exacting*

EXILIO, *exile*

EXISTENCIA, *existence*

EXISTENCIAL, *existential*

EXISTENTE, *existing, in existence*

ÉXODO, *exodus*

EXONERACIÓN, *exoneration, vindication*

EXORBITANTE, *exorbitant, extreme, outrageous*

EXORCISTA, *exorcist*

EXÓTICO (A), *exotic, unique, extraordinary*

EXPANSIVO (A), *expansive, effusive, extensive*

EXPECTACIÓN, *expectation, excitement*

EXPECTANTE, *expectant, excited*

EXPECTATIVA, *prospect, anticipation*

EXPEDICIÓN, *expedition*

EXPEDIENTE, *dossier, record; proceedings*

EXPEDITIVO (A), *expeditious, efficient, ready, fast*

EXPENSAS, *expenses, costs*

EXPERIENCIA, *experience*

EXPERIMENTACIÓN, *experimentation*

EXPERIMENTADO (A), *experienced*

EXPERIMENTO, *experiment*

EXPERTO (A), *expert*

EXPIACIÓN, *expiation, atonement*

EXPIRACIÓN, *expiration, termination, conclusion*

EXPLICACIÓN, *explanation, description, account*

EXPLICATIVO (A), *explanatory, interpretive*

EXPLÍCITO, *explicit*

EXPLORACIÓN, *examination* (MED), *prospecting; reconnaissance* (MIL); *exploration*

EXPLORADOR (A), *explorer; scout* (MIL)

EXPLORATORIO (A), *exploratory*

EXPLOSIVO (A), *explosive*

EXPLOTACIÓN, *exploitation; running, operating, working*

EXPLOTADOR (A), *exploiter, manipulator*

EXPONENCIAL, *exponential* (MAT)

EXPONENTE, *exponent, practitioner, promoter*

EXPORTACIÓN, *export; exportation*

EXPORTADOR (A), *exporting (adj), exporter (n)*

EXPOSICIÓN, *exposure, exhibition, display; show, fair*

EXPRÉS, *express*

EXPRESAMENTE, *expressly, explicitly, specifically*

EXPRESIÓN, *expression*

EXPRESIVO (A), *expressive; tender, warm, affectionate*

EXPRESO (A), *specific, clear; express*

EXPROPIACIÓN, *expropriation*

EXQUISITO (A), *exquisite, delicious, superb, perfect*

ÉXTASIS, *ecstasy, rapture*

EXTÁTICO (A), *ecstatic, rapturous*

EXTEMPORÁNEO, *unseasonable, untimely*

EXTENDIDO, *spread out; outstretched, stretched out*

EXTENSAMENTE, *extensively, widely*

EXTENSIVO (A), *extensive, includes, encompasses*

EXTENSO (A), *extensive, long, lengthy*

EXTERMINIO, *extermination, destruction*

EXTERNO (A), *external, outside*

EXTINCIÓN, *extinction, loss, termination*

EXTINTO (A), *extinct*

EXTIRPACIÓN, *extirpation, eradication; removal* (MED)

EXTORSIÓN, *extortion; trouble, bother*

EXTRACCIÓN, *extraction, removal, uprooting*

EXTRACTO, *summary, abstract, extract*

EXTRADICIÓN, *extradition*

EXTRAFINO (A), *super fine*

EXTRALARGO (A), *king-sized*

EXTRAÑO (A), *strange, odd, weird, bizarre, curious*

EXTRAOFICIAL, *unofficial, informal*

EXTRAORDINARIO (A), *extraordinary; supplementary*

EXTRAPOLACIÓN, *extrapolation*

EXTRASENSORIAL, *extrasensory*

EXTREMADO (A), *excessive, extreme*

EXTREMO (A), *extreme; furthest, outermost*

EXTRÍNSECO (A), *extrinsic*

EXTROVERTIDO (A), *extrovert; outgoing*

EXUBERANCIA, *exuberance*

EXUBERANTE, *exuberant; lush, luxuriant, abundant*

EXULTANTE, *exultant, elated, overjoyed*

Easily Recognizable Verbs

ECLIPSAR, *to eclipse, outshine, surpass*

EDIFICAR, *to build, construct; edify*

EDITAR, *to publish, release, edit*

EDUCAR, *to educate, bring up, train*

EFECTUAR, *to make, carry out, go on, take place*

EJECUTAR, *to execute, perform, carry out*

ELABORAR, *to make, draw up, produce*

ELECTRIFICAR, *to electrify*

ELEVAR, *to raise, uplift, increase*

ELIMINAR, *to eliminate, remove, get rid of*

ELOGIAR, *to praise, eulogize*

ELUCIDAR, *to elucidate, explain*

ELUDIR, *to elude, avoid, escape*

EMANAR, *to emanate, come from*

EMANCIPAR, *to emancipate, liberate, release*

EMBARCAR, *to embark, board*

EMBELLECER, *to embellish, adorn*

EMERGER, *to emerge*

EMIGRAR, *to emigrate, move, relocate, resettle*

EMITIR, *to emit, issue*

ENCENDER, *to light, turn on, switch on*

ENCONTRAR, *to find, encounter, meet*

ENDOSAR, *to endorse*

ENFOCAR, *to focus on, look at*

ENMENDAR, *to put right, correct, reform*

ENROLAR, *to enroll, enlist, join up*

ENROLLAR, *to roll up, coil up*

ENTRAR, *to go in, come in, enter*

ENUMERAR, *to list, enumerate, specify, count*

ENUNCIAR, *to enunciate, articulate*

ENVIDIAR, *to envy, desire, covet*

ENVOLVER, *to wrap up, cover up*

EQUIPAR, *to equip, fit out*

EQUIVALER, *to be equal to, equivalent*

EROSIONAR, *to erode, wear away, destroy*

ERRADICAR, *to eradicate, root out, remove*

ESCALAR, *to climb, move up, scale, rise*

ESCAPAR, *to escape, run away*

ESCRIBIR, *to write*

ESPECIALIZAR, *to specialize*

ESPECIFICAR, *to specify, list, itemize*

ESPECULAR, *to speculate, consider; guess, gamble*

ESTANDARIZAR, *to standardize*

ESTERILIZAR, *to sterilize*

ESTIMAR, *to estimate, calculate, evaluate*

ESTUDIAR, *to study*

EVACUAR, *to evacuate, move, relocate, transfer*

EVADIR, *to evade, avoid, escape*

EVALUAR, *to evaluate, assess*

EVAPORAR, *to evaporate, vanish, disappear*

EVITAR, *to avoid, avert, prevent*

EVOCAR, *to evoke, conjure up*

EVOLUCIONAR, *to evolve, develop; progress* (MED)

EXAGERAR, *to exaggerate*

EXAMINAR, *to examine, test, study*

EXASPERAR, *to exasperate, infuriate*

EXCAVAR, *to dig, dig out, excavate*

EXCEDER, *to exceed, surpass*

EXCEPTUAR, *to except, exclude*

EXCITAR, *to excite, stimulate, inspire, motivate*

EXCLAMAR, *to exclaim, cry out*

EXCLUIR, *to exclude, reject, rule out*

EXCUSAR, *to excuse, apologize, exempt*

EXHIBIR, *to show, exhibit, screen*

EXHORTAR, *to exhort*

EXHUMAR, *to exhume, disinter*

EXILIAR, *to exile*

EXISTIR, *to exist*

EXPANDIR, *to expand, spread, extend, enlarge*

EXPENDER, *to expend, spend, consume, exhaust*

EXPIRAR, *to expire*

EXPLICAR, *to explain, expound*

EXPLORAR, *to explore, examine; reconnoiter* (MIL)

EXPLOSIONAR, *to explode, to blow up*

EXPLOTAR, *to exploit*

EXPOLIAR, *to pillage, plunder*

EXPORTAR, *to export* (COM) (INFORM)

EXPRESAR, *to express, voice*

EXPULSAR, *to expel, send off, reject*

EXTENDER, *to spread out, stretch out*

EXTERMINAR, *to exterminate, wipe out*

EXTINGUIR, *to extinguish, put out*

EXTRACTAR, *to extract, summarize*

EXTRADITAR, *to extradite*

EXUDAR, *to exude*

EXULTAR, *to exult, rejoice, celebrate*

STUDY NOTES:

F

Interchangeable Words

FACIAL

FACSÍMILE

FACTOR

FACTÓTUM

FAIR PLAY (DEP)

FAKIR ó, FAQUIR

FAMILIAR

FAN (DEP)

FANDANGO

FASHION, *trendy*

FAST FOOD

FATAL; *awful, terrible*

FAUCES (ZOOL)

FAUNA

FAVOR

FAVORABLE

FAX

FEBRIL (MED); *hectic, feverish*

FECAL

FEDERAL

FEMORAL

FÉMUR

FERRY

FERVOR (RELIG)

FESTIVAL (RELIG)

FETAL

FEUDAL

FIASCO

FIBROSIS

FIESTA

FILIAL

FILM ó FILME, *movie, film*

FINAL

FISCAL

FÍSTULA, (MED); *tube*

FLASH, *photo flash, newsflash, inspiration*

FLEXIBLE

FLIRT, *fling*

FLORA

FLORAL

FLOTILLA

FLUVIAL

FOCAL

FOIE-GRAS

FOLDER

FOLIO

FOLK, *folk music*

FOLKLORE

FÓRCEPS

FORMAL, *requirement*

FORMIDABLE

FÓRMULA

FÓRUM ó FORO

FOUL (DEP)

FOX TERRIER, *the dog*

FOXTROT

FRATERNAL ó FRATERNO

FREELANCE

FREEZER ó CONGELADOR

FRONTAL, *direct*

FRUGAL

FUEL ó FUEL-OIL

FULL CONTACT (DEP)

FUNDAMENTAL

FUNERAL, *burial*

FUNICULAR, *cable car*

FUROR

FUSIBLE; *fuse*

FUSIÓN, *uniting, merger, nuclear fusion*

FUTÓN

Easily Recognizable Nouns, Adjectives and Adverbs

FÁBRICA, *factory*

FABRICACIÓN, *production*

FABRICANTE, *manufacturer*

FÁBULA, *fable, legend, myth*

FABULOSO (A), *fabulous, incredible*

FACCIÓN, *faction* (POL); *features* (ANAT); *guerrilla band*

FACETA, *facet, aspect, characteristic, feature*

FÁCIL, *easy, simple, uncomplicated, basic*

FÁCILMENTE (adv), *easily, simply, effortlessly*

FACTIBLE, *feasible, viable, practicable, possible*

FACTORÍA, *factory*

FACTURA, *invoice, bill, receipt*

FACULTAD, *faculty; authority*

FALACIA, *fallacy, deceit, mistake, error*

FALAZ, *false, wrong, incorrect, spurious, sham*

FALIBLE, *fallible, deceitful, misleading, erroneous*

FALLA, *defect, fault; fault* (GEOL); *failing, flaw*

FALLO, *mistake, error; miss* (DEP)

FALLUTO (A), *phony, hypocritical, two-faced, unreliable*

FALSEDAD, *falseness, falsity*

FALSETE, *falsetto* (MUS)

FALSIFICACIÓN, *falsification, forgery*

FALSO (A), *false, untrue; fake, counterfeit; spurious*

FALTA, *lack, need, absence; shortcoming, fault; default*

FALTO (A), *lacking in, short of, deficiency*

FAMA, *fame, glory*

FAMILIA, family

FAMOSO (A), *famous person, celebrity*

FANÁTICO (A), *fanatic; fanatical, compulsive, rabid*

FANATISMO, *fanaticism, hysteria, frenzy*

FANFARRIA, *fanfare, flourish* (MUS); *fuss, commotion, stir*

FANTASÍA, *imagination, fantasy*

FANTASIOSO (A), *dreamy*

FANTASMA, *ghost, phantom; boaster, braggart*

FANTASMAL, *illusory, ghostly*

FANTÁSTICO (A), *fantastic, extraordinary, marvelous, spectacular, splendid, wonderful, tremendous*

FARMACÉUTICO (A), *pharmaceutical*

FARMACIA, *pharmacy*

FÁRMACO, *drug, medicine*

FARMACOLOGÍA, *pharmacology*

FARSA, *farce (TEATRO), sham*

FASCINACIÓN, *fascination*

FASCINANTE, *fascinating, intriguing, beguiling, engrossing, enthralling, spellbinding*

FASE, *phase, stage*

FATALIDAD, *misfortune, destiny, providence; doom, downfall, fate*

FATALISMO, *fatalism*

FATALISTA, *fatalistic (adj), fatalist (n); pessimist*

FATIGA, *fatigue, weariness, tiredness*

FATIGADO (A), *tired, weary, worn-out*

FATIGOSO (A), *tiring, fatiguing, exhausting; painful, difficult, labored*

FATUIDAD, *fatuousness, foolishness, conceit; immodesty*

FATUO (A), *fatuous, foolish, conceited*

FAUL, *foul* (DEP)

FAUNO, *fawn*

FAVORECIDO, *favored, beloved, preferred*

FAVORITISMO, *favoritism, bias, prejudice, partiality*

FAVORITO (A), *favorite, best-liked, most-liked*

FEBRERO, *February*

FECUNDO, *fecund, fertile, rich, productive*

FEDERACIÓN, *federation*

FELACIÓN, *fellatio*

FELINO (A), *feline; catlike; cat*

FELONÍA, *treachery, betrayal; felony*

FEMENINO (A), *feminine, female* (BOT) (ZOOL)

FÉMINA, *female, woman*

FEMINIDAD ó FEMINEIDAD, *femininity*

FEMINISMO, *feminism*

FEMINISTA, *feminist*

FÉNIX, *phoenix*

FENOMENAL, *fantastic, phenomenal*

FENÓMENO, *phenomenon; freak, genius*

FERMENTACIÓN, *fermentation*

FERMENTO, *fermenting agent, cause; ferment*

FEROCIDAD, *fierceness, ferociousness, savageness, brutality, barbarous*

FEROZ, *fierce, ferocious, cruel, savage, brutal, frenzied; intense, truculent, barbaric*

FÉRREO (A), *iron, railroad*

FERROCARRIL, *railroad system*

FERROSO (A), *ferrous*

FÉRTIL, *fertile, rich, productive, prolific, fruitful*

FERTILIDAD, *fertility*

FERTILIZACIÓN, *fertilization*

FERVIENTE ó FERVOROSO (A), *fervent, passionate*

FESTIVIDAD, *festivity; feast* (RELIG)

FESTIVO (A), *festive, cheerful, merry*

FETICHE, *fetish, obsession, mania, compulsion*

FÉTIDO (A), *fetid, stinking, foul smelling*

FETO, *fetus*

FEUDALISMO, *feudalism*

FIBRA, *fiber*

FIBROSO (A), *fibrous*

FICCIÓN, *fiction, pretense, fanciful, imaginary*

FICTICIO (A), *fictitious, imaginary, fabricated*

FIDELIDAD, *fidelity, loyalty; accuracy*

FIERO (A), *savage, ferocious, wild, feral* (ZOOL)

FIGURA, *shape, figure, form*

FIGURATIVO (A), *figurative, metaphorical*

FILAMENTO, *electric filament; thread*

FILARMÓNICO (A), *philharmonic*

FILETE, *fillet; strip, band*

FILME, *film, a film* (CINE), *movie*

FILOLOGÍA, *philology*

FILOSOFÍA, *philosophy*

FILOSÓFICO (A), *philosophical*

FILÓSOFO (A), *philosopher*

FILTRACIÓN, *filtration; leak, seepage*

FILTRO, *filter, screening*

FIN, *end, extreme limit; purpose, aim*

FINALIDAD, *aim, purpose; finality*

FINALISTA, *finalist*

FINALIZACIÓN, *termination, conclusion, completion*

FINALMENTE, *finally, in the end*

FINANCIACIÓN, *financing, funding*

FINANCIERA, *finance company*

FINANCIERO (A), *financial (adj), financier (n)*

FINITO (A), *finite, bounded, restricted, delimited*

FINO (A), *fine, thin, slim*

FINURA, *fineness, excellence; refinement, politeness*

FIORDO, *fiord*

FIRMAMENTO, *firmament*

FIRME, *firm, stable, secure, solid, compact; resolute, determined, steadfast; resolved, purposeful*

FIRMEMENTE, *securely, firmly, solidly, rigidly*

FIRMEZA, *firmness, stability, resolution, strength*

FÍSICO (A), *physical (adj); physicist (n); physique*

FISIÓN, *fission*

FISURA, *fissure, crack; fracture* (MED)

FLACIDEZ ó FLACCIDEZ, *flabbiness*

FLÁCIDO (A) ó FLÁCCIDO (A), *flaccid, flabby; loose, slack, sagging, limp, drooping*

FLAGRANTE, *flagrant, glaring, notorious, scandalous, blatant, obvious; arrant, outrageous, egregious*

FLAMA, *flame*

FLAMANTE, *brand-new; new, brilliant, fabulous*

FLANCO, *flank, side; flank* (MIL)

FLATULENCIA, *flatulence* (MED)

FLAUTA, *flute*

FLAUTÍN, *piccolo*

FLAUTISTA, *flutist*

FLEBITIS, *phlebitis*

FLEMA, *phlegm*

FLEMÁTICO (A), *phlegmatic, unruffled*

FLEXIBILIDAD, *flexibility, suppleness, pliancy, resiliency; adaptability, manageability, tractability*

FLIRTEO, *flirtation, flirting*

FLOREADO (A), *flowered, floral*

FLORECIENTE, *flourishing, thriving*

FLORECIMIENTO, *flowering, blooming; blossoming*

FLORERO, *vase*

FLORIDO (A), *florid, flowery; choice, select*

FLORISTA, *florist*

FLORISTERÍA, *flower shop*

FLOTA, *fleet*

FLOTACIÓN, *flotation* (ECON); *buoyancy*

FLOTADOR, *rubber ring, a float, life preserver*

FLUCTUACIÓN, *fluctuation*

FLUCTUANTE, *fluctuating, wavering*

FLUIDEZ, *fluency; fluidity, smoothness*

FLUIDO (A), *fluent; fluid, smooth; free flowing*

FLUORESCENTE, *fluorescent*

FOBIA, *phobia, aversion, dread, loathing*

FOCO, *focus* (MED) (MAT); *center, focal point, spotlight*

FOFO (A), *soft, spongy; flabby, limp, flaccid; drooping*

FOLIACIÓN, *foliation*

FOLÍCULO, *follicle*

FONÉTICO (A), *phonetic*

FORENSE, *forensic*

FORESTAL, *forest woodland; lumber*

FORMA, *shape, form, way*

FORMACIÓN, *formation, creation; training; group*

FORMAL, *formal, well-behaved, serious or reliable person; dependable*

FORMALIDAD, *formality, seriousness, correctness*

FORMALITO, *respectable, well-behaved*

FORMATIVO (A), *formative, educational, instructive, developmental, organizational*

FORMATO, *format* (INFORM)

FORMULACIÓN, *formulation*

FORNICACIÓN, *fornication*

FOROFO (A), *fan* (DEP), *supporter, buff*

FORTIFICACIÓN, *fortification*

FORTUITAMENTE, *fortuitously, accidentally*

FORTUITO (A), *chance, accidental; casual*

FORTUNA, *fortune, luck, destiny; prosperity, wealth*

FOSFATO, *phosphate*

FOSFORESCENCIA, *phosphorescence*

FOSFORESCENTE, *phosphorescent*

FÓSFORO, *phosphorus; match*

FÓSIL, *fossil*

FOTO, *photo, picture*

FOTOCOPIA, *photocopy, print*

FOTOCOPIADORA, *photocopier*

FOTOELÉCTRICO, *photoelectric*

FOTOGÉNICO (A), *photogenic*

FOTOGRAFÍA, *photography*

FOTOGRÁFICO (A), *photographic*

FOTÓGRAFO (A), *photographer*

FOTOMODELO, *photographic model*

FOTOSÍNTESIS, *photosynthesis*

FRACCIÓN, *fraction, division; part, fragment*

FRACCIONARIO (A), *fractional* (MAT) (POL); *incomplete*

FRACTURA, *fracture* (MED); *break, separation, division, breach, rupture; fault (GEOL)*

FRAGANCIA, *fragrance*

FRAGANTE, *fragrant, scented*

FRÁGIL, *breakable, fragile, frail; tenuous, shaky*

FRAGMENTACIÓN, *fragmentation*

FRAGMENTARIO (A), *fragmentary*

FRAGMENTO*, fragment, piece, chip, splinter, sliver, shard; extract, excerpt; remnant*

FRANCO (A), *frank, open, direct; generous, free*

FRASE*, phrase, sentence, expression*

FRATERNIDAD, *brotherhood, fraternity*

FRATERNO (A), *fraternal, brotherly*

FRATRICIDA, *fratricidal*

FRATRICIDIO, *fratricide*

FRAUDE, *fraud, deception, hoax, swindle, scam*

FRAUDULENTO (A), *fraudulent, dishonest*

FRECUENCIA (adv), *frequency, commonness*

FRECUENTE, *often, frequent; rife, common; habitual, constant, persistent, regular, recurrent, continual*

FRECUENTEMENTE, *frequently, often*

FRENESÍ, *frenzy; wildness*

FRENÉTICO (A), *furious, mad, frantic, frenzied*

FRESCO (A), *fresh, cool; clean, clear*

FRESCOR, *coolness, freshness*

FRICCIÓN, *friction, rub; massage*

FRÍGIDO (A), *frigid, frosty, frozen, wintery, cold*

FRIGIDEZ, *frigidity, sexually unresponsive; austere, unemotional, apathetic, unenthusiastic*

FRÍO (A), *cold*

FRIVOLIDAD, *frivolity, frivolousness, insouciance*

FRÍVOLO (A), *frivolous, superficial, trivial, insignificant, paltry, trumpery, nugatory; puerile, flippant*

FRONTERA, *border area; frontier*

FRONTIS, *facade; outward appearance*

FRUCTOSA, *fructose*

FRUCTUOSO (A), *fruitful*

FRUGALIDAD, *frugality*

FRUICIÓN, *delight, relish*

FRUSTRACIÓN, *frustration, disappointment, discontentment*

FRUSTRADO (A), *frustrated, failed; disappointed, discontented, forestalled, foiled; sexually unfulfilled*

FRUSTRANTE, *frustrating, disappointing, discouraging*

FRUTA, *fruit*

FRUTERÍA, *fruit shop/store*

FUGITIVO (A), *fugitive, escapee, runaway*

FULGURANTE, *bright, shining; rapid, intense*

FUMIGACIÓN, *fumigation; crop dusting/spraying*

FUNCIÓN, *function, duty, task, chore; purpose, aim*

FUNCIONAL, *functional, working, running, operational*

FUNCIONARIO (A), *civil servant, employee*

FUNDACIÓN, *foundation; founding, establishment*

FUNDADO (A), *well-founded, justified*

FUNDADAMENTE, *with good reason, on good grounds*

FUNDADOR (A), *founder, originator, developer*

FUNDAMENTO, *foundation, basis, reason, grounds*

FUNERARIA, *funeral parlor*

FUNERARIO, *funeral*

FUNGICIDA, *fungicidal (adj), fungicide (n)*

FURIA, *anger, fury, rage; cross, irate, madness; incensed, infuriated, enraged*

FURIBUNDO (A) ó FURIOSO (A), *furious, frenzied, unrestrained, savage, wild, violent*

FURTIVO (A), *furtive, poacher; secretive, clandestine; cunning, foxy, crafty, shifty*

FUSELAJE, *fuselage*

FUSIÓN, *merging, merger; joining, uniting*

FÚTBOL ó FUTBOL, *football*

FÚTIL, *futile; trivial, trifling*

FUTILIDAD, *triviality*

FUTURIBLE, *potential, possible, likely*

FUTURO (A), *intended; future*

Easily Recognizable Verbs

FABRICAR, *to make, manufacture, fabricate*

FALSEAR, *to falsify, doctor*

FALSIFICAR, *to forge, falsify*

FAMILIARIZAR, *to familiarize, acquaint*

FANTASEAR, *to fantasize, dream*

FASCINAR, *to fascinate, captivate*

FATIGAR, *to tire, weary, wear out*

FAVORECER, *to favor, prefer*

FELICITAR, *to congratulate, be glad about*

FERMENTAR, *to ferment, work up*

FERTILIZAR, *to fertilize*

FIGURAR, *to figure; appear, pose*

FILMAR, *to film*

FILTRAR, *to filter*

FINALIZAR, *to finish, complete, conclude, end*

FINANCIAR, *to finance*

FLEXIONAR, *to bend, flex, limber*

FLIRTEAR, *to flirt*

FLUCTUAR, *to fluctuate, waver, change, shift*

FLUIR, *to flow, run*

FOMENTAR, *to promote, encourage*

FORJAR, *to forge, build, invent*

FORMALIZAR, *to formalize, put in order*

FORMAR, *to form, train, educate, make*

FORMULAR, *to formulate, get an opinion, draw up, express, make*

FORNICAR, *to fornicate*

FORZAR, *to force, compel, coerce*

FOTOCOPIAR, *to photocopy*

FOTOGRAFIAR, *to photograph*

FRACCIONAR, *to divide, break up, split up*

FRACTURAR, *to fracture, break, force*

FRAGMENTAR, *to fragment, divide*

FRECUENTAR, *to frequent, haunt, hang out*

FRICCIONAR, *to rub, massage*

FRUSTRAR, *to frustrate, thwart*

FUMAR, *to smoke*

FUNCIONAR, *to work, function*

FUNDAMENTAR, *to base, lay a foundation* (CONSTR)

FUNDAR, *to found, set up, establish*

FUSIONAR, *to merge* (ECON), *fuse*

STUDY NOTES:

G

Interchangeable Words

GAG, *to silence*

GAMMA

GÁNGSTER

GARAGE ó GARAJE

GARDENIA

GARROTE ó GAROTTE

GAS, *as carbonated or natural gas*

GASTRITIS

GASTROENTERITIS

GASTROINTESTINAL

GAY, *homosexual*

GAZPACHO

GEISHA, *geisha girl*

GEL

GENE ó GEN, *gene*

GENERAL, *overall, widespread, universal; general* (MIL)

GÉNESIS

GENIAL

GENITAL (ES), *genital, genitals*

GEYSER

GHETTO ó GUETO

GIGABYTE

GIGOLÓ

GINGIVITIS

GINSENG

GIN-TONIC, *gin and tonic*

GLACIAL

GLAMOR ó GLAMOUR

GLANDULAR

GLAUCOMA

GLOBAL, *overall, total*

GLOBULAR

GLUTEN

GO GO, *dancer*

GOLF

GÓNDOLA

GONG ó GONGO

GÓSPEL, *gospel music*

GOURMET ó GURMET

GRADUAL

GRANULAR; *also the verb to granulate*

GRATIS, *free*

GRAVE, *serious, heavy*

GRILL, *grillroom, grill*

GRIPE, *flu*

GROGGY ó GROGUI, *slang for shocked, in a state of shock*

GUACAMOLE

GUANO

GUARDIÁN; *security guard*

GUERRILLA, *as a group, warfare*

GURÚ

Easily Recognizable Nouns, Adjectives and Adverbs

GALA, *ceremony, show, event; elegance*

GALÁCTICO (A), *galactic*

GALANTE, *gallant (only to describe men)*

GALAXIA, *galaxy*

GALEÓN, *galleon*

GALERÍA, *gallery, department store, mall*

GALÓN, *gallon*

GAMBITO, *gambit, strategy, ploy, device*

GANGLIO, *ganglion, gland*

GANGRENA, *gangrene*

GARAJE, *garage, a parking space*

GARANTE, *guarantor (n); responsible (adj)*

GARANTÍA, *guarantee, warranty*

GARRAFA, *carafe; demijohn*

GASEODUCTO, *gas pipeline*

GASEOSO (A), *gaseous; carbonated*

GASOIL, *diesel oil*

GASOLINA, *gasoline*

GASOLINERA, *gas station*

GASTADO (A), *worn, old, stale, hackneyed*

GÁSTRICO (A), *gastric*

GASTRONOMÍA, *gastronomy*

GASTRONÓMICO (A), *gastronomic*

GASTRÓNOMO (A), *gourmet, gastronome*

GÉISER, *geyser*

GELATINA, *gelatin (e)*

GEMA, *gem, jewel*

GEN, *gene*

GENEALOGÍA, *genealogy*

GENEALÓGICO (A), *genealogical*

GENERACIÓN, *generation; descendant*

GENERALIZACIÓN, *generalization*

GENERALIZADO (A), *widespread*

GENERALMENTE, *generally, widely*

GENERADOR (A), *generator*

GENÉRICO (A), *generic*

GÉNERO, *genus; sort, kind, type*

GENEROSIDAD, *generosity*

GENEROSO (A), *generous, unstinting, bountiful*

GENÉTICO (A), *genetic (adj); geneticist (n)*

GENIO, *temper, mood; genius; genie*

GENOCIDIO, *genocide*

GENOMA, *genome*

GENTIL, *kind, nice, dashing, helpful; also means Gentile*

GENTILEZA, *courtesy, kindness, elegance*

GENUFLEXIÓN, *genuflection*

GENUINO (A), *genuine, authentic, real, legitimate*

GEOFÍSICA, *geophysics*

GEOFÍSICO, *geophysical*

GEOGRAFÍA, *geography*

GEOGRÁFICO (A), *geographical*

GEÓGRAFO (A), *geographer*

GEOLOGÍA, *geology*

GEOLÓGICO (A), *geological*

GEÓLOGO (A), *geologist*

GEOMETRÍA, *geometry*

GEOMÉTRICO (A), *geometric*

GEOPOLÍTICO (A), *geopolitical*

GERANIO, *geranium*

GERIÁTRICO (A), *geriatric*

GERMEN, *germ; source*

GERMICIDA, *germicide (n); germicidal (adj)*

GERMINACIÓN, *germination*

GERUNDIO, *gerund*

GESTA, *exploit, feat, heroic deed*

GESTACIÓN, *gestation*

GESTICULACIÓN, *gesticulation, signal, sign*

GESTUAL, *gestural, body language*

GIGANTE, *giant, gigantic; person of exceptional ability, courage, integrity*

GIGANTESCO (A), *gigantic, towering, immense huge, massive, enormous*

GIMNASIA, *gymnastics*

GIMNASIO, *gymnasium, gym*

GIMNASTA, *gymnast*

GIMNÁSTICO, *gymnastic*

GLACIAR, *glacier*

GLADIADOR, *gladiator*

GLADIOLO, *gladiolus*

GLAMOROSO (A), *glamorous, elegance, allure, charm*

GLOBALIZACIÓN, *globalization*

GLOBO, *globe, earth, sphere; balloon*

GLÓBULO (A), *corpuscle* (MED)

GLORIA, *glory, delight*

GLORIFICACIÓN, *glorification*

GLORIOSO (A), *glorious*

GLOSA, *marginal note, explanation; gloss*

GLOSARIO, *glossary*

GLOTIS, *glottis*

GLOTONERÍA, *gluttony, greed, greediness*

GLUCOSA, *glucose*

GNOMO, *gnome*

GOBERNABILIDAD, *governability*

GOBERNABLE, *governable; navigable*

GOBERNACIÓN, *governing, government*

GOL, *goal*

GOLERO (A), *goalkeeper*

GOLFISTA, *golfer*

GOLFO, *gulf*

GÓNADA, *gonad*

GONDOLERO (A), *gondolier*

GONORREA, *gonorrhea*

GORILA, *gorilla or bodyguard, bouncer, thug*

GRÁCIL, *graceful, delicate*

GRACILIDAD, *gracefulness*

GRADACIÓN, *gradation*

GRADIENTE, *gradient*

GRADO, *degree*

GRADUACIÓN, *adjustment; proof grading; graduation*

GRADUALMENTE, *gradually*

GRADUADO (A), *graduated; graduate*

GRAFÍA, *written symbol; spelling*

GRÁFICA, *graph, chart*

GRÁFICAMENTE, *graphically*

GRÁFICO (A), *written, illustrated, graphic; graphite*

GRAFITI, *graffiti*

GRAFITO, *graphite, black lead*

GRAMÁTICA, *grammar*

GRAMATICAL, *grammatical (adj)*

GRAMÁTICO (A), *grammatical (adj), grammarian (n)*

GRAMO, *gram*

GRANADO, *choice, select; cream of society; a pomegranate tree*

GRANDE, *big, large, tall*

GRANDILOCUENCIA, *grandiloquence*

GRANDILOCUENTE, *grandiloquent*

GRANDIOSIDAD, *grandeur, impressiveness*

GRANDIOSO (A), *splendid, impressive, grandiose*

GRANERO, *granary; barn*

GRANITO, *granite*

GRANO, *grain; bean, seed*

GRATIFICACIÓN, *recompense, reward*

GRATIFICANTE, *gratifying, rewarding, satisfying*

GRATIS, *free, for nothing*

GRATITUD, *gratitude, appreciation, thanksgiving*

GRAVAMEN, *burden; tax, duty*

GRAVEDAD, *seriousness, gravity; magnitude, urgency*

GRAVEMENTE, *seriously, gravely*

GRAVILLA, *gravel*

GRAVOSO (A), *costly, burdensome, stressful, oppressive*

GRAVITACIÓN, *gravitation*

GREGARIO (A), *gregarious, sociable*

GROSERO, *coarse, rude, vulgar; gross, disgusting*

GROTESCO (A), *grotesque, deformed, unnatural, monstrous, repulsive; ludicrous, bizarre*

GRUPO, *group*

GUARDA, *keeper, security guard*

GUARDIA, *police; guardsman* (MIL); *national guard; guard/sentry duty; bodyguard*

GUERRILLERO (A), *guerrilla*

GUETO, *ghetto*

GUILLOTINA, *guillotine; paper cutter*

GUITARRA, *guitar*

GUITARRISTA, *guitarist*

GUTURAL, *guttural, throaty; gruff*

Easily Recognizable Verbs

GALOPAR, *to gallop*

GALVANIZAR, *to galvanize, rouse; to coat* (QUIM)

GARANTIZAR, *to guarantee, vouch for*

GENERALIZAR, *to generalize; spread, widen*

GENERAR, *to generate, create, cause, evolve*

GERMINAR, *to germinate, originate, develop*

GESTICULAR, *to gesticulate, grimace*

GLORIFICAR, *to glorify, exalt, enhance, dignify*

GLOSAR, *to gloss, annotate, explain*

GOBERNAR, *to govern, manage, handle, run*

GRADUAR, *to adjust, regulate, calibrate*

GRAVITAR, *to gravitate to, lean towards*

GUARDAR, *to put away, guard, keep*

GUSTAR, *to like, enjoy*

STUDY NOTES:

H

Interchangeable Words

HÁBEAS CORPUS

HÁBITAT

HABITUAL, *regular*

HACIENDA

HACKER, *computer hacker*

HALIBUT

HALITOSIS

HALL, *entrance hall, foyer*

HALO, *for stars, saints, angels*

HÁMSTER

HANDICAP(s), *golf, horse racing*

HANGAR, *airport*

HARDWARE, (INFORM)

HARAKIRI ó HARAQUIRI

HAREM ó HARÉM

HEMATOMA

HEPATITIS

HEPTAGONAL

HERCULES, *very strong man*

HERNIA

HERPES (MED)

HETEROSEXUAL

HEXAGONAL

HI-FI

HIPPY ó HIPPIE

HIT(s), *a blow, a success*

HOBBY

HOCKEY

HOMO, *gay*

HOMOSEXUAL

HONOR, *privilege*

HONORABLE

HORIZONTAL

HORMONAL, *hormone*

HORRIBLE

HORROR

HOSPITAL

HOTEL

HUMOR, *mood, temperament*

HUMUS

Easily Recognizable Nouns, Adjectives and Adverbs

HABITABLE, *inhabitable*

HABITADO, *inhabited, manned*

HABITANTE, *inhabitant*

HABITO, *habit; religious clothing* (RELIG)

HACHÍS, *hashish, hash*

HALCÓN, *falcon*

HAMACA, *hammock, swing*

HAMBURGUESA, *hamburger*

HANDLING, *baggage handling*

HARÉN, *harem*

HASTIÓ, *weariness, boredom; disgust*

HEDONISMO, *hedonism*

HEDONISTA, *hedonistic, hedonist*

HEGEMONÍA, *dominance, hegemony*

HEGEMÓNICO (A), *dominant*

HELICÓPTERO, *helicopter*

HELIO, *helium*

HELIPUERTO, *heliport*

HEMATOLOGÍA, *hematology*

HEMICICLO, *semicircle; semicircular theater*

HEMISFÉRICO (A), *hemispherical*

HEMISFERIO, *hemisphere*

HEMOFILIA, *hemophilia*

HEMOFÍLICO (A), *hemophiliac*

HEMOGLOBINA, *hemoglobin*

HEMORRAGIA, *hemorrhage* (MED)

HEMORROIDES, *hemorrhoids*

HEPTÁGONO, *heptagon*

HERÁLDICO (A), *heraldic*

HERALDO, *herald*

HERBARIO (A), *herbal*

HERBICIDA, *herbicide*

HERBÍVORO (A), *herbivore*

HERCÚLEO (A), *Herculean, incredibly strong*

HERÉTICO (A), *heretical*

HERMÉTICO (A), *airtight, hermetic, watertight*

HÉROE, *hero*

HEROICO (A), *heroic*

HEROÍNA, *heroine*

HETERODOXIA, *unorthodox nature, heterodoxy*

HEXÁGONO, *hexagon*

HIATO, *hiatus, interval, break, interruption*

HIBERNACIÓN, *hibernation*

HIBERNAL, *winter*

HIBISCO, *hibiscus*

HÍBRIDO (A), *hybrid*

HIDRANTE, *hydrant*

HIDRATANTE (adj), *moisturizing*

HIDRÁULICO (A), *hydraulic*

HIDROCARBURO, *hydrocarbon*

HIDROELÉCTRICA, *hydroelectric power station*

HIDROELÉCTRICO, *hydroelectric*

HIDRÓFILO (A), *absorbent; absorbent cotton*

HIDROFOBIA, *hydrophobia; rabies*

HIDROFOIL, *hydrofoil*

HIDRÓGENO, *hydrogen*

HIDROPLANO, *seaplane*

HIDROSOLUBLE, *water-soluble*

HIDROSTÁTICO (A), *hydrostatic*

HIENA, *hyena*

HIERBA, *grass; herb*

HIGIENE, *hygiene*

HIGIÉNICO (A), *hygienic, sanitary, clean*

HILARANTE, *hilarious, uproarious, hysterical*

HILARIDAD, *hilarity, exuberance, jubilation, glee*

HIMEN, *hymen*

HIMNO, *hymn*

HIPERACTIVO (A), *hyperactive*

HIPÉRBOLA, *hyperbola* (MAT)

HIPÉRBOLE, *hyperbole*

HIPERSENSIBLE, *hypersensitive*

HIPERTENSIÓN, *hypertension*

HIPERTENSO (A), *having high blood pressure*

HIPNOSIS, *hypnosis*

HIPNÓTICO (A), *hypnotic; a sedative* (MED)

HIPNOTISMO, *hypnotism*

HIPOCENTRO, *focus, hypocenter*

HIPOCONDRÍA, *hypochondria*

HIPOCRESÍA, *hypocrisy, deceit, duplicity, insincerity*

HIPÓCRITA, *hypocrite (n), hypocritical (adj)*

HIPÓDROMO, *race course, racetrack*

HIPOPÓTAMO, *hippopotamus*

HIPOTERMIA, *hypothermia*

HIPÓTESIS, *hypothesis*

HIPOTÉTICO (A), *hypothetical*

HIRSUTO, *hirsute, hairy; surly, brusque*

HISTAMÍNICO (A), *histamine*

HISTERIA, *hysteria*

HISTÉRICO (A), *hysterical, frantic; irrational; hilarious, uproarious*

HISTORIA, *history; story, excuse*

HISTORIADOR (A), *historian*

HISTORIAL, *historical record, personal record*

HISTÓRICO (A), *historical; historic*

HISTORIETA, *cartoon, anecdote, comic strip*

HOLOCAUSTO, *the Holocaust, holocaust*

HOLOGRAMA, *hologram*

HOMÉRICO (A), *Homeric*

HOMICIDA, *homicidal*

HOMICIDIO, *murder, homicide*

HOMILÍA, *homily, sermon*

HOMÍNIDO, *hominid*

HOMOFOBIA, *homophobia*

HOMOGÉNEO (A), *homogeneous, uniform*

HONDO, *deep; profound; insightful, extreme*

HONDURA, *depth; profundity; deeply felt*

HONESTIDAD ú HONRADEZ, *honesty, modesty, decency, fairness; honor*

HONESTO (A), *honest, modest, decent*

HONORABILIDAD, *honor*

HONORARIO (A), *honorary*

HONORÍFICO (A), *honorable, honorific*

HONRA, *pride, toast of, proud of*

HONRADEZ, *honesty, integrity*

HONRADO (A), *honest, upright, honorable*

HORDA, *horde*

HORIZONTE, *horizon*

HORMONA, *hormone*

HORÓSCOPO, *horoscope*

HORRENDO (A), *horrendous, awful, hideous, terrible, horrific, ghastly, shocking, appalling*

HORROROSO (A), *awful, dreadful, nasty, unpleasant*

HOSPITALIDAD, *hospitality*

HOSTAL, *guest house, boarding house, cheap hotel*

HOSTEL, *youth residence*

HOSTIA, *consecrated host*

HOSTERÍA, *country hotel, inn*

HOSTIL, *hostile, contrary, adverse, opposing; combative, warring, inhospitable, unfriendly, averse*

HUMANIDAD, *humanity, mankind*

HUMANAMENTE, *humanely*

HUMANO (A), *human, humane*

HUMEDAD, *humidity, moisture, dampness*

HÚMEDO (A), *humid, damp, wet*

HUMILDAD, *humility, meekness*

HUMILDE, *humble, modest, meek, self-effacing, deferential; lowly, inferior, mean, low-born*

HUMILLACIÓN, *humiliation, disgrace, shame, dishonor, embarrassment*

HUMILLADO (A), *humiliated, embarrassed, shamed*

HUMILLANTE, *humiliating, humbling*

HUMORISTA, *comic, humorist; cartoonist*

HURACÁN, *hurricane*

HURACANADO (A), *violent, tempestuous, intense, fierce, raging; wild, brutal, severe, extreme, harsh, forceful*

HURAÑO (A), *unsociable, introverted, unfriendly*

HURRA, *hooray*

HURTO, *stealing, shoplifting*

Easily Recognizable Verbs

HABITAR, *to live in, inhabit, occupy*

HABITUAR, *to become accustomed to, get use to*

HIBERNAR, *to hibernate*

HIPNOTIZAR, *to hypnotize, mesmerize*

HOMOGENEIZAR, *to homogenize, standardize, equalize*

HONRAR, *to be honored*

HORRORIZAR, *to horrify, terrify*

HOSTIGAR, *to harass, pester, bother, plague*

HUMANIZAR, *to humanize*

HUMIDIFICAR, *to humidify*

HUMILLAR, *to humiliate, humble*

STUDY NOTES:

I

Interchangeable Words

IBIDEM ó IBIDEM

ICEBERG

IDEA

IDEAL

IGUANA

IMAGINABLE, *conceivable*

IMITABLE

IMPALPABLE

IMPASSE ó IMPASE

IMPENETRABLE

IMPERCEPTIBLE

IMPERIAL

IMPERMEABLE

IMPERSONAL

IMPERTURBABLE

IMPLACABLE

IMPONDERABLE

IMPOSTOR (A); *also means fraudulent*

IMPRACTICABLE; *impassable*

IMPRECISIÓN

IMPROBABLE

IMPUTABLE

IN SITU

IN VITRO

INALIENABLE

INALTERABLE

INAUDIBLE

INAUGURAL

INCALCULABLE

INCIDENTAL

INCISIÓN

INCLUSIÓN

INCLUSIVE

INCÓGNITO (A); *unknown*

INCOMBUSTIBLE

INCOMPARABLE

INCOMPATIBLE

INCONSOLABLE

INCONTESTABLE

INCORRUPTIBLE

INCURABLE

INCURSIÓN

INDECISIÓN

INDESTRUCTIBLE

INDIGESTIÓN

ÍNDIGO

INDISPENSABLE

INDIVIDUAL; *single*

INDIVISIBLE

INDUSTRIAL

INELUCTABLE

INESTIMABLE

INEVITABLE

INEXCUSABLE

INEXORABLE
INEXPLICABLE
INEXTRICABLE
INFERIOR
INFERNAL
INFINITESIMAL
INFLEXIBLE
INFLEXIÓN
INFLUENZA
INFORMAL; *unreliable*
INFUSIÓN
INGESTIÓN
INGUINAL
INIMITABLE
INNUMERABLE
INPUT
INQUISITORIAL
INSENSIBLE
INSEPARABLE
INSIGNIA, *badge, decoration, flag*
INSOLUBLE
INSPECTOR (A)
INSTRUCTOR (A)
INSTRUMENTAL
INSULAR
INSUPERABLE
INTANGIBLE
INTEGRAL; *whole-grain*
INTERIOR
INTERLOCUTOR (A)
INTERMINABLE
INTERNET
INTERPERSONAL
INTESTINAL
INTOLERABLE
INTRUSIÓN
INVARIABLE
INVASIÓN
INVENTOR (A)
INVERSIÓN, *reversal; investment*
INVIOLABLE
INVISIBLE
INVULNERABLE
ION
IRASCIBLE
IRIS (ANAT)
IRREFUTABLE
IRREGULAR
IRREMEDIABLE
IRREPARABLE
IRRESISTIBLE
IRREVERSIBLE
IRREVOCABLE
IRRITABLE
ISÓSCELES
ITEM

ÍCONO, *icon*

ICONOCLASTA, *iconoclastic (adj), iconoclast (n)*

IDEALISMO, *idealism*

IDEALISTA, *idealistic, idealist*

ÍDEM, *ditto*

IDEARIO, *ideology*

IDÉNTICO (A), *identical, duplicate, twin, same, matching, interchangeable*

IDENTIDAD, *identity*

IDENTIFICABLE, *identifiable*

IDENTIFICACIÓN, *identification, computer password*

IDEOGRAMA, *ideogram*

IDEOLOGÍA, *ideology*

IDEÓLOGO (A), *ideologist*

IDÍLICO (A), *idyllic, peaceful, blissful, pastoral*

IDIOMÁTICO (A), *idiomatic*

IDIOSINCRASIA, *idiosyncrasy*

IDIOTA, *idiotic; stupid*

IDIOTEZ, *stupid thing, stupidity, idiocy*

IDÓLATRA, *idolatress (f), idolater (m); idolatrous*

ÍDOLO, *idol*

IGLÚ, *igloo*

IGNICIÓN, *ignition*

IGNOMINIA, *ignominy, disgrace, dishonor*

IGNOMINIOSO (A), *ignominious, disgraceful*

IGNORADO (A), (LITER) *unknown, obscure*

IGNORANCIA, *ignorance, unawareness, inexperience*

IGNORANTE, *ignorant, ignoramus, unaware, uneducated, uninformed*

IGNOTO (A), *undiscovered, unknown*

IGUAL, *the same (as), similar to; identical*

IGUALADA, *tie, draw; even score*

IGUALADO (A), *level, evenly matched*

IGUALDAD, *equality, equal rights*

IGUALITARIO (A), *egalitarian*

IGUALITARISMO, *egalitarianism*

IGUALMENTE, *also, likewise; equally*

ILEGAL, *illegal, unlawful*

ILEGALIDAD, *unlawful act, illegality*

ILEGALMENTE, *illegally*

ILEGIBLE, *illegible, unreadable, scrawled, scribbled*

ILEGITIMIDAD, *illegitimacy*

ILEGÍTIMO (A), *illegitimate, illegal*

ILETRADO (A), *illiterate, uncultured, uneducated*

ILÍCITO (A), *illicit, illegal, forbidden, unlawful; secret, furtive, clandestine*

ILIMITADO (A), *unlimited, limitless*

ILOCALIZABLE, *cannot be found/ located*

ILÓGICO (A), *illogical, unreasonable, absurd*

ILUMINACIÓN, *lighting, illumination*

ILUMINADO (A), *enlightened, illuminated, lit*

ILUSIÓN, *excitement, hope, illusion*

ILUSIONANTE, *exciting*

ILUSIONISTA, *illusionist*

ILUSO (A), *gullible, unwary, unsuspecting, innocent, unsophisticated, credulous*

ILUSORIO (A), *illusory; empty*

ILUSTRACIÓN, *illustration, instance, example; sample*

ILUSTRADO (A), *illustrated, explained, depicted; erudite*

ILUSTRADOR (A), *illustrator*

ILUSTRATIVO (A), *illustrative*

ILUSTRE, *illustrious, distinguished, famous*

IMAGEN, *image, TV picture*

IMAGINACIÓN, *imagination*

IMAGINARIO (A), *imaginary*

IMAGINATIVO (A), *imaginative*

IMBATIBLE, *unbeatable*

IMBEBIBLE, *undrinkable*

IMBÉCIL, *imbecile*

IMBECILIDAD, *imbecility* (MED)

IMITACIÓN, *imitation, copy, counterfeit, fake, reproduction, forgery, alteration*

IMITADOR (A), *imitator, impersonator; follower*

IMITATIVO (A), *imitative, simulation, parody, replica, facsimile, caricature, duplicate*

IMPACIENCIA, *impatience, abrupt, testy, curt, short; irritable, grumpy, crabby, touchy*

IMPACIENTE, *impatient, restless, eager, intolerant*

IMPACIENTEMENTE, *impatiently*

IMPACTO, *impact, collision, crash, smash; meaning, bearing, effect, import*

IMPARABLE, *unstoppable; inexorable, implacable*

IMPARCIAL, *impartial, fair, equitable, unbiased, evenhanded, disinterested*

IMPARCIALIDAD, *impartiality*

IMPASIBILIDAD, *impassivity, impassiveness*

IMPASIBLE, *impassive, serene, stolid, unemotional*

IMPECABLE, *impeccable, faultless*

IMPECABLEMENTE, *impeccably*

IMPEDIDO (A), *disabled; disabled person*

IMPEDIMENTO, *obstacle, impediment, hindrance*

IMPENETRABILIDAD, *impenetrability*

IMPENITENTE, *impenitent, unrepentant*

IMPENSABLE, *unthinkable*

IMPENSADO (A), *unexpected, unforeseen*

IMPERATIVO (A), *imperative, commanding*

IMPERDONABLE, *unforgivable, inexcusable*

IMPERFECCIÓN, *imperfection, flaw, fault*

IMPERFECTO (A), *imperfect, flawed, defective*

IMPERIALISMO, *imperialism*

IMPERIALISTA, *imperialist*

IMPERIO, *empire*

IMPERIOSO (A), *imperious; pressing, urgent*

IMPERMEABILIDAD, *impermeability*

IMPERTINENCIA, *impertinence*

IMPERTINENTE, *impertinent, impudent*

ÍMPETU, *force, impetus, vehemence*

IMPETUOSIDAD, *impetuosity, rashness*

IMPETUOSO (A), *violent, impulsive, impetuous, rash*

IMPLANTE, *implant*

IMPLEMENTO, *implement, tool*

IMPLICACIÓN, *involvement, implication*

IMPLÍCITAMENTE, *implicitly*

IMPLÍCITO (A), *implicit, implied*

IMPOLUTO (A), *unpolluted, pure, unblemished*

IMPONENCIA, *impressiveness*

IMPONENTE, *imposing, impressive, stunning*

IMPOPULAR, *unpopular*

IMPOPULARIDAD, *unpopularity*

IMPORTACIÓN, *importation, import*

IMPORTANCIA, *importance*

IMPORTANTE, *important, significant, major*

IMPOSIBILIDAD, *impossibility*

IMPOSIBILITADO (A), *disabled, impeded, prevented*

IMPOSIBLE, *impossible*

IMPOSICIÓN, *imposition, taxation*

IMPOTENCIA, *impotence, incapacity*

IMPOTENTE, *impotent, powerless, helpless*

IMPRECACIÓN, *curse, imprecation*

IMPRECISO (A), *imprecise, vague*

IMPRECISIÓN, *vagueness*

IMPREDECIBLE, *unpredictable, unforeseeable*

IMPREMEDITADO (A), *unpremeditated, inadvertent*

IMPRESCINDIBLE, *indispensable, essential*

IMPRESENTABLE, *not presentable, disgraceful*

IMPRESIÓN, *impression, imprint*

IMPRESIONABLE, *impressionable*

IMPRESIONANTE, *impressive, striking*

IMPREVISIBLE, *unforeseeable, unpredictable*

IMPREVISIÓN, *careless, thoughtless, imprudent, indiscreet, inconsiderate*

IMPREVISTO (A), *unexpected, unforeseen*

IMPROBABILIDAD, *improbability, unlikelihood*

IMPRODUCTIVO (A), *unproductive, unprofitable*

IMPRONUNCIABLE, *unpronounceable*

IMPROPERIO, *insult, offense*

IMPROPIEDAD, *impropriety, unsuitability*

IMPROPIO (A), *improper, unfitting, inappropriate*

IMPROVISACIÓN, *improvisation*

IMPROVISADO (A), *improvised, makeshift*

IMPROVISO (A), *unexpectedly, suddenly*

IMPRUDENCIA, *imprudence, carelessness, indiscretion, rashness, inattentiveness*

IMPRUDENTE, *careless, rash, imprudent*

IMPUGNABLE, *contestable*

IMPUGNACIÓN, *challenge, contest*

IMPULSIVO (A), *impulsive, hothead*

IMPULSO, *stimulus, momentum, boost, impulse*

IMPULSOR (A), *driving force (adj), catalyst*

IMPUNE, *unpunished*

IMPUNEMENTE, *with impunity (adv)*

IMPUNIDAD, *impunity*

IMPUNTUAL, *unpunctual*

IMPUNTUALIDAD, *unpunctuality*

IMPUREZA, *impurity*

IMPURO (A), *impure*

IMPUTACIÓN, *accusation, imputation*

INACCESIBLE, *inaccessible, prohibitive; aloof*

INACEPTABLE, *unacceptable*

INACTIVIDAD, *inactivity, unemployment*

INACTIVO (A), *inactive, dormant, jobless*

INADAPTACIÓN, *maladjustment (socially)*

INADAPTADO (A), *maladjusted (adj), misfit (n)*

INADECUADO (A), *inadequate*

INADMISIBLE, *inadmissible, unacceptable*

INADVERTIDO (A), *unnoticed, unobserved; inattentive*

INALTERADO (A), *unchanged*

INAMOVIBLE, *immovable, fixed*

INANIMADO (A), *inanimate*

INAPELABLE, *not appealable, final*

INAPLICABLE, *inapplicable*

INAPRECIABLE, *imperceptible, indiscernible*

INAPTITUD, *unsuitability*

INATENCIÓN, *inattention*

INAUDITO (A), *unprecedented, unheard of*

INAUGURACIÓN, *inauguration, opening, unveiling*

INCANDESCENTE, *incandescent*

INCAPACIDAD, *inability, incompetence, incapacity*

INCAPACITADO (A), *disqualified* (DER), *incapacitated*

INCAPAZ, *incapable; incompetent*

INCENDIARIO (A), *incendiary, inflammatory*

INCENDIO, *fire*

INCENTIVO (A), *incentive, motivation, inducement*

INCESANTE, *incessant, unceasing, continual*

INCESTO, *incest*

INCIDENCIA, *incidence* (MAT); *impact, repercussion*

INCIDENTE, *incident, episode, happening*

INCIERTO (A), *doubtful, uncertain*

INCINERACIÓN, *incineration, cremation*

INCINERADORA, *garbage incinerator*

INCINERADOR, *crematorium*

INCIPIENTE, *incipient, early*

INCISIVO (A), *sharp, cutting, incisive*

INCÍVICO (A), *antisocial*

INCLASIFICABLE, *unclassifiable*

INCLEMENCIA, *harshness, inclemency*

INCLEMENTE, *harsh, inclement weather*

INCLINACIÓN, *slant, inclination, slope; propensity, fondness, preference*

INCLINADO (A), *inclined, sloping; inclined to do sthg*

INCIVILIZADO (A), *uncivilized*

INCLUIDO (A), *included*

INCLUSO (A) (adj), *enclosed, included*

INCLUSO (adv), *inclusively, including*

INCÓGNITA, *unknown quantity* (MAT); *enigma*

INCÓGNITO (A), *unknown*

INCOHERENCIA, *incoherence*

INCOHERENTE, *incoherent*; *inconsistent, disconnected*

INCOLORO (A), *colorless*

INCOMIBLE, *inedible*

INCÓMODO (A), *inconvenient place, uncomfortable*

INCOMPATIBILIDAD, *incompatibility*

INCOMPETENCIA, *incompetence*

INCOMPETENTE, *incompetent*

INCOMPLETO (A), *incomplete*

INCOMPRENDIDO (A), *misunderstood*

INCOMPRENSIBLE, *incomprehensible*

INCOMPRENSIÓN, *incomprehension*

INCOMUNICADO (A), *isolated, cut off, incommunicado*

INCONCEBIBLE, *inconceivable, unthinkable*

INCONCILIABLE, *irreconcilable*

INCONCLUSO (A), *unfinished*

INCONCRETO (A), *imprecise, inexact, inaccurate*

INCONDICIONAL, *unconditional, complete*

INCONEXO (A), *unconnected, disjointed, unrelated*

INCONFESABLE, *shameful, disgraceful*

INCONFORMISTA, *nonconformist*

INCONGRUENCIA, *incongruity, contradiction*

INCONGRUENTE, *incongruous, inconsistent*

INCONMENSURABLE, *immeasurable, vast*

INCONSCIENCIA, *unconsciousness, thoughtlessness*

INCONSCIENTE, *unconscious, thoughtless*

INCONSECUENCIA, *inconsistency*

INCONSECUENTE, *inconsistent*

INCONSIDERADO (A), *inconsiderate, thoughtless*

INCONSISTENCIA, *flimsiness, weakness*

INCONSISTENTE, *flimsy, weak, uneven*

INCONSTANCIA, *unreliability, changeability*

INCONSTANTE, *unreliable, weak, flimsy, changeable*

INCONSTITUCIONAL, *unconstitutional*

INCONSTITUCIONALIDAD, *unconstitutionality*

INCONTABLE, *countless, innumerable*

INCONTENIBLE, *uncontainable, unstoppable*

INCONTINENCIA, *incontinence* (MED)

INCONTINENTE, *incontinent*

INCONTROLABLE, *uncontrollable*

INCONVENIENCIA, *inappropriateness*

INCONVENIENTE, *inappropriate; problem; disadvantage*

INCORPORACIÓN, *incorporation (into), induction*

INCORPORADO (A), *built-in* (TECNOL*)*

INCORPÓREO, *incorporeal*

INCORRECCIÓN, *incorrectness, inaccuracy*

INCORRECTO (A), *incorrect*, *wrong; discourteous*

INCORREGIBLE, *incorrigible; evil, immoral*

INCORRUPTO (A), *uncorrupted, incorrupt*

INCREDULIDAD, *incredulity*

INCRÉDULO (A), *skeptical, incredulous*

INCREÍBLE, *incredible, unconvincing, unbelievable*

INCREÍBLEMENTE, *incredibly*

INCREMENTO, *increase, increment*

INCRIMINACIÓN, *accusation, incrimination*

INCRUSTACIÓN, *incrustation* (MED); *inlay work*

INCUBACIÓN, *incubation*

INCUESTIONABLE, *irrefutable, unquestionable, indisputable*

INCULTO (A), *uneducated; uncultivated* (AGRIC)

INDECENCIA, *indecency, obscenity; indecent*

INDECENTE, *indecent, shameless, obscene*

INDECIBLE*, indescribable, unspeakable*

INDECISO (A), *indecisive, undecided, irresolute*

INDECOROSO (A), *indecorous, unseemly*

INDEFECTIBLE, *unfailing*

INDEFENDIBLE, *indefensible*

INDEFINIBLE, *indefinable*, *uncertain*

INDEFINIDO (A), *indefinite*, *vague, undefined*

INDELEBLE, *indelible, permanent, enduring*

INDEMNIDAD, *indemnity*

INDEPENDENCIA, *independence*

INDEPENDIENTE, *independent*

INDESCRIPTIBLE, *indescribable, inexpressible*

INDESEABLE, *undesirable, unwanted; repugnant*

INDETERMINACIÓN, *indecisiveness, vagueness*

INDETERMINADO (A), *indeterminate, indecisive*

INDICACIÓN, *sign, signal, indication*

INDICADO (A), *advisable, indicated, suitable, specified*

ÍNDICE, *index, catalog*

INDICIO, *sign, clue, trace, indication*

INDIFERENCIA, *indifference, apathy, disregard*

INDIFERENTE, *indifferent, impartial, unconcerned*

INDÍGENA, *indigenous, native*

INDIGENCIA, *destitution, poverty, indigence*

INDIGENTE, *destitute, poor, indigent*

INDIGESTO (A), *indigestible*

INDIGNACIÓN, *indignation, anger*

INDIGNADO (A), *indignant, angry*

INDIGNANTE, *shocking, outrageous, infuriating*

INDIGNO (A), *unworthy; despicable*

INDIRECTA, *hint, suggestion; clue*

INDIRECTAMENTE, *indirectly*

INDIRECTO (A), *indirect, oblique, veiled*

INDISCIPLINA, *insubordination* (MIL)

INDISCIPLINADO (A), *undisciplined, insubordinate*

INDISCRECIÓN, *indiscretion*

INDISCRETO (A), [illegible], *tactless*

INDISCRIMINADO (A), *indiscriminate*

INDISCRIMINADAMENTE, *indiscriminately*

INDISCUTIBLE, *indisputable, irrefutable*

INDISOLUBLE, *insoluble; indissoluble*

INDISPOSICIÓN, *indisposition, unwillingness*

INDISPUESTO (A), *indisposed, unwell; unwilling*

INDIVIDUALIDAD, *individuality*

INDIVIDUALISMO, *individualism*

INDIVIDUO, *individual, character*

INDOLENCIA, *laziness, indolence*

INDOLENTE, *indolent, lazy*

INDOMABLE, *untamable, rebellious, unruly, indomitable; unmanageable, boundless*

INDUCCIÓN, *induction* (FIS), *inducement*

INDUDABLE, *undoubted, unquestionable*

INDULGENCIA, *indulgence*

INDULGENTE, *indulgent, lenient, tolerant*

INDULTO, *pardon, reprieve*

INDUSTRIA, *industry*

INDUSTRIALISMO, *industrialism*

INDUSTRIALIZACIÓN, *industrialization*

INDUSTRIOSO (A), *industrious*

INEFABLE, *ineffable, inexpressible*

INEFICAZ, *inefficient, ineffective, incompetent*

INEFICIENCIA, *inefficiency, incompetence*

INEFICIENTE, *inefficient*

INELUDIBLE, *unavoidable, inescapable*

INEPTITUD, *ineptitude*

INEPTO (A), *inept, incompetent*

INEQUÍVOCO (A), *unequivocal*

INERCIA, *inertia, immobility; apathy*

INERTE, *inert, lifeless, motionless*

INESCRUTABLE, *inscrutable, mysterious*

INESTABILIDAD, *instability, unpredictability*

INESTABLE, *unstable, unsteady*

INEXACTITUD, *inaccuracy*

INEXACTO, *inaccurate, incorrect, wrong, inexact*

INEXISTENTE, *nonexistent*

INEXPERIENCIA, *inexperience*

INEXPERTO (A), *inexperienced, unskilled*

INEXPRESIVO (A), *inexpressive*

INEXPUGNABLE, *unassailable, impregnable*

INEXTINGUIBLE, *unquenchable, undying, eternal*

INFALIBILIDAD, *infallibility*

INFALIBLE, *infallible*

INFAME, *odious, thankless*

INFAMIA, *infamy, slur, disgrace, shame, ignominy*

INFANCIA, *infancy*

INFANTE (A), *infant*

INFANTERÍA, *infantry* (MIL)

INFANTICIDA, *infanticide*

INFANTIL, *infantile, childish*

INFATIGABLE, *indefatigable, tireless, untiring*

INFECCIÓN, *infection, disease*

INFECCIOSO (A), *infectious, malignant, virulent*

INFECTO (A), *putrid, foul; infected, tainted*

INFERENCIA, *inference, deduction, surmise*

INFERIORIDAD, *inferiority; disadvantage*

INFÉRTIL, *infertile*

INFESTADO (A), *infested*

INFIDELIDAD, *infidelity*

INFIEL, *unfaithful; heathen, pagan*

INFILTRACIÓN, *seeping, infiltration*

INFILTRADO (A), *infiltrated*

INFINIDAD, *infinity, infinite extent; eternity*

INFINITIVO, *infinitive*

INFINITO (A), *infinite, limitless, boundless, endless*

INFINITO (n) (MAT), *infinite quantity or number*

INFLACIÓN, *inflation*

INFLAMABLE, *inflammable*

INFLABLE, *inflatable*

INFLAMACIÓN, *inflammation* (MED); *ignition*

INFLAMATORIO (A), *inflammatory*

INFLEXIBILIDAD, *inflexibility*

INFLEXIÓN, *inflection*

INFLUENCIA (n), *influence, sway, control*

INFLUENCIABLE, *easily influenced, impressionable*

INFLUYENTE (adj), *influential, powerful, dominant, weighty, authoritative; effective*

INFORMACIÓN, *information*; *news, data*

INFORMADO, *informed*

INFORMADOR (A), *reporting; reporter; inquiry*

INFORMANTE, *informant*

INFORMATIVO (A), *informative*

INFORME, *shapeless; report*

INFORTUNADO (A), *unfortunate*

INFORTUNIO, *misfortune; mishap*

INFRACCIÓN, *infringement, violation, infraction*

INFRACTOR (A), *offender*

INFRAESTRUCTURA, *infrastructure*

INFRAHUMANO (A), *subhuman*

INFRECUENTE, *infrequent, occasional, rare, seldom*

INFUNDADO (A), *unfounded, groundless*

INGENIO, *ingenuity, aptitude, wit; device*

INGENIOSO (A), *clever, resourceful*

INGENUO (A), *ingenuous; candid*

INGRATITUD, *ingratitude*

INGRATO (A), *ungrateful, thankless*

INGRÁVIDO (A), *weightless; very light*

INGREDIENTE, *ingredient, constituent, component*

INGRESO, *entry, admission*

INHABITABLE, *uninhabitable*

INHABITADO (A), *uninhabited*

INHABITUAL, *unusual, uncommon, rare*

INHERENTE, *inherent, inborn, innate, intrinsic, implicit*

INHIBICIÓN, *inhibition, repression; abstention* (MED)

INHÓSPITO (A), *inhospitable, unsociable; grim, bleak*

INHUMANO (A), *inhuman*

INICIACIÓN, *initiation, beginning, commencement*

INICIADO (A), *initiated*

INICIAL, *initial, first, prime, primary, original*

INIMAGINABLE, *unimaginable*

ININTELIGIBLE, *unintelligible*

ININTERRUMPIDO (A), *uninterrupted, continuous*

INIQUIDAD, *iniquity, wickedness*

INJURIOSO (A), *insulting, offensive*

INJUSTICIA, *injustice, disparity, unfairness, bias*

INJUSTIFICADO (A), *unjustified*

INJUSTO (A), *unfair, unjust*

INMACULADO (A), *immaculate, spotless*

INMATERIAL, *immaterial*

INMEDIATAMENTE, *immediately, at once*

INMEDIATO (A), *immediate, instant, prompt, spontaneous, instantaneous*

INMEMORIAL, *immemorial*

INMENSAMENTE, *immensely, vastly*

INMENSIDAD, *immensity, vastness*

INMENSO (A), *immense, vast, enormous*

INMERSIÓN, *immersion, submersion*

INMERSO (A), *immersed, involved, absorbed, engrossed, occupied*

INMIGRACIÓN, *immigration*

INMIGRANTE, *immigrant*

INMINENCIA, *imminence*

INMINENTE, *imminent, impending, looming, threatening, menacing, immediacy, soon*

INMODERADO (A), *immoderate, extreme, exorbitant*

INMODESTIA, *immodesty, impudence, indecency*

INMOLACIÓN, *immolation*

INMORAL, *immoral, depraved, dissolute*

INMORALIDAD, *immorality*

INMORTAL, *immortal, eternal, everlasting*

INMORTALIDAD, *immortality*

INMUNE, *immune (*MED*), exempt (n)*

INMUNIDAD, *immunity*

INMUNITARIO (A) (adj), *immune*

INMUNIZACIÓN, *immunization*

INMUTABLE, *immutable, unchanging, impassive*

INNECESARIO (A), *unnecessary*

INNOBLE, *ignoble, dishonorable; mean, base*

INNOVACIÓN, *innovation*

INNOVADOR (A), *innovative (adj), innovator (n)*

INOCENCIA, *innocence, ingenuous, virtuous, guiltless, blameless, faultless, irreproachable*

INOCENTE, *innocent, trusting, naive, good, pure*

INOCENTÓN (A), *gullible; simpleton*

INOCULACIÓN, *inoculation*

INOCUO (A), *innocuous, harmless, inoffensive*

INODORO (A), *odorless*

INOFENSIVO (A), *inoffensive, harmless*

INOPERANTE, *ineffective, inoperative, useless*

INOPORTUNO (A), *inopportune, inconvenient time*

INORGÁNICO (A), *inorganic*

INQUIETANTE (adj), *worrisome*

INQUIETO (A) (adj), *worried, anxious, unsettled*

INQUIETUD, *worry, anxiety, concern; interest*

INSACIABLE, *insatiable, unsatisfied; extremely greedy*

INSALUBRE, *insalubrious, unhealthy*

INSANO (A), *unhealthy, insane; mad*

INSATISFACCIÓN, *dissatisfaction*

INSATISFACTORIO, *unsatisfactory*

INSATISFECHO (A), *dissatisfied; unacceptable*

INSATURADO (A), *unsaturated*

INSCRIPCIÓN, *inscription; enrollment, entry*

INSECTICIDA, *insecticide*

INSECTO, *insect*

INSEGURO (A), *unsafe, insecure, unsteady*

INSEMINACIÓN, *insemination*

INSENSATEZ, *foolishness, stupidity*

INSENSATO (A), *foolish, stupid; insensitive, unfeeling, crass, boorish; thoughtless*

INSERCIÓN, *insertion*

INSERVIBLE, *useless, unserviceable*

INSIDIA, *maliciousness; trap, deception*

INSIDIOSO (A), *insidious, deceptive, treacherous*

INSIGNIFICANCIA, *insignificance*

INSIGNIFICANTE, *insignificant, unimportant, trifling*

INSINCERO (A), *insincere, dishonest, deceitful*

INSINUACIÓN, *insinuation, suggestion, hint, intimation*

INSINUANTE, *suggestive, insinuating*

INSÍPIDO (A), *insipid, tasteless; dull person*

INSISTENCIA, *insistence, compelling attention, demanding*

INSISTENTE, *insistent, emphatic, firm, assertive*

INSOBORNABLE, *incorruptible, moral, upright, noble, pure, upstanding*

INSOCIABLE, *unsociable, introverted; shy*

INSOLENCIA, *insolence, disrespect, impertinence*

INSOLENTE, *insolent, haughty, rude*

INSOLVENCIA, *insolvency, bankruptcy*

INSOLVENTE, *insolvent, bankrupt*

INSOMNE, *sleepless; insomniac*

INSOMNIO, *insomnia*

INSOPORTABLE, *unbearable, intolerable*

INSPECCIÓN, *inspection, examination*

INSPIRACIÓN, *inspiration, revelation, vision*

INSTALACIÓN, *installation*

INSTANTÁNEO (A), *instantaneous, immediate, direct, instantly, unhesitatingly, spontaneous*

INSTANTE, *moment, instant*

INSTIGACIÓN, *instigation, urge on, incite; persuade*

INSTIGADOR (A), *instigator*

INSTINTIVO (A), *instinctive, tendency, reflex action; flair, knack; aptitude, skill, faculty*

INSTINTO, *instinct, intuition*

INSTITUCIÓN, *institution*

INSTITUCIONAL, *institutional*

INSTITUTO, *institute, high school*

INSTRUCCIÓN, *education, teaching, instruction*

INSTRUCTIVO (A), *instructive, educational*

INSTRUIDO (A), *educated*

INSTRUMENTO, *musical instrument*

INSUBORDINACIÓN, *insubordination*

INSUBORDINADO (A), *insubordinate, unruly*

INSUFICIENCIA, *lack, shortage, insufficiency*

INSUFICIENTE, *insufficient, inadequate*

INSUFRIBLE, *insufferable, unbearable*

INSULINA, *insulin*

INSULTANTE, *insulting, offensive*

INSULTO, *insult, abuse, affront; defame, vilify*

INSURGENTE, *insurgent, rebel*

INSURRECCIÓN, *insurrection, revolt, rebellion*

INSUSTANCIAL, *insubstantial, flimsy, fragile, weak*

INSUSTITUIBLE, *irreplaceable, invaluable, priceless*

INTACHABLE, *irreproachable, faultless, blameless*

INTACTO (A), *untouched, intact, unimpaired, unscathed*

INTEGRACIÓN, *integration, unite, unify, merge*

INTEGRADO, *integrated*

ÍNTEGRAMENTE, *entirely, in full, completely*

INTEGRANTE, *integral, constituent, essential, basic*

INTEGRIDAD, *integrity, wholeness; totality, entirety*

INTEGRO (A), *whole, entire; upright, honest*

INTELECTO, *intellect, insight, intelligence*

INTELECTUAL, *intellectual, insightful, analytical, scholarly*

INTELIGENCIA, *intelligence*

INTELIGENTE, *intelligent, logical, bright, brilliant, smart, astute, quick, wise*

INTELIGIBLE, *intelligible*

INTEMPORAL, *timeless, perpetual, eternal, endless*

INTENCIÓN, *intention, motive, design, goal, aim*

INTENCIONAL (adj), *intentional*

INTENCIONADO (A), *deliberate, premeditated*

INTENSIVAMENTE, *intensively*

INTENSIDAD, *intensity, force, strength*

INTENSIFICACIÓN, *intensification*

INTENSIVO (A), *intensive, thorough, vigorous, concentrated, rigorous, dynamic*

INTENSO (A), *intense, strong, vehement*

INTENTO, *intent, aim; attempt*

INTERACCIÓN, *interaction, cooperation*

INTERACTIVO (A), *interactive, mutual*

INTERCAMBIABLE, *interchangeable, alternate*

INTERCESIÓN, *intercession, plea, intervention*

INTERCONEXIÓN, *interconnection*

INTERDICTO, *prohibition,*

INTERÉS, *interest, concern; attraction, appeal*

INTERESADO (A) (adj), *interested*

INTERESANTE, *interesting; attractive*

INTERJECCIÓN, *interjection, interruption*

INTERLUDIO, *interlude, interval, pause*

INTERMEDIARIO (A), *intermediary*

INTERMEDIO (A), *intermediate, halfway*

INTERMITENTE, *intermittent, sporadic, random*

INTERNACIONAL, *international*

INTERNADO (A), *boarder; inmate; patient, intern*

INTERNO (A), *internal, domestic*

INTERPRETACIÓN, *interpretation; performance*

INTERRELACIÓN, *interrelation*

INTERROGATORIO, *interrogation, questioning*

INTERROGATIVO (A), *interrogative*

INTERRUPCIÓN, *interruption, disruption, suspension*

INTERSECCIÓN, *intersection*

INTERURBANO (A), *intercity*

INTERVALO, *interval* (MUS); *space, gap, break*

INTERVENCIÓN, *intervention, hindrance, interruption*

INTERVIÚ, *interview*

INTESTINO, *intestine*

INTIMACIÓN, *intimation, announcement*

INTIMIDACIÓN, *intimidation, scare, terrify, unnerve*

INTIMIDAD, *private life, privacy; private parts*

ÍNTIMO (A), *private, intimate; personal*

INTOCABLE, *untouchable; sacred; taboo*

INTOLERANCIA, *intolerance, impatience, bias, bigotry*

INTOLERANTE, *intolerant, inflexible, biased*

INTOXICACIÓN, *intoxication*

INTRANSFERIBLE, *non-transferable*

INTRANSIGENCIA, *intransigence, stubbornness*

INTRANSIGENTE, *intransigent, stubborn, obstinate*

INTRANSITIVO (A), *intransitive*

INTRASCENDENCIA, *insignificance, pointlessness*

INTRASCENDENTE, *insignificant, paltry, trivial*

INTRATABLE, *difficult, impossible; untreatable* (MED)

INTRÉPIDO (A), *intrepid, unafraid; valiant; daring*

INTRIGA, *curiosity, intrigue, plot, scheme, suspense*

INTRIGANTE, *scheming, contriving, conniving*

INTRINCADO (A), *thick, dense, intricate*

INTRÍNSECO (A), *intrinsic, inherent, implicit, basic*

INTRODUCCIÓN, *introduction*

INTRODUCTORIO (A), *introductory*

INTROSPECCIÓN, *introspection*

INTROSPECTIVO (A), *introspective*

INTROVERTIDO (A), *introverted, bashful, coy, withdrawn*

INTRUSO (A), *intrusive (adj), intruder (n)*

INTUICIÓN, *intuition, instinct, presentiment*

INTUITIVO (A), *intuitive*

INUNDACIÓN, *inundation, flood, flooding*

INUSUAL, *unusual*

INUTILIDAD, *uselessness*

INUTILIZABLE, *unusable*

INÚTILMENTE, *uselessly, vainly, fruitlessly*

INVÁLIDO (A), *invalid, disabled* (MED)

INVECTIVA, *invective, tirade, insulting/ abusive language*

INVENCIBLE, *invincible, indomitable, unbeatable*

INVENCIÓN ó INVENTO, *invention; fabrication*

INVENTARIO, *inventory*

INVENTIVA, *inventiveness*

INVENTIVO (A), *inventive*

INVERSO (A), *opposite, inverse*

INVERTEBRADO (A), *invertebrate*

INVERTIDO (A), *inverted, upside-down*

INVESTIGACIÓN, *research, inquiry, investigation*

INVETERADO (A), *inveterate*

INVIABILIDAD, *impracticability*

INVIABLE, *impractical, unfeasible*

INVISIBILIDAD, *invisibility*

INVITACIÓN, *invitation*

INVITADO (A), *invited (adj), guest (n)*

INVOCACIÓN, *invocation*

INVOLUNTARIO (A), *involuntary*

IRA, *anger, rage, ire*

IRIDISCENTE, *iridescent*

IRONÍA, *irony, ridicule; satire*

IRÓNICO (A), *ironic, ironical, sarcastic, derisive*

IRRACIONAL, *irrational number* (MAT); *unreasonable*

IRRACIONALIDAD, *irrationality*

IRRADIACIÓN, *irradiation*

IRRAZONABLE, *irrational* (MAT); *illogical*

IRREAL, *unreal*

IRREALIDAD, *unreality*

IRREALIZABLE, *unattainable, impractical*

IRREBATIBLE, *irrefutable, incontrovertible, unalterable, immutable, conclusive, decisive*

IRRECONCILIABLE, *irreconcilable*

IRRECONOCIBLE, *unrecognizable*

IRRECUPERABLE, *irretrievable, hopeless, irreparable*

IRREDENTISTA, *irredentist*

IRREFLEXIÓN, *rashness, thoughtlessness*

IRREFLEXIVO (A), *rash, thoughtless*

IRREGULARIDAD, *irregularity*

IRRELEVANCIA, *irrelevance*

IRRELEVANTE, *irrelevant, inapplicable*

IRREPARABLEMENTE, *irreparably*

IRREPETIBLE, *unique, unrepeatable*

IRREPRIMIBLE, *irrepressible, incorrigible*

IRREPROCHABLE, *irreproachable*

IRREPRODUCIBLE, *irreplaceable*

IRRESOLUBLE, *unsolvable*

IRRESOLUTO (A), *irresolute, indecisive, uncertain*

IRRESPETUOSO (A), *disrespectful*

IRRESPONSABILIDAD, *irresponsibility*

IRRESPONSABLE, *irresponsible*

IRREVERENTE, *irreverent, impious, profane*

IRRIGACIÓN, *irrigation*

IRRITABILIDAD, *irritability; irascible, testy, touchy*

IRRITACIÓN, *irritation*

IRRITANTE, *irritating, maddening, exasperating*

IRRUPCIÓN, *irruption; invasion* (MIL)

ISOBARA ó ISÓBARA, *isobar*

ISÓTOPO, *isotope*

ITINERANTE, *itinerant, roving, traveling*

ITINERARIO, *route, itinerary*

Easily Recognizable Verbs

IDEALIZAR, *to idealize*

IDEAR, *to think up, devise, conceive*

IDENTIFICAR, *to identify*

IDOLATRAR, *to worship, idolize*

IGNORAR, *to ignore*

ILUMINAR, *to illuminate, enlighten*

ILUSTRAR, *to illustrate*

IMAGINAR, *to imagine, suppose*

IMPACTAR, *to have an impact on, to hit, strike*

IMPARTIR, *to give, impart*

IMPEDIR, *to prevent, stop*

IMPELER, *to propel, drive, urge*

IMPLANTAR, *to introduce, impose, bring in*

IMPLEMENTAR, *to implement, introduce; install*

IMPLICAR, *to involve, implicate*

IMPLORAR, *to implore, beg*

IMPORTAR, *to import; to matter, mind*

IMPORTUNAR, *to bother, pester*

IMPOSIBILITAR, *to make impossible, prevent*

IMPREGNAR, *to impregnate, pervade; soak*

IMPRESIONAR*, to impress, be impressed*

IMPROVISAR*, to improvise, ad-lib*

IMPUGNAR*, to challenge, contest*

IMPULSAR, *to drive, propel; promote*

IMPUTAR*, to accuse, impute, attribute*

INAUGURAR, *to inaugurate, open*

INCITAR, *to incite, stir up*

INCLINAR*, to bend, tilt, persuade, lean*

INCORPORAR, *to incorporate*

INCREMENTAR, *to increase*

INCRIMINAR, *to accuse, incriminate*

INCUBAR, *to incubate*

INCULCAR, *to inculcate, instill*

INCULPAR*, to accuse, charge*

INCURRIR*, to commit, incur*

INDEMNIZAR, *to compensate, indemnify*

INDEXAR, *to index*

INDICAR*, to indicate, register, show; prescribe* (MED)

INDIGNAR*, to anger, infuriate, outrage*

INDIVIDUALIZAR, *to single people out*

INDUCIR, *to induce, lead sb into sthg*

INDULTAR*, to pardon, reprieve*

INDUSTRIALIZAR, *to industrialize*

INFAMAR, *to defame, slander*

INFECTAR*, to infect, transmit; to become infected*

INFESTAR, *to infest, corrupt*

INFILTRAR, *to inject, infiltrate, penetrate*

INFLAMAR, *to inflame, arouse, ignite*

INFLUENCIAR, *to influence, persuade, motivate*

INFLUIR, *having the influence to control, change*

INFORMAR*, to inform, plead*

INFORMATIZAR, *to computerize*

INFRINGIR, *to infringe, contravene*

INMORTALIZAR, *to immortalize, be immortalized*

INMUNIZAR, *to immunize*

INNOVAR, *to improve on, innovate*

INOCULAR, *to inoculate*

INSCRIBIR, *to engrave, inscribe*

INSERTAR, *to insert*

INSINUAR, *to insinuate, imply*

INSISTIR, *to insist, persist*

INSPIRAR, *to inspire; inhale*

INSTALAR*, to install, fit, settle*

INSTIGAR, *to instigate, incite*

INSTILAR, *to instill*

INSTITUIR, *to establish, found, set up, create*

INSULTAR*, to insult*

INTEGRAR, *to integrate, incorporate, blend in*

INTENSIFICAR, *to intensify, heighten*

INTERACCIONAR, *to interact*

INTERCEDER, *to intercede, plead*

INTERCEPTAR, *to intercept, stop, hold up*

INTERFERIR, *to interfere*

INTERMEDIAR, *to mediate*

INTERPRETAR, *to interpret*

INTERROGAR, *to question, interrogate*

INTIMAR, to *become intimate, very friendly*

INTIMIDAR, *to intimidate*

INTRIGAR, *to intrigue, scheme, plot*

INTRODUCIR, *to put in, insert*

INVADIR, *to invade, violate, enter*

INVALIDAR, *to invalidate*

INVENTAR, *to invent*

INVERTIR, *to reverse*

INVESTIGAR, *to research, investigate*

INVESTIR, *to invest sb with sthg*

INVITAR, *to invite*

INVOCAR, *to invoke*

IRONIZAR, *to ridicule*

IRRITAR, *to irritate*

STUDY NOTES:

J

Interchangeable Words

JADE

JAGUAR

JAZZ

JEANS

JEEP

JERSEY ó JERSEI

JET (plane)

JET LAG

JET-SET

JET-SKI

JITTERBUG

JOCKEY ó JOCKETA

JOGGING, *also means track suit*

JOKER (in cards)

JOVIAL

JUDAS, *a traitor*

JUDICIAL

JUDO ó YUDO

JUMBO (jet)

JUMPER, *a dress*

JUNIOR

JÚPITER, *the planet* (ASTROL)

Easily Recognizable Nouns, Adjectives and Adverbs

JAMBA, *door jamb*

JAZMÍN, *jasmine*

JIRAFA, *giraffe*

JOCOSO (A), *jocular*

JOVIALIDAD, *joviality*

JUBILEO, *jubilee* (RELIG)

JÚBILO, *joy, jubilation*

JUBILOSO (A), *joyous, jubilant*

JUGOSO (A), *juicy*

JUICIOSO (A), *wise, sensible, judicious*

JUJITSU, *jiu-jitsu*

JULIO, *July*

JUNIO, *June*

JUNCO, *junk*

JUNGLA, *jungle*

JUNTA, *committee, council, military junta*

JUNTO (A), *together*

JUNTURA, *joint*

JURADO (A), *jury; juror*

JURAMENTO, *oath*

JURISDICCIÓN, *jurisdiction*

JURISDICCIONAL, *jurisdictional*

JURISPRUDENCIA, *jurisprudence*

JURISTA, *jurist*

JUSTAMENTE, *justly, exactly*

JUSTICIA, *justice, equity, fairness*

JUSTICIERO (A), *righteous, just*

JUSTIFICABLE, *justifiable*

JUSTIFICACIÓN, *justification*

JUSTIFICADO (A), *justified*

JUSTIFICANTE, *receipt; sick note*

JUSTO (A), *fair, just, deserved*

JUVENIL, *youthful* (DEP)

JUVENTUD, *youth*

Easily Recognizable Verbs

JURAMENTAR, *to swear in*

JURAR, *to swear, pledge*

JUSTIFICAR, *to justify*

STUDY NOTES:

K

Interchangeable Words

KAMIKAZE

KAPUT

KARAOKE

KARMA

KARATE ó CARATE

KAYAK ó KAYAC

KEPI ó KEPIS

KÉTCHUP

KILO ó QUILO

KILOBYTE

KIMONO ó QUIMONO

KIT, *also means assembly kit*

KIWI, *the fruit*

KNOCKOUT ó KO

KOALA, *a bear*

Easily Recognizable Nouns, Adjectives and Adverbs

KART, *go cart*

KAKI ó CAQUI, *khaki*

KEROSÉN, *kerosene*

KIBUTZ, *kibbutz*

KILOGRAMO ó QUILIGRAMO, *kilogram*

KILOMÉTRICO (A) ó QUILOMÉTRICO (A), *kilometric*

KILÓMETRO ó QUILÓMETRO, *kilometer*

KÍNDER, *kindergarten*

KLAXON, *horn, claxon*

STUDY NOTES:

L

Interchangeable Words

LABIAL, *of the lips*

LABOR

LABORAL

LAMA*; also means mud, slime*

LAMBADA

LAMENTABLE

LAPISLÁZULI, *lapis lazuli*

LARVA

LÁSER

LATERAL

LÁTEX

LATÍN, *the language*

LAUDABLE ó LOABLE

LAUREL, *the plant*

LAVA

LEASING

LEGAL

LEGIBLE

LEGIÓN, *many*

LEO (ASTROL)

LESIÓN, *also means injury*

LEXICÓN

LIBERAL

LIBIDO

LIBRA (ASTROL)

LIGHT, *low calorie, low tar*

LIMBO

LINEAL

LITERAL

LLAMA, *the animal; also means flame*

LOBBY, *pressure group*

LOCAL

LOCKER

LOGO

LONGITUDINAL

LUMBAGO

LUMBAR

LUMPEN, *underclass*

LUNAR; *mole, beauty mark*

Easily Recognizable Nouns, Adjectives and Adverbs

LABORABLE, *working*

LABORATORIO, *laboratory*

LABORERO, *foreman*

LABORIOSIDAD, *industry*

LABORIOSO (A), *industrious*

LABURO, *job, work*

LACÓNICO (A), *laconic, terse, precise, concise*

LACRIMOSO (A), *tearful, sorrowful*

LACTOSA, *lactose*

LÁGRIMA, *tear*

LAGUNA, *lagoon, pool*

LAMENTACIÓN, *moaning, sorrow; grief, regret*

LAMENTO, *moan, cry of pain*

LAMINADO (A), *laminated*

LÁMPARA, *lamp, light*

LANOLINA, *lanolin*

LAPSO, *space, interval, lapse; omission*

LAPSUS, *slip, mistake, oversight; blunder*

LARINGITIS, *laryngitis*

LASAÑA, *lasagna*

LASCIVIA, *lust, lewdness, lecherous, salacious*

LASITUD, *lassitude, languor, weariness*

LÁSTIMA, *pity, shame*

LASTIMERO (A), *pitiful, pathetic*

LATENTE, *latent, concealed, dormant*

LATITUD, *latitude*

LAUDATORIO (A), *laudatory*

LAUREADO (A), *honored, acclaimed*

LAURELES, *laurels, distinction, tribute*

LAVANDA, *lavender*

LAVATIVA, *enema*

LAXANTE, *laxative*

LAXITUD, *laxity, laxness*

LAXO (A), *slack, lax (morals)*

LECCIÓN, *lesson, class*

LEGACIÓN, *legation*

LEGALIDAD, *legality*

LEGALISMO, *legalism*

LEGALISTA, *legalistic*

LEGALIZACIÓN, *legalization*

LEGALMENTE, *legally, lawfully*

LEGENDARIO (A), *legendary*

LEGISLACIÓN, *legislation*

LEGISLADOR (A) (adj), *legislative*

LEGITIMACIÓN, *legitimization, authentication*

LEGÍTIMO (A), *legitimate, rightful*

LENTAMENTE, *slowly*

LENTO (A), *slow*

LEÓN, *lion*

LEÓNA, *lioness*

LEOPARDO (A), *leopard*

LEOTARDO (s), *leotards, tights*

LÉPERO (A), *coarse, rotten*

LEPRA, *leprosy*

LEPROSO (A), *leprous (adj), leper (n)*

LESBIANA, *lesbian*

LETAL, *lethal, deadly, mortal, fatal*

LETANÍA, *litany*

LETÁRGICO (A), *lethargic, sluggish, slow, dull, lazy, idle, listless; indolent, shiftless*

LETARGO, *lethargy, indolence, indifference, sloth, apathy; languid, torpid, stagnant*

LETRINA, *latrine*

LEUCEMIA, *leukemia*

LEVA, *levy* (MIL)

LEVANTISCO (A), *rebellious, turbulent, troubled*

LÉXICO, *vocabulary*

LIBELO, *libel, lampoon*

LIBACIÓN, *libation*

LIBERACIÓN, *liberation, release*

LIBERADO (A), *liberated*

LIBERALIDAD, *liberality*

LIBERALISMO, *liberalism*

LIBERALIZACIÓN, *liberalization*

LIBERTAD, *freedom*

LIBRETA, *notebook, notepad*

LIBRETO, *libretto* (MUS)

LICENCIA, *license, permit*

LICENCIOSO (A), *licentious, immoral, promiscuous*

LICITACIÓN, *tender, bid*

LÍCITO (A), *lawful, allowed; fair*

LICOR, *liquor*

LIFTING, *face-lift*

LIGAMENTO, *ligament*

LIMITACIÓN, *limitation, limit, minimal*

LIMITADO, *scant, limited, restricted, curbed*

LÍMITE, *maximum, limit, fixed, end*

LIMÓN, *lemon*

LIMONADA, *lemonade*

LÍMPIDO (A), *limpid, clear, transparent*

LIMUSINA, *limousine*

LÍNEA, *line*

LINFA, *lymph*

LINIMENTO, *liniment*

LIPOSUCCIÓN, *liposuction*

LIQUIDACIÓN, *sale, clearance, liquidation*

LIQUIDEZ, *liquidity*

LÍQUIDO (A), *liquid; cash*

LISTA, *list, register, inventory, index*

LISTÍN, *directory, register, roster, list*

LISTO (A), *ready, finished; clever, smart*

LITERATURA, *literature*

LITERALMENTE, *literally*

LITIGANTE, *litigant*

LITORAL, *littoral, seacoast*

LITURGIA, *liturgy* (RELIG)

LÍVIDO (A), *livid, ashen, pale, leaden, gray*

LIVING, *living room, lounge*

LÓBULO, *lobe* (ANAT)

LOCALIDAD, *place, town, locality*

LOCALISMO, *parochialism, provincialism*

LOCALISTA, *parochial, local, indigenous, native; regional*

LOCAMENTE, *madly, wildly*

LOCIÓN, *lotion*

LOCALIZADO, *localized, restricted, assigned*

LOCOMOCIÓN, *locomotion*

LOCOMOTORA, *engine, locomotive*

LOCUACIDAD, *loquacity, garrulous; verbose, wordy*

LOGARITMO, *logarithm*

LÓGICA, *logic, obvious*

LÓGICO (A), *logical, natural, rational, credible, believable, reasonable, plausible*

LOGÍSTICA, *logistics*

LOGÍSTICO (A), *logistic*

LOGOTIPO, *logo, logotype*

LONGEVIDAD, *longevity*

LONGEVO (A), *long-lived*

LONGITUD, *length; long jump* (DEP)

LOTE, *batch, share, lot, piece of land*

LOTERÍA, *lottery*

LOTO, *lotus*

LUBRICACIÓN, *lubrication*

LUBRICANTE, *lubricating, lubricant*

LUCIDEZ, *lucidity, clarity*

LÚCIDO (A), *lucid, clear*

LUCIDO (A), *splendid, magnificent*

LUCRATIVO (A), *lucrative, profitable*

LUCRO, *profit*

LUMINOSIDAD, *brightness, luminosity*

LUMINOSO (A), *luminous, bright, illuminated*

LUNA, *moon*

LUNÁTICO (A), *lunatic, madman; mad, foolish*

LUSTRE, *luster, gloss, brilliance*

LUSTROSO (A), *shiny, glossy*

LUZ, *light*

Easily Recognizable Verbs

LACAR ó LAQUEAR, *to lacquer*

LACERAR, *to lacerate, wound*

LAMENTAR, *to lament, regret, bemoan*

LAMINAR, *to laminate*

LANZAR, *to throw, hurl, fling*

LAPIDAR, *to stone*

LAXAR, *to loosen, loosen up*

LEGALIZAR, *to legalize, authenticate*

LEGISLAR, *to legislate*

LEGITIMAR, *to legitimize*

LEVANTAR, *to raise, lift, hoist; build up*

LEVITAR, *to levitate*

LIBERAR, *to liberate, set free, release; exempt*

LIBRAR, *to free sb, save, deliver from*

LICITAR, *to bid for, tender*

LIMITAR, *to limit, restrict*

LINCHAR, *to lynch*

LITIGAR, *to litigate, dispute*

LOCALIZAR, *to locate, track down, find*

LUBRICAR, *to lubricate*

LUCIR, *to shine, look good, excel*

LUSTRAR, *to polish, shine*

STUDY NOTES:

M

Interchangeable Words

MACHETE

MACHISMO

MACRO

MADRIGAL

MAESTRO, *teacher*

MAFIA

MAFIOSO (A)

MAGENTA

MAGMA

MAGNATE

MAGNESIA

MAGNOLIA

MAIL, *e-mail*

MAJORETTE

MALARIA

MAMBO

MANAGER ó MÁNAGER

MANDARÍN

MANÍA

MANIFESTÓ

MANSIÓN

MANTILLA

MANTIS

MANTRA

MANUAL

MARGARITA, the *drink; daisy*

MARGINAL, *apart; secondary*

MARIMBA

MARITAL

MARKETING

MARSUPIAL

MASÓN (Freemason)

MASS MEDIA

MATCH (DEP)

MATERIAL

MATERNAL

MATINÉE ó MATINÉ, *matinee*

MATRIMONIAL

ME, *as the personal pronoun: my, mine*

MEDICINAL

MEDIEVAL

MEDIOCRE

MÉDIUM

MEGABYTE

MELANOMA

MELODRAMA

MELÓN

MEMO; *also means silly, stupid*

MEMORABLE

MEMORÁNDUM

MEMORIAL

MENINGITIS

MENSTRUAL

MENTAL; *intellectual*

MENTOR (A)

MENÚ

METAL; *brass* (MUS)

METÁSTASIS (MED)

METRÓPOLIS

MIASMA

MICA; *a chamber pot*

MICRO (INFORM); *a mike*

MICROCHIP

MICROFILM

MIMOSA

MINERAL

MINI, *miniskirt*

MINIBÚS

MINISTERIAL

MISERABLE, *poor, pitiful*

MODAL

MÓDEM

MODULAR

MOHAIR

MOLAR, *tooth; grinding*

MOLECULAR

MOLOTOV CÓCTEL, *Molotov cocktail*

MONUMENTAL, *tremendous*

MORAL; *a mulberry tree*

MORGUE

MORMÓN (A), *Mormon*

MORSE *(code)*

MORTAL

MOSQUITO

MOTEL

MOTOR

MOUSSE

MULTICULTURAL

MULTIDIMENSIONAL

MULTILATERAL

MULTIMEDIA

MÚLTIPLE

MUNICIPAL

MURAL

MUSCULAR

MUSICAL

MUTABLE

MUTUAL

Easily Recognizable Nouns, Adjectives and Adverbs

MACABRO (A), *macabre*

MACADÁN, *macadam*

MACARRONES, *macaroni*

MACERACIÓN, *maceration, soaking, softening*

MAGIA (n), *magic*

MÁGICO (A) (adj), *magical*

MAGISTRADO (A), *judge, magistrate*

MAGNÁNIMO (A), *magnanimous*

MAGNESIO, *magnesium*

MAGNÉTICO (A), *magnetic*

MAGNETISMO, *magnetism*

MAGNIFICENCIA, *magnificence*

MAGNÍFICO (A), *wonderful, magnificent*

MAGNITUD, *magnitude, extent, immensity; significance*

MAHONESA ó MAYONESA, *mayonnaise*

MAÍZ, *corn*

MAL, *harm, wrong*

MALDAD, *wickedness, evil*

MALDICIÓN, *curse*

MALEABLE, *malleable, adaptable; pliable, flexible*

MALEDUCADO (A), *uneducated, ill-mannered; rude*

MALHUMORADO (A), *bad-tempered*

MALICIA, *malice, spite*

MALICIOSO (A), *malicious, spiteful, vicious*

MALIGNIDAD, *malignancy; invasive, pernicious*

MALIGNO (A), *evil, harmful, malignant* (MED)

MALINTERPRETACIÓN, *misinterpretation*

MALNUTRICIÓN, *malnutrition*

MALTA, *malt, beer*

MANATÍ, *manatee*

MANDARINA, *mandarin, tangerine*

MANDATO, *mandate*

MANDÍBULA, *jaw, mandible*

MANDOLINA, *mandolin*

MANERA, *manner, way*

MANGANESO, *manganese*

MANICURA, *manicure*

MANIFESTANTE, *demonstrator*

MANIQUÍ, *mannequin, dummy, model*

MANIFESTACIÓN, *show, display, manifestation*

MANIFIESTO (A), *evident, clear, manifest*

MANIPULACIÓN, *manipulation, handling*

MANUFACTURA, *product*

MANUFACTURADO (A), *manufactured*

MANUSCRITO (A) (adj), *handwritten*

MANUSCRITO (n), *manuscript*

MAPA, *map*

MAQUINACIÓN, *machination, plot*

MARAVILLA, *marvel, wonder*

MARAVILLOSO (A), *marvelous, wonderful*

MARCA, *mark*

MARCIAL, *martial* (MIL)

MARGARINA, *margarine*

MARGEN, *margin*

MARGINADO (A), *marginalized, alienated, deprived*

MÁRTIR, *martyr*

MARZO, *March*

MASACRE, *massacre*

MASAJE, *massage*

MÁSCARA, *mask*

MASCOTA, *mascot*

MASCULINO (A), *male, manly, masculine*

MASIVO (A), *massive, huge*

MATEMÁTICAS, *mathematics*

MATERIALISMO, *materialism*

MATERIALISTA, *materialistic*

MATERNIDAD, *motherhood, maternity*

MATERNO (A), *maternal/blood relationship*

MATRIMONIO, *marriage, matrimony*

MAXILAR, *maxillary, jaw*

MÁXIMA, *maximum, high; maxim*

MÁXIMO (A) (adj), *highest, maximum*

MAYO, *May*

MAYORAL, *foreman, overseer*

MECÁNICO (A), *mechanical (adj); mechanic (n)*

MECANISMO, *mechanism, way of working*

MECANIZACIÓN, *mechanization*

MECANIZADO (A), *mechanized*

MEDALLA, *medal* (DEP) (MIL)

MEDALLÓN, *medallion*

MEDIA, *average; knee-high socks, pantyhose*

MEDIACIÓN, *mediation, intercession*

MEDIADO, *half-full, halfway through*

MEDICACIÓN, *medication, treatment*

MEDICAMENTO, *medicine*

MÉDICO (A), *medical*

MEDIO (A) (adj) (adv), *half*

MEDIO (adj), *middle*

MEDIOCRIDAD, *mediocrity; indifferent, ordinary*

MEDIODÍA, *noon, midday*

MEDITACIÓN, *meditation, contemplation, study*

MEGAFONÍA, *public address system*

MEGÁFONO, *megaphone*

MEGALITO, *megalith*

MEGALÓMANO (A), *megalomaniac*

MELANCOLÍA, *melancholy, sadness*

MELANCÓLICO, *sad, wistful*

MELANINA, *melanin*

MELODÍA, *melody*

MELÓDICO (A), *melodic*

MELODIOSO (A), *melodious, tuneful, musical*

MELODRAMÁTICO (A), *melodramatic*

MELÓMANO (A), *music lover*

MEMBRANA, *membrane*

MEMORIA, *memory*

MEMORIZACIÓN, *memorization*

MENCIÓN, *mention, reveal, disclose*

MENDACIDAD, *mendacity, untruthfulness*

MENDAZ, *mendacious, untruthful, lying*

MENDICANTE, *mendicant; beggar*

MENSTRUACIÓN, *menstruation*

MENSUAL, *monthly*

MENTALIDAD, *mentality*

MENTOL, *menthol*

MERCANTE, *merchant*

MERCANTIL, *mercantile, commercial*

MERCANTILISMO, *mercantilism*

MERCURIO, *mercury*; *Mercury* (ASTROL)

MÉRITO, *merit, worth*

MERO (A), *mere, simple, bare, basic, sheer*

METABÓLICO (A), *metabolic*

METABOLISMO, *metabolism*

METADONA, *methadone*

METÁFORA, *metaphor*

METAFÓRICO (A), *metaphorical*

METÁLICO (A), *metal, metallic*

METALIZADO (A), *metallic*

METALURGIA, *metallurgy*

METALÚRGICO (A), *metallurgical*

METAMORFOSIS, *metamorphosis*

METANO, *methane*

METEÓRICO (A), *meteoric, brief, temporary, transient*

METEORITO, *meteorite*

METEORO, *meteor*

METEOROLOGÍA, *meteorology*

METEOROLÓGICO (A), *meteorological*

METEORÓLOGO (A), *meteorologist*

METICULOSIDAD, *meticulousness*

METICULOSO (A), *meticulous, fastidious; thorough*

METÓDICO (A), *methodical, organized, systematic*

MÉTODO, *method, way, means, manner, approach*

METODOLOGÍA, *methodology, system, procedure*

METODOLÓGICO (A), *methodological*

MÉTRICO (A), *metric*

METRO, *meter*

METRÓNOMO, *metronome*

METRÓPOLI, *metropolis*

METROPOLITANO (A), *metropolitan*

MICROBIO, *microbe*

MICROBIOLOGÍA, *microbiology*

MICROBÚS, *minibus*

MICROFICHA, *microfiche*

MICRÓFONO, *microphone*

MICROSCÓPICO (A), *microscopic*

MICROSCOPIO, *microscope*

MIGRACIÓN, *migration*

MIGRAÑA, *migraine*

MILITANTE, *militant, politically active*

MILITAR (adj), *military*

MILLÓN, *million*

MINA, *mine, strip mine*

MINERO (A), *miner*

MINIATURA, *miniature, small, tiny, diminutive, little*

MINIGOLF, *miniature golf*

MÍNIMO (A), *minimum, minimal, least, slightest*

MINISTERIO, *ministry*

MINÚSCULO (A), *minuscule, minute, tiny*

MINUTO, *minute of time*

MINISTRO (A), *minister*

MIOPÍA, *myopia*

MISAL, *missal* (RELIG)

MISCELÁNEA, *miscellany*

MISCELÁNEO, *miscellaneous, varied, diverse, mixed*

MISERIA, *poverty, destitution*

MISERICORDIA, *compassion, mercy, forgiveness, pity*

MÍSERO (A), *wretched, stingy, miserly, mean*

MISIL, *missile* (MIL)

MISIÓN, *mission, task, assignment, work, job*

MISIONERO (A), *missionary*

MISIVA, *missive*

MISTERIO, *mystery, puzzle, enigma, riddle, conundrum*

MISTERIOSO (A), *mysterious*

MÍSTICO (A), *mystical (adj), mystic (n)*

MIXTO (A), mixed*; joint*

MIXTURA, *mixture, combination, blend, amalgam*

MOCASÍN, *moccasin*

MOCIÓN, *motion* (POL)

MODELO, *model, brand, design, replica*

MODÉLICO, *model, exemplary person*

MODERACIÓN, *moderation, restraint*

MODERADO (A), *moderate, reasonable*

MODERADOR (A), *moderator, chairperson*

MODERNIDAD, *modernity*

MODERNISMO, *modernism*

MODERNISTA, *modernist (n), modernistic (adj)*

MODERNIZACIÓN, *modernization*

MODERNO (A), *modern*

MODESTIA, *modesty*

MODESTO (A), *modest, restrained, diffident; humble*

MÓDICO (A), *modest, reasonable*

MODIFICACIÓN, *modification, alteration, change*

MODO, *way, manner, procedure, method*

MODOS, *manners, behavior*

MODOSO (A), *demure, well-mannered*

MODULACIÓN, *modulation, temper, soften, balance; lower, modify, reduce, diminish, lessen*

MOL, *mole*

MOLÉCULA, *molecule*

MOLESTIA, *nuisance, inconvenience, bother; trouble*

MOLESTO (A), *inconvenient, unpleasant, irritating, embarrassing, annoying, uncomfortable*

MOLESTOSO (A), *annoying, irritating, irksome*

MOMENTO, *moment*

MOMENTÁNEO (A), *momentary, temporary, brief*

MONACAL, *monastic*

MONASTERIO, *monastery*

MONETARIO (A), *monetary*

MONITOR (A), *coach, trainer, instructor*

MONOCORDE, *single-stringed* (MUS); *monotonous, unvaried; boring, dull, tiresome*

MONÓCULO, *monocle*

MONOGAMIA, *monogamy*

MONÓGAMO (A), *monogamous*

MONOGRAFÍA, *monograph*

MONOLÍTICO (A), *monolithic, massive, huge; rigid*

MONOLITO, *monolith*

MONÓLOGO, *monologue, soliloquy*

MONOPLANO, *monoplane*

MONOPOLIO, *monopoly*

MONOPOLIZACIÓN, *monopolization*

MONOSÍLABO (A), *monosyllabic*

MONOTONÍA, *monotony, tedious, dull, routine*

MONÓTONO (A), *monotonous, dreary, humdrum*

MONÓXIDO, *monoxide*

MONSTRUO, *enormous, monster; superstar*

MONSTRUOSIDAD, *monstrosity; gigantic; outrageous*

MONSTRUOSO (A), *monstrous; disfigured; absurd*

MONUMENTO, *monument, memorial*

MONTAÑA, *mountain*

MONTAÑERO (A), *mountaineer*

MONTAÑOSO (A) (adj), *mountainous*

MONZÓN, *monsoon*

MORATORIA, *moratorium, halt, delay, stay*

MORBO, *morbid pleasure, illness; macabre*

MORBOSIDAD, *morbidity, disordered, unsound*

MORBOSO (A), *morbid, unhealthy, sickly; grim*

MORDACIDAD, *mordacity, sharpness*

MORDAZ, *caustic, biting, scathing*

MORFINA, *morphine*

MORTALIDAD, *mortality*

MORTIFICACIÓN, *torture, humiliation, mortification*

MORTUORIO (A), *mortuary*

MOSAICO, *mosaic*

MOSCATEL, *muscatel*

MOSTAZA, *mustard*

MOTIVACIÓN, *motivation, motive*

MOTIVO, *reason, cause*

MOVEDIZO (A), *moving, shifting, restless*

MOVILIDAD, *mobility*

MOVILIZACIÓN, *mobilization*

MÓVIL, *motive, reason*

MOVIMIENTO, *movement, motion, relocation*

MUCOSA, *mucus*

MUDO (A), *mute*

MULATO (A), *mulatto*

MULO, *mule*

MULTICOLOR, *multicolored*

MULTICONFERENCIA, *conference call*

MULTIPLICACIÓN, *multiplication*

MULTIPLICIDAD, *multiplicity*

MÚLTIPLO (A), *multiple*

MULTITUD, *crowd, multitude*

MULTIUSO, *multipurpose*

MUNDANAL *worldly, temporal, secular*

MUNDANO (A), *worldly, fashionable, sophisticated, suave, cosmopolitan, refined, elegant, poised*

MUNDIAL, *worldwide*

MUNDIALIZACIÓN, *globalization*

MUNICIÓN, *ammunition*

MUNICIPIO, *municipality*

MUNIFICENCIA, *munificence, generous, bountiful*

MURMULLO, *whisper, murmur*

MURMURACIÓN, *gossip*

MURMURADOR (A), *gossiping, backbiting; backbiter*

MÚSCULO, *muscle*

MUSCULOSO (A), *muscular*

MUSEO, *museum*

MÚSICA, *music*

MÚSICO (A), *musician (n), musical (adj)*

MUTACIÓN, *sudden, change, mutation*

MUTUALIDAD, *mutuality; a mutual benefit society*

MUTANTE, *mutant*

MUTILACIÓN, *mutilation; deface, vandalize, ruin*

MUTILADO (A), *mutilated; disabled; mangled, maimed*

MUTUAL, *benefit society*

MUTUO (A), *mutual, joint*

Easily Recognizable Verbs

MAGNIFICAR, *to exaggerate*

MANIFESTAR, *to show, declare, demonstrate*

MANIPULAR, *to operate, manipulate*

MANUFACTURAR, *to manufacture*

MASTICAR, *to masticate, chew*

MATERIALIZAR, *to produce, bring into being, carry out, materialize*

MATRICULAR, *to register, enroll*

MAXIMIZAR, *to maximize*

MECANIZAR, *to mechanize*

MEDICAR, *to be on medication, take medication*

MEDICINAR, *to give medication*

MEDITAR, *to ponder, meditate on, think about*

MEMORIZAR, *to memorize*

MENCIONAR, *to mention*

MICROFILMAR, *to microfilm*

MIMETIZAR, *to imitate*

MODELAR, *to mold, shape, model, fashion*

MODERNIZAR, *to modernize*

MODIFICAR, *to alter, modify, adapt*

MOLER, *to grind*

MOLESTAR, *to annoy, bother, molest, inconvenience*

MONITORIZAR, *to monitor*

MONOPOLIZAR, *to monopolize*

MORTIFICAR, *to mortify, torment*

MOTIVAR, *to cause, motivate*

MOTORIZAR, *to motorize*

MOVER, *to move, drive, provoke, rouse*

MULTIPLICAR, *to multiply, increase; multiply* (MAT)

MURMURAR, *to murmur, whisper, gossip*

MUTAR, *to mutate*

MUTILAR, *to mutilate*

STUDY NOTES:

N

Interchangeable Words

NAPALM

NARCOSIS

NASAL

NATURAL

NÁUSEA

NAVAL

NAVE, *in a church; ship, vessel*

NAZI

NECRÓPOLIS

NECROSIS

NÉCTAR

NEÓN

NEONAZI

NEURALGIA

NEUROSIS

NEUTRAL

NEUTRÓN

NICK, *internet nickname*

NIRVANA

NO; *not, non*

NOBLE, *nobleman or woman*

NOMINAL

NORMAL

NOSTALGIA

NOTABLE, *remarkable, outstanding, considerable*

NOTARIAL; *legal, lawyer's*

NOVEL, *new, first time, inexperienced*

NOVENA, (RELIG)

NUCLEAR

NUMERAL; *number*

NUNCIO

NYLON ó NILÓN

Easily Recognizable Nouns, Adjectives and Adverbs

NACIENTE, *nascent, rising; east, spring*

NACIÓN, *nation, people*

NACIONAL, *national, domestic*

NACIONALIDAD, *nationality*

NACIONALISMO, *nationalism*

NACIONALISTA, *nationalist*

NADA, *nothing*

NADIE, *nobody, no one*

NAFTA, *naphtha* (QUIM)

NARCISISMO, *narcissism*

NARCISISTA, *narcissistic (adj), narcissist (n)*

NARCÓTICO (A), *narcotic*

NARRACIÓN, *narration, account, story*

NARRADOR (A), *narrator*

NARRATIVA, *literature, fiction*

NARRATIVO (A) (adj), *narrative*

NATAL (adj), *native of a country, locality, etc.*

NATIVIDAD, *the Nativity*

NATIVO (A), *native*

NATURA, *nature*

NATURALIDAD, *naturalness*

NATURALIZACIÓN, *naturalization*

NATURALIZADO (A), *naturalized*

NATURALMENTE, *naturally; of course!*

NATURISTA, *natural, alternative*

NÁUTICA (n), *seamanship, navigation*

NÁUTICO (A), *nautical*

NAVEGABLE, *navigable, seaworthy*

NAVEGACIÓN, *navigation*

NAVEGADOR, *browser on internet*

NAVEGANTE, *navigator, seafarer*

NAVIDAD, *Christmas (day) (time)*

NAVÍO, *ship*

NEBLINA, *mist, mistiness, haze*

NEBULOSA, *nebula*

NEBULOSO (A), *vague, misty, cloudy, obscure*

NECESARIAMENTE, *necessarily*

NECESARIO (A), *necessary*

NECESIDAD, *need for/to do sthg*

NECESITADO (A), *to be needy, in need of*

NECESITADOS, *the needy*

NECROFILIA, *necrophilia*

NECTARINA, *nectarine*

NEFASTO (A), *ill-fated, bad, harmful, awful*

NEFRITIS, *nephritis*

NEGACIÓN, *denial, refusal, negation*

NEGADO (A), *useless at something*

NEGATIVA, *refusal*

NEGATIVO, *photo negative; negative* (MAT)

NEGATIVO (A) (adj), *negative*

NEGLIGENCIA, *negligence*

NEGLIGENTE, *negligent, careless person*

NEGOCIABLE, *negotiable*

NEGOCIACIÓN, *negotiation*

NEGOCIANTE, *businessman or woman, dealer*

NEGOCIO, *business*

NEGRO (A), *black; pessimistic; color/person*

NEOCLÁSICO (A), *neoclassical*

NEÓFITO (A), *neophyte*

NEOLÍTICO (A), *Neolithic (period)*

NEPOTISMO, *nepotism*

NERVIO, *nerve* (ANAT)

NERVIOSISMO (adj), *nervousness*

NERVIOSO (A), *nervous* (ANAT); *excitable*

NETAMENTE, *clearly; purely*

NETO (A), *net* (COM) (ECON); *clear, concluding*

NEUMÁTICO (A), *pneumatic*

NEUMONÍA, *pneumonia*

NEUROLOGÍA, *neurology*

NEUROLÓGICO (A), *neurological*

NEURÓLOGO (A), *neurologist*

NEURONA, *neuron, brain cell*

NEURÓTICO (A), *neurotic*

NEUTRALIDAD, *neutrality*

NEUTRALIZACIÓN, *neutralization*

NEUTRO (A), *neutral* (QUIM)

NEVADA, *snowfall*

NEVADO (A), *snow covered or capped*

NEVERA, *refrigerator*

NEXO, *link, connection, nexus*

NICHO, *niche*

NICOTINA, *nicotine*

NIEBLA, *fog*

NIHILISMO, *nihilism*

NIMBO, *nimbus* (METEO), *halo*

NIMIEDAD, *insignificance*

NIMIO (A), *insignificant, trivial, petty*

NINFA, *nymph*

NINFÓMANA, *nymphomaniac*

NITRATO, *nitrate*

NÍTRICO (A), *nitric*

NITRÓGENO, *nitrogen*

NITROSO (A), *nitrous*

NOBLEZA, *nobility*

NOCIÓN, *notion, concept, idea*

NOCIONAL, *notional*

NOCTURNO, *nocturne* (MUS)

NOCTURNO (A), *night, nocturnal*

NODO, *node*

NÓDULO, *nodule*

NÓMADA, *nomadic (adj), nomad (n)*

NOMBRADO (A), *famous*

NOMBRE, *name*

NOMENCLATURA, *nomenclature*

NOMINACIÓN, *nomination*

NOMINADO (A), *nominated*

NON (adj), *odd number, uneven*

NORMA, *rule, norm, standard; regulation*

NORMALIDAD, *normality, normalcy*

NORMALIZACIÓN, *normalization*

NORMALMENTE, *normally, usually*

NORMATIVA, *regulations, guidelines*

NORMATIVO (A) (adj), *normative, prescriptive*

NOROESTE, *northwestern (direction), north west (region)*

NORORIENTAL, *northeastern (direction), north east (region)*

NORTE (adj), *north, northern*

NOSTÁLGICO (A), *nostalgic; homesick*

NOTA, *note*

NOTABLEMENTE, *significantly, considerably*

NOTACIÓN, *notation*

NOTARIO (A), *notary*

NOTICIA, *the news*

NOTICIERO, *news bulletin*

NOTIFICACIÓN, *notification*

NOTORIO (A), *obvious, widely-known*

NOVATO (A), *inexperienced, novice, beginner*

NOVELA, *novel*

NOVELISTA, *novelist*

NOVELÍSTICA, *fiction, unreal, imaginary, fanciful*

NOVICIO (A), *novice* (RELIG)

NOVIEMBRE, *November*

NOVIO (A), *bridegroom, bride*

NOVÍSIMO (A), *newest, latest, brand new*

NUBE, *cloud*

NÚBIL, *nubile*

NUBLADO (A) (adj), *cloudy, overcast*

NUBOSIDAD, *cloudiness*

NÚCLEO, *nucleus; center, hub*

NUDISMO, *nudism*

NUDISTA, *nudist*

NUEVO, *new; original; fresh, latest; novel*

NULIDAD, *nullity, incompetence*

NULO (A), *invalid, null and void*

NUMERACIÓN, *numbering system, numeration*

NUMERADOR, *numerator*

NUMÉRICO, *numerical*

NÚMERO, *number; aggregate; digit, figure*

NUMEROSO (A), *numerous, many, profuse, myriad*

NUMISMÁTICA, *numismatics*

NUPCIAL, *nuptial (adj)*

NUTRICIÓN, *nutrition*

NUTRICIONAL, *nutritional*

NUTRICIONISTA, *dietician*

NUTRIENTE, *nutrient*

NUTRITIVO (A), *nutritious*

Easily Recognizable Verbs

NACIONALIZAR, *to nationalize*

NARCOTIZAR, *to drug*

NARRAR, *to recount, tell, narrate*

NATURALIZAR, *to naturalize, become naturalized*

NAVEGAR, *to sail*

NECESITAR, *to need, want; to need to do sthg*

NEGAR, *to deny, refuse*

NEGOCIAR, *to do business, negotiate, deal*

NEUTRALIZAR, *to neutralize*

NOMINAR, *to nominate*

NORMALIZAR, *to return to normal, standardize*

NOTAR, *to notice, point out*

NOTIFICAR, *to notify, inform*

NOVELAR, *to fictionalize, write a novel*

NUBLAR, *to blur, cloud, mar*

NUMERAR, *to number*

STUDY NOTES:

O

Interchangeable Words

¡OH!
OASIS
OBOE
OCCIDENTAL
OCCIPITAL
OCTAGONAL
OCULAR
OMBUDSMAN
OMEGA
ÓMNIBUS
ON-LINE
ÓPERA; *opera house*
OPINIÓN
OPUS (MUS)
ORAL; *orally* (MED)
ORANGUTÁN
ORCA
ORDINAL
ORÉGANO
ORIENTAL
ORIGINAL
ORNAMENTAL
ÓSCAR (CINE)
ÓSMOSIS
OSTENSIBLE, *obvious*
OUTPUT (INFORM)
OVAL ú OVALADO ú ÓVALO
OVERBOOKING

Easily Recognizable Nouns, Adjectives and Adverbs

OBEDIENCIA, *obedience*
OBEDIENTE, *obedient, compliant, subservient*
OBELISCO, *obelisk*
OBERTURA, *overture* (MUS); *advance*
OBESIDAD, *obesity, corpulence, plumpness*
OBESO (A), *obese, overweight, stout*
OBITUARIO, *obituary*
OBJECIÓN, *objection*
OBJETIVAMENTE, *objectively*
OBJETIVIDAD, *objectivity*
OBJETIVO (n), *objective* (MIL)
OBJETIVO (A) (adj), *objective*
OBJETO, *object*
OBJETOR (A), *objector*
OBLICUO (A), *oblique, slanted; oblique* (GEOM)
OBLIGACIÓN, *obligation*
OBLIGADO (A) (adj), *obligated, forced*

OBLIGATORIEDAD, *an obligation, requirement*

OBLIGATORIO (A) (adj), *obligatory, compulsory*

OBLONGO, *oblong*

OBSCENIDAD, *obscenity*

OBSCENO (A), *obscene, vulgar, coarse, dirty*

OBSEQUIOSO (A), *obsequious, obliging, attentive, deferential; servile, toadying*

OBSERVACIÓN, *observation*

OBSERVADOR (A), *observant* (adj), *observer* (n)

OBSERVANCIA, *observance, compliance, regard*

OBSERVATORIO, *observatory*

OBSESIÓN, *obsession, fixation, mania*

OBSESIVO (A), *obsessive, dominating*

OBSESO (A), *obsessed; obsessed person*

OBSOLETO (A), *obsolete, dated*

OBSTÁCULO, *obstacle; hurdle* (DEP)

OBTENCIÓN, *obtaining*

OBTENIBLE, *obtainable, available, accessible*

OBSTETRICIA, *obstetrics*

OBSTINACIÓN, *perseverance, obstinacy*

OBSTINADO (A), *persistent, obstinate, stubborn, mulish*

OBSTRUCCIÓN, *obstruction*

OBSTRUCCIONISMO, *obstructionism, stonewalling*

OBSTRUCCIONISTA, *obstructionist*

OBTURACIÓN, *blockage, obstruction*

OBTUSO (A), *blunt, obtuse, stupid, insensitive*

OBVIAMENTE, *obviously*

OBVIO (A) (adj), *obvious, apparent, evident, conspicuous*

OCASIÓN, *occasion, opportunity, chance*

OCASIONAL, *accidental, occasional*

OCCIDENTAL (adj), *western*

OCEÁNICO (A), *oceanic*

OCÉANO, *ocean*

OCEANOGRAFÍA, *oceanography*

OCELOTE, *ocelot*

OCLUSIÓN, *occlusion, blockage*

OCLUSIVO (A), *occlusive*

OCRE, *ocher*

OCTÁGONO, *octagon*

OCTANO, *octane*

OCTAVA, *octave*

OCTETO, *octet*

OCTUBRE, *October*

OCULISTA, *ophthalmologist*

OCULTO (A), *hidden, secret; occult, esoteric*

OCUPACIÓN, *occupation*

OCUPACIONAL, *occupational*

OCUPADO (A), *busy, occupied, engaged*

OCUPANTE, *occupying (adj), occupant (n)*

OCURRENCIA, *bright idea, witty remark*

OCURRENTE, *witty, entertaining, amusing*

ODIO, *hatred, dislike, loathe, detest*

ODIOSO (A), *hateful, horrible, nasty*

ODONTOLOGÍA, *dentistry*

ODONTÓLOGO (A), *dentist, dental surgeon*

OFENDIDO (A), *offended (adj), offended party (n)*

OFENSA, *offense (against), slight, insult*

OFENSIVA (n), *offensive*

OFENSIVO (A) (adj), *offensive*

OFENSOR (A), *offender*

OFERTA, *offer*

OFERTORIO, *offertory* (RELIG)

OFICIAL (A) (n), *worker, clerk*

OFICIAL (adj), *official*

OFICIALIDAD, *official nature*

OFICIALMENTE, *officially*

OFICIANTE, *celebrant*

OFICINA, *office*

OFICINISTA, *office worker*

OFICIO, *profession, trade; religious service*

OFICIOSO (A), *unofficial, informal*

OFTALMOLOGÍA, *ophthalmology*

OFTALMÓLOGO (A), *ophthalmologist*

OFUSCACIÓN, *blindness, confusion*

OGRO, *ogre*

OKEY, *okay, OK!*

OLEAGINOSO (A), *oleaginous, oily*

ÓLEO, *oil, oil paint* (ARTE)

OLEODUCTO, *oil pipeline*

OLEOSO (A) (adj), *oily*

OLFATIVO (A), *olfactory*

OLFATO, *sense of smell, instinct*

OLIGARCA, *oligarch*

OLIGARQUÍA, *oligarchy (government by a few)*

OLIGÁRQUICO (A), *oligarchic*

OLÍMPICO (A), *Olympic* (DEP*); Olympian, haughty*

OLIVA (n), *olive*

OLIVÁCEO (A) (adj), *olive*

OLIVAR, *olive grove*

OLIVO, *olive tree*

OMBLIGO, *navel, belly button*

OMISO (A), *negligent, lax, indifferent, derelict*

OMISIÓN, *omission, deletion*

OMNIPOTENCIA, *omnipotence*

OMNIPOTENTE, *omnipotent, supreme*

OMNIPRESENTE, *omnipresent, ubiquitous; universal*

OMNÍVORO (A), *omnivorous (adj), omnivore (n)*

ONCOLOGÍA, *oncology*

ONCÓLOGO (A), *oncologist*

ONDULACIÓN, *rippling, ripple, wave*

ONDULADO (A), *wavy*

ONDULANTE, *undulating*

ONEROSO (A), *burdensome, onerous*

ONOMATOPEYA, *onomatopoeia*

ONTOLOGÍA, *ontology*

OPACIDAD, *opacity*

OPACO (A), *opaque, dull, gloomy; obscure*

ÓPALO, *opal*

OPCIÓN, *option, choice*

OPCIONAL, *optional,*

OPERACIÓN, *operation* (MED); *activity*

OPERACIONAL, *operational*

OPERADOR (A), *operator, (in a general sense)*

OPERANTE (adj), *operating, working*

OPERARIO (A) (n), *worker*

OPERÍSTICO, *operatic; opera*

OPERATIVO (n), *operation* (MIL) (POL)

OPERETA, *operetta*

OPIÁCEO, *opiate*

OPIO, *opium*

OPONENTE, *opponent*

OPORTUNAMENTE, *opportunely*

OPORTUNIDAD, *opportunity, chance*

OPORTUNISMO, *opportunism*

OPORTUNISTA, *opportunist (n), opportunistic (adj)*

OPORTUNO (A), *opportune, timely*

OPOSICIÓN, *opposition*

OPOSITOR (A), *opponent*

OPRESIÓN, *oppression, anxiety*

OPRESIVO (A), *oppressive*

OPRESOR (A), *oppressive (adj), oppressor (n)*

OPROBIO, *shame, disgrace, opprobrium*

OPROBIOSO (A), *disgraceful*

OPTATIVO (A), *optional*

ÓPTICO(A), *optic (adj), optician (n)*

OPTIMISMO, *optimism*

OPTIMISTA, *optimistic (adj), optimist (n)*

OPTIMIZACIÓN, *optimization*

ÓPTIMO (A), *optimum*

OPUESTO (A), *opposite, contrary; conflicting*

OPULENCIA, *opulence, abundance*

OPULENTO (A), *opulent, wealthy, luxurious*

ORACIÓN, *prayer, moral speech* (RELIG)

ORÁCULO, *oracle*

ORADOR (A), *orator, speaker*

ORATORIA, *oratory*

ORATORIO, *chapel*

ORBE, *globe, world*

ÓRBITA, *orbit*

ORDEN, *order, decree; religious order*

ORDENACIÓN, *order, arrangement; ordination* (RELIG)

ORDENADA, *ordinate* (MAT)

ORDENADO (A) (n), *ordained person* (RELIG)

ORDENADO (A), *tidy, neat, organized*

ORDENANZA, *ordinance, decree; orderly* (MIL)

ORDENAMIENTO, *legislation, regulations*

ORDINARIEZ, *commonness, coarseness*

ORDINARIO (A), *ordinary, usual*

ORFELINATO, *orphanage*

ORGÁNICO (A), *organic*

ORGANISMO, *organism* (BIOL); *organization* (POL)

ORGANISTA, *organist*

ORGANIZACIÓN, *organization*

ORGANIZADOR (A), *organizer (n); organizing (adj)*

ORGANIZADO (A), *organized, structured, arranged*

ÓRGANO, *organ* (ANAT); *organ* (MUS)

ORGANISTA, *organist*

ORGASMO, *orgasm*

ORGÍA, *orgy, wildness*

ORGIÁSTICO (A), *orgiastic*

ORIENTACIÓN, *orientation, situation*

ORIENTE, *east, (el oriente = the East)*

ORIFICIO, *hole, opening, orifice*

ORIGEN, *origin, origin of birth*

ORIGINALIDAD, *originality*

ORIGINARIO (A), *indigenous, native; original, initial, first; authentic, genuine*

ORINA, *urine*

ORINAL, *chamber pot*

ORNAMENTACIÓN, *ornamentation*

ORNAMENTO, *ornament*

ORNATO, *decoration*

ORQUESTA, *orchestra*

ORQUESTACIÓN, *orchestration*

ORTODONCIA, *orthodontics*

ORTODOXIA, *orthodoxy*

ORTODOXO (A), *orthodox*

ORTOPÉDICO (A), *orthopedic (adj), orthopedist (n)*

ORTOPEDISTA, *orthopedics*

OSCILACIÓN, *oscillation*

OSCILADOR, *oscillator*

OSCURIDAD ú OBSCURIDAD, *darkness, obscurity*

OSCURO(A) ú OBSCURO (A), *dark, overcast, obscure*

OSOBUCO, *osso bucco*

OSTENTACIÓN, *ostentation, show*

OSTENTOSO (A), *ostentatious, showy, pretentious*

OSTEÓPATA, *osteopath*

OSTEOPATÍA, *osteopathy*

OSTIÓN, *large oyster*

OSTRA, *oyster*

OSTRACISMO, *ostracism, blacklist, isolate, shun*

OTOÑAL, *autumnal*

OVACIÓN, *ovation*

ÓVALO (n), *oval*

OVARIO, *ovary*

OVEROL ú OVEROLS, *dungarees, overalls*

OVINO (A), (adj), *ovine*

OVÍPARO (A), *oviparous*

OVULACIÓN, *ovulation*

OXIDACIÓN, *oxidation*

OXIDADO (A), *rusty*

ÓXIDO, *oxide*

OXÍGENO, *oxygen*

OZONO, *ozone*

Easily Recognizable Verbs

OBJETAR, *to object*

OBJETIVAR, *to treat objectively*

OBLIGAR, *to oblige, force*

OBSERVAR, *to observe, watch*

OBSESIONAR, *to obsess, haunt*

OBSTACULIZAR, *to hinder, hamper*

OBSTINARSE, *to refuse, to give way, persist*

OBSTRUIR, *to block, obstruct*

OBTENER, *to get, win, obtain*

OBTURAR, *to block, fill, close*

OBVIAR, *to avoid*

OCASIONAR, *to cause*

OCULTAR, *to hide, conceal*

OCUPAR, *to occupy, take up, fill*

OCURRIR, *to happen*

ODIAR, *to hate; pester, annoy*

OFENDER, *to insult, offend*

OFERTAR, *to offer, tender*

OFICIALIZAR, *to make official*

OFUSCAR, *to dazzle, blind*

OMITIR, *to omit*

ONDULAR, *to ripple, undulate*

OPERAR, *to produce, bring about; operate, use*

OPINAR, *to think, give an opinion*

OPONER, *to oppose, confront, object*

OPTAR, *to choose, opt for*

OPTIMIZAR, *to optimize*

ORAR, *to pray*

ORDENAR, *to arrange, put in order, tidy up*

ORDEÑAR, *to milk*

ORGANIZAR, *to organize*

ORIENTAR, *to direct, orient*

ORIENTARSE, *to point towards, get one's bearings, find one's way around*

ORIGINAR, *to cause*

ORNAMENTAR ú ORNAR, *to decorate, adorn*

ORQUESTAR, *to orchestrate*

OSCILAR, *to swing, fluctuate*

OSCURECER, *to darken, confuse, cloud, obscure*

OSTENTAR, *to hold, have, show off*

OVACIONAR, *to give an ovation*

OXIDAR, *to oxidize, rust*

STUDY NOTES:

P

Interchangeable Words

PAGODA

PALADÍN

PALATAL

PALPABLE

PANACEA

PANAMÁ, *hat*

PÁNCREAS

PANDA (ZOOL)

PANEL

PANORAMA

PAPAL

PAPARAZZI

PAPAYA

PAR (MAT) (DEP)

PARÁBOLA

PARANOIA

PARANORMAL

PARASOL; *sunshade, sun visor*

PARIETAL; *parietal bone*

PARQUET, *a floor*

PARKING (lot), *car park*

PARTICULAR; *special*

PASTEL, *drawing; cake, pie, color*

PASTOR (A), *shepherd, clergyman*

PASTORAL

PATÉ

PATERNAL

PÁTINA

PATIO; *courtyard, backyard, playground*

PECTORAL

PECULIAR, *typical, particular, distinctive*

PEDAL

PEDESTAL

PEDIGREE ó PEDIGRÍ

PELVIS

PENAL

PENALTY ó PENALTI, *kick* (DEP)

PENÍNSULA (n)

PENINSULAR (adj)

PENSIÓN; *allowance, alimony*

PENUMBRA

PER CÁPITA

PERCEPTIBLE

PERFORMANCE

PERFUME

PERINATAL

PERITONITIS

PERMEABLE

PERPENDICULAR

PERSONAL

PERSUASIÓN

PERVERSIÓN, *sexual*

PETUNIA

PI (MAT)

PIANO

PICKUP (truck)

PICNIC

PING-PONG

PIQUÉ

PISTÓN (MECAN)

PÍVOT (DEP)

PIXEL

PIZZA

PIZZERÍA

PLACEBO

PLACENTA, *afterbirth*

PLACER (GEOL)

PLAN

PLASMA

PLAUSIBLE

PLAYBOY ó PLAY-BOY

PLAZA, *a square*

PLURAL

PLUVIAL

PÓKER ó PÓQUER

POLAR

POLIO

POLO (DEP); *a polo shirt, a pole or a pole* (GEOG)

PONCHO

POP (MUS)

POPULAR; *traditional*

PORNO

PÓRTICO

POSE

POST MERÍDIEM

POSTAL, *order, money order*

POSTDOCTORAL ó POST-DOCTORAL

PÓSTER

POSTERIOR

POSTURAL

POTABLE

PRACTICABLE

PRAXIS (RELIG); *practice*

PRECISIÓN

PRECURSOR (A)

PRECONCILIAR

PREMENSTRUAL

PREMIER, *prime minister*

PREMIERE

PREMOLAR

PRENATAL

PRENUPCIAL

PRESENTABLE

PRIMATE (ZOOL)

PRIMORDIAL; *fundamental, essential*

PRINCIPAL

PRIOR (A) (RELIG), *prioress*

PRO

PROBABLE

PROFUSIÓN

PRONOMINAL

PROPAGANDA, *electoral, advertising*

PROPULSIÓN

PROTECTOR (A) (adj)

PROTÓN

PROVERBIAL

PROVINCIAL

PROVISIÓN

PROVISIONAL

PUB, *bar*

PUBIS

PULLMAN ó PULMAN, *sleeping car*

PUMA, *cougar*

PUS

PUZZLE

Easily Recognizable Nouns, Adjectives and Adverbs

PACIENCIA, *patience*

PACIENTE (adj), *patient, tolerant, diligent, stoical*

PACIFICACIÓN, *pacification*

PACÍFICO (A), *peaceful*

PACTO, *pact, agreement, contract*

PADRE, *father* (RELIG)

PAGINACIÓN, *pagination*

PALACIO, *palace*

PALIATIVO (A) (MED), *palliative*

PALEOLÍTICO (A), *Paleolithic, Stone Age*

PALMA, *palm*

PALMO, *span of a hand, few inches, small amount*

PALPITACIÓN, *palpitation, beat, throb*

PALPITANTE, *beating, throbbing; exciting*

PAN, *bread*

PANERA, *bread box*

PÁNICO, *panic*

PANORÁMICO (A), *panoramic*

PANTEÓN, *pantheon; tomb, cemetery vault*

PANTERA, *panther*

PANTOMIMA, *pantomime, mime*

PAPÁ, *dad, daddy; potato; pope*

PAPEL, *paper*

PAPELEO, *paperwork, red tape*

PARABÓLICO (A), *parabolic*

PARADIGMA, *paradigm, example*

PARAFERNALIA, *paraphernalia*

PARAFINA, *paraffin*

PARÁFRASIS, *paraphrase*

PARALELO (A), *parallel*

PARAÍSO, *paradise, heaven*

PARÁLISIS, *paralysis*

PARÁMETRO, *parameter*

PARAMILITAR, *paramilitary*

PARANGÓN, *paragon, incomparable*

PARANOICO (A), *paranoid*

PARAPLÉJICO (A), *paraplegic*

PARAPETO, *parapet* (MIL), *barricade; defense*

PARCIAL, *partial, incomplete; biased*

PARCIALIDAD, *partiality, bias*

PARÉNTESIS, *parenthesis, bracket*

PARIA, *pariah*

PARIDAD, *parity, equality*

PARODIA, *parody*

PARQUE, *park*

PARQUÉ, *floor*

PÁRRAFO ó PARÁGRAFO, *paragraph*

PARTE, *part; also means report*

PARTICIÓN, *partition; division* (MAT)

PARTICIPACIÓN, *participation*

PARTICIPANTE, *participating*

PARTICIPIO, *participle*

PARTÍCULA, *particle*

PASABLE, *passable, tolerable; fordable*

PASADO (A), *past; stale, overripe*

PASAPORTE, *passport*

PASIÓN, *passion; the Passion*

PASIONAL, *passionate*

PASIVIDAD, *passivity; pension*

PASIVO (A), *passive; liabilities* (COM)

PASTA, *putty, paste; pastry, filler*

PASTEURIZADO (A), *pasteurized*

PATENA, *paten*

PATERNALISMO, *paternalism*

PATERNALISTA, *paternalistic*

PATERNO (A), *paternal*

PATÉTICO (A), *pathetic, moving*

PATOLOGÍA, *pathology*

PATOLÓGICO (A), *pathological*

PATRIARCA, *patriarch*

PATRIARCAL, *patriarchal*

PATRIOTA, *patriot*

PATRIÓTICO (A), *patriotic*

PATRÓN (A), *boss, master*

PAUSA, *pause, break*

PAUSADO (A), *slow, deliberate*

PAVIMENTO, *pavement, road surface, paving*

PECTINA, *pectin*

PECULIARIDAD, *uniqueness, peculiarity*

PEDAGOGÍA, *education, pedagogy*

PEDAGÓGICO (A), *educational*

PEDAGOGO (A), *teacher, educator*

PEDANTE, *pedantic, pretentious; pedant*

PEDERASTA, *pederast*

PEDESTRE, *pedestrian*

PELÍCANO, *pelican*

PENABLE, *punishable*

PENALIDAD, *punishment, hardship*

PENALIZACIÓN, *penalization, penalty*

PENETRACIÓN, *penetration*

PENICILINA, *penicillin*

PENITENTE, *penitent*

PENSADOR (A), *thinker*

PENÚLTIMO (A), *penultimate*

PENURIA, *penury, poverty, destitution*

PÉPTICO, *peptic*

PERCEPCIÓN, *perception*

PERCUSIÓN, *percussion*

PERDICIÓN, *ruin, undoing; perdition*

PERDIDAMENTE, *hopelessly, madly*

PERDÓN, *pardon; forgiveness; write-off* (COM)

PERFECCIÓN, *perfection*

PERFECCIONISTA, *perfectionist*

PERFECTAMENTE, *perfectly*

PERFECTO (A), *perfect (adj); perfect tense (n)*

PERFIDIA, *perfidy, treachery, betrayal*

PÉRFIDO (A), *perfidious, treacherous*

PERFORACIÓN, *perforation, drilling, piercing*

PERIFERIA, *periphery, outskirts*

PERIFÉRICO (A), *peripheral, outlying*

PERÍMETRO, *perimeter* (MAT)

PERIODICIDAD, *frequency, periodicity* (TECNOL)

PERIÓDICO, *periodic*

PERÍODO, *period,* (DEP) (MED); *time period* (GEOL)

PERISCOPIO, *periscope*

PERJUDICIAL, *harmful, damaging*

PERJUICIO, *harm, damage*

PERJURIO, *perjury, lying, mendacity, deception*

PERLA, *pearl*

PERLADO (A), *pearly*

PERMANENCIA, *staying, continued stay, continuation*

PERMANENTE, *permanent, fast*

PERMEABILIDAD, *permeability*

PERMISIBLE, *permissible*

PERMISIVIDAD, *permissiveness*

PERMISIVO (A), *permissive*

PERMISO, *permission*

PERMUTACIÓN, *permutation*

PERNICIOSO (A), *damaging, harmful, pernicious*

PERÓXIDO, *peroxide*

PERPETUIDAD, *perpetuity, permanence, forever*

PERPETUO (A), *perpetual, uninterrupted, ageless*

PERPLEJIDAD, *perplexity, bewilderment, confusion*

PERPLEJO (A), *perplexed, bewildered, puzzled*

PERSECUCIÓN, *pursuit; persecution* (POL) (RELIG)

PERSEVERANCIA, *perseverance, determination*

PERSISTENCIA, *persistence*

PERSISTENTE (adj), *persistent, tenacious, steadfast*

PERSONA, *person*

PERSONAJE, *important person, celebrity*

PERSONALIDAD, *personality*

PERSONALISMO, *partiality, preference; choice, pick*

PERSONALMENTE, *personally*

PERSONIFICACIÓN, *personification*

PERSPECTIVA, *perspective, view, prospect*

PERSPICACIA, *perceptiveness, insight*

PERSPICAZ, *sharp, perceptive, shrewd, attentive*

PERSUASIVO (A), *persuasive, convincing, compelling*

PERTINENCIA, *appropriateness, relevance*

PERTINENTE, *appropriate, pertinent, relevant*

PERTURBACIÓN, *disquiet, unease, perturbed*

PERTURBADO (A), *mentally disturbed* (MED)

PERVERSIDAD, *wickedness, perversity, depravity*

PERVERSO (A), *depraved, wicked, perverse*

PERVERTIDO (A), *perverted, deviant*

PERVERTIDOR (A), *pernicious, corrupting, fatal*

PESIMISMO, *pessimism*

PESIMISTA, *pessimistic (adj), pessimist (n)*

PÉSIMO (A) (adj), *terrible, awful, dreadful*

PESTICIDA, *pesticide*

PESTILENCIA, *plague, pestilence*

PESTILENTE (adj), *foul-smelling, stink, stench*

PÉTALO, *petal*

PETICIÓN, *request, petition*

PETRÓLEO, *petroleum, crude oil*

PETULANCIA, *arrogance, conceit, insolence, pride*

PETULANTE, *opinionated, arrogant, brazen*

PIANISTA, *pianist*

PICTÓRICO (A), *pictorial*

PIGMENTACIÓN, *pigmentation*

PIGMENTO, *pigment*

PIGMEO (A), *pygmy*

PIJAMA ó PIYAMA, *pajama (s)*

PILAR, *pillar, post*

PILOTO, *pilot, driver; raincoat*

PINO, *pine*

PINTA, *spot; pint*

PINTO, *speckled, spotted, dappled*

PIONERO (A), *pioneer (n); pioneering (adj)*

PIPA, *pipe for smoking; cask, barrel*

PIRAMIDAL, *pyramidal*

PIRÁMIDE, *pyramid*

PIRAÑA, *piranha*

PIRATA, *pirate*

PIROMANÍA, *pyromania*

PISTACHO, *pistachio*

PISTILO, *pistil*

PISTOLA, *pistol, gun*

PISTOLERA, *holster*

PISTOLERO (A), *gunman*

PISTÓN, *piston; cornet, bugle; percussion cap, key* (MUS)

PLAGA, *plague, blight* (AGRIC); *epidemic*

PLANCTON, *plankton*

PLANTA, *plant*

PLANTACIÓN, *plantation*

PLÁSTICO (A), *plastic*

PLATA, *silverware; silver*

PLATAFORMA, *platform* (POL)

PLATO, *plate*

PLATÓNICO (A), *platonic, chaste, asexual, detached*

PLAZOLETA, *small square*

PLEBE, *the masses; mob, rabble*

PLEBISCITO, *plebiscite*

PLENARIO (A), *plenary* (POL)

PLENITUD, *completeness, fullness*

PLENO (A), *full, complete*

PLEURESÍA, *pleurisy*

PLUMA, *feather*

PLURALIDAD, *plurality*

PLUS, *bonus, extra pay*

PLUTOCRACIA, *plutocracy*

PLUTÓCRATA, *plutocrat*

POCIÓN, *potion, elixir, tonic; brew*

POEMA, *poem*

POLARIDAD, *polarity*

POLARIZACIÓN, *polarization*

POLCA, *polka*

POLÉMICA, *controversy (n); polemic (adj)*

POLÉMICO, *polemical*

POLEN, *pollen*

POLICÍA, *police officer, police*

POLIÉSTER, *polyester*

POLIGAMIA, *polygamy*

POLÍGONO, *polygon* (MAT)

POLÍTICO (A), *political,* (POL); *tactful*

POLUCIÓN, *pollution*

POMPOSO (A), *pompous, splendid*

PONEY ó PONI, *pony*

PONTIFICIO, *papal, pontifical*

POPULARIDAD, *popularity*

POPURRÍ, *potpourri*

PORCELANA, *porcelain*

PORCIÓN, *portion, piece*

PORCHE, *arcade, porch*

PORNOGRÁFICO (A), *pornographic*

PORO, *pore*

POROSO (A), *porous*

PORTAFOLIOS, *briefcase, attaché case*

PORTAL, *entrance, main door*

PORTÁTIL, *portable*

PORTILLO, *gap, opening, side entrance*

POSESIÓN, *possession*

POSESIVO (A), *possessive*

POSIBLE, *possible*

POSIBILIDAD, *possibility, chance*

POSICIÓN, *position*

POSIMPRESIONISMO, *post-impressionism*

POSIMPRESIONISTA, *post-impressionist*

POSINDUSTRIAL, *post-industrial*

POSITIVA, *photographic print*

POSITIVO (A), *positive, practical*

POSMODERNISMO, *post-modernism*

POSNATAL, *postnatal*

POSTDATA ó POSDATA, *postscript*

POSTE, *post, pole*

POSTERIDAD, *posterity*

POSTERIORIDAD, *subsequently, later*

POSTGRADUADO (A), *postgraduate*

POSTRACIÓN (A), *prostration*

POSTRERO, *last*

POSTULADO, *postulate; assumption*

PÓSTUMO (A), *posthumous*

POSTURA, *posture, position, stance*

POTASIO, *potassium*

POTE, *pot*

POTENCIA, *power*

POTENCIAL, *potential, conditional*

POTENTE, *powerful*

PRÁCTICA, *practice (as in golf, tennis, any sport)*

PRÁCTICO (A) (adj), *practical, dandy; sensible*

PRÁCTICO, *pilot* (NAUT)

PRAGMÁTICO (A), *pragmatic (adj), pragmatist (n)*

PREÁMBULO, *preamble, preface*

PREBENDA, *prebend* (RELIG), *special favor, perk*

PRECARIO (A), *precarious*

PRECAUCIÓN; *precaution; caution, care*

PRECEDENTE, *preceding, previous, foregoing*

PRECEPTIVO (A), *compulsory, obligatory*

PRECEPTO, *precept, order, rule*

PRECIOSO (A), *precious*

PRECIPICIO, *precipice*

PRECIPITACIÓN, *precipitation, haste; rain*

PRECIPITADO (A), *hasty, headlong*

PRECISAMENTE, *precisely*

PRECISO (A), *precise*

PRECOCIDAD, *precociousness, precocity*

PRECONCEBIDO (A), *preconceived*

PRECOZ, *premature, early; precocious*

PREDADOR (A), *predatory (adj), predator (n)*

PREDATORIO (A), *predatory instincts, animal instincts*

PREDECESOR (A), *predecessor, ancestor*

PREDESTINACIÓN, *predestination*

PREDESTINADO (A), *predestined, ordained, fated*

PREDICADO, *predicate*

PREDICAMENTO, *standing, prestige*

PREDICATIVO (A), *predicative, predicates*

PREDICCIÓN, *prediction, forecast; prognosis*

PREDILECCIÓN, *predilection, preference*

PREDILECTO (A) (adj), *favorite*

PREDISPOSICIÓN, *predisposition* (MED); *tendency*

PREDISPUESTO (A), *predisposed, inclined to, liable to*

PREDOMINANCIA, *predominance*

PREDOMINANTE, *predominant, controlling, ruling*

PREDOMINIO, *preponderance, predominance*

PREEMINENCIA, *preeminence*

PREEMINENTE, *preeminent, peerless, unequaled*

PREESTABLECIDO (A), *preestablished*

PREEXISTENTE, *preexisting*

PREFABRICADO (A), *prefabricated*

PREFACIO, *preface, foreword*

PREFECTO (A), *prefect, administrator*

PREFECTURA, *prefecture*

PREFERENCIA, *preference, partiality, inclination, bent*

PREFERENCIAL, *preferential*

PREFERENTE, *priority, preference*

PREFERENTEMENTE, *preferably*

PREFERIBLE, *preferable (to)*

PREFERIDO (A), *preferred, favored*

PREFORMATEADO, *preformatted*

PREHISTORIA, *prehistory*

PREHISTÓRICO (A), *prehistoric*

PREINSTALACIÓN, *standard equipment*

PREINSTALADO, *pre-installed*

PREJUICIO, *prejudice*

PRELADO, *prelate*

PRELIMINAR (adj), *preliminary; qualifying* (DEP)

PRELUDIO, *prelude*

PREMATRIMONIAL, *premarital*

PREMATURO (A), *premature*

PREMEDITACIÓN, *premeditation*

PREMEDITADO (A), *premeditated, deliberate*

PREMISA, *premise*

PREMONICIÓN, *premonition*

PREMONITORIO (A), *warning*

PREMURA, *haste, urgency*

PREOCUPACIÓN, *concern, worry*

PREOCUPADO (A), *worried, concerned*

PREOCUPANTE, *worrisome*

PREPARACIÓN, *preparation*

PREPARADO (A), *ready, prepared*

PREPARADOR (A), *trainer, coach, tutor*

PREPARATIVO (A), *preparatory, preliminary*

PREPARATIVOS, *preparations*

PREPARATORIO (A), *introductory, warm-up*

PREPONDERANCIA, *preponderance*

PREPONDERANTE, *prevailing, preponderant*

PREPOSICIÓN, *preposition*

PREPOSICIONAL, *prepositional*

PREPOTENCIA, *arrogance*

PREPOTENTE, *domineering, overbearing, high-handed*

PRERREQUISITO, *prerequisite*

PRERROGATIVA, *prerogative*

PRESAGIO, *omen, portent; presage*

PRESCRIPCIÓN, *prescription*

PRESCRIPTIVO, *prescriptive*

PRESCRITO (A), *prescribed*

PRESELECCIÓN, *short list, short listing*

PRESENCIA, *presence*

PRESENTACIÓN, *presentation, introduction*

PRESENTADOR (A), *presenter, hostess/host*

PRESENTE, *present*

PRESENTIMIENTO, *presentiment, feeling, premonition*

PRESERVACIÓN, *preservation*

PRESIDENCIAL, *presidential*

PRESIDIO, *prison*

PRESIÓN, *pressure, under pressure, squeeze*

PRESTANCIA, *excellence, distinction, poise*

PRESTIDIGITACIÓN, *conjuring, sleight of hand*

PRESTIGIO, *prestige*

PRESTIGIOSO (A), *prestigious, famous*

PRESTO (A) (adv), *ready; quickly, swiftly*

PRESUMIBLE, *probable, likely, presumable*

PRESUMIDO (A), *conceited, vain*

PRESUNCIÓN, *presumption, conceit, vanity*

PRESUNTAMENTE, *supposedly, allegedly*

PRESUNTO (A), *presumed, supposed, suspected*

PRESUNTUOSO (A), *conceited, presumptuous*

PRESUPOSICIÓN, *assumption, presupposition*

PRETENCIOSO (A), *pretentious, showy, snobbish, vain*

PRETENDIDO (A), *supposed, alleged*

PRETENSIÓN, *aim, intention, aspiration*

PRETEXTO, *pretext, excuse*

PREVARICACIÓN, *prevarication*

PREVENCIÓN, *prevention*

PREVENIDO (A), *to be cautious, alert, prepared*

PREVENTIVO (A), *preventive* (MED)

PREVIO (A), *prior, previous*

PREVISIBLE, *foreseeable, predictable*

PREVISIÓN, *forecast, foresight, anticipation*

PREVISOR (A), *prudent, farsighted*

PREVISTO (A), *anticipated, predicted; planned*

PRIMA, *premium; bonus*

PRIMACÍA, *primacy, supremacy*

PRIMADO, *primate* (RELIG)

PRIMARIO (A), *primary; elementary, basic*

PRIMERO (A), *first*

PRIMITIVO (A), *primitive; first, original*

PRIMO, *prime*

PRINCESA, *princess*

PRINCIPADO, *principality*

PRINCIPIO, *beginning; outset, start*

PRIORIDAD, *right of way* (AUTO), *priority*

PRISIÓN, *prison*

PRISIONERO (A), *prisoner*

PRISMA, *prism*

PRISMÁTICOS, *binoculars, field glasses*

PRÍSTINO, *pristine, original*

PRIVACIDAD, *privacy*

PRIVACIÓN, *loss, privation*

PRIVADO (A), *private, confidential*

PRIVATIVO (A), *exclusive*

PRIVATIZACIÓN, *privatization*

PRIVILEGIADO (A), *privileged; exceptional*

PRIVILEGIO, *privilege*

PROBABILIDAD, *probability, likelihood*

PROBABLEMENTE, *probably, likely, possible*

PROBADO (A), *proven, tested*

PROBIDAD, *integrity, honesty*

PROBLEMA, *problem*

PROBLEMÁTICO (A), *problematic*

PROCACIDAD, *insolence, imprudence*

PROCAZ, *insolent, imprudent*

PROCESIÓN (RELIG), *procession*

PROCESO, *process*

PROCLAMA, *bands, address*

PROCLAMACIÓN, *proclamation*

PROCLIVE (adj), *inclined*

PROCLIVIDAD, *proclivity, inclination*

PROCREACIÓN, *procreation*

PROCURADOR (A), *attorney* (DER)

PRODIGIO, *wonder, marvel, prodigy*

PRODIGIOSO (A), *prodigious, marvelous*

PRODUCCIÓN, *production*

PRODUCTIVIDAD, *productivity*

PRODUCTIVO (A), *productive*

PRODUCTO, *product (*MAT) (AGRIC)

PRODUCTOR (A) (adj), *producing*

PROFANACIÓN, *desecration, profanation*

PROFANO (A), *profane, secular*

PROFESIÓN, *profession*

PROFESIONAL, *professional*

PROFESO (A) (adj), *professed*

PROFESOR (A), *teacher, instructor, lecturer*

PROFETA, *prophet*

PROFÉTICO (A), *prophetic*

PROFUNDIDAD, *depth*

PROFUNDAMENTE, *deeply, profoundly*

PROFUNDO (A), *deep, profound*

PROFUSO (A), *profuse, extravagant*

PROGENIE, *progeny, offspring*

PROGRAMA, *program* (INFORM); *program, schedule*

PROGRESIÓN, *progression*

PROGRESIVO (A), *progressive, gradual*

PROGRESO, *progress, advance*

PROHIBICIÓN, *ban, prohibition*

PROHIBIDO (A), *prohibited, banned*

PROHIBITIVO (A), *prohibitive*

PROHOMBRE, *great, outstanding man*

PROLIFERACIÓN, *proliferation, escalation, buildup*

PROLÍFICO (A), *prolific, productive, creative*

PROLONGACIÓN, *extension, prolongation*

PROLONGADO (A), *long, lengthy, extended*

PROMEDIO, *an average of*

PROMESA, *promise, pledge*

PROMETEDOR (A), *promising, encouraging, positive*

PROMINENCIA, *protuberance, bump; prominence*

PROMINENTE, *protruding, prominent*

PROMISCUIDAD, *promiscuity*

PROMISCUO (A), *promiscuous*

PROMOCIÓN, *promotion, advance*

PROMOCIONAL, *promotional*

PROMONTORIO, *promontory, headland*

PROMOTOR (A), *promoter, instigator*

PROMULGACIÓN, *enactment*

PRONOMBRE, *pronoun*

PRONÓSTICO, *forecast, prediction, prognosis*

PRONTAMENTE, *promptly*

PRONTITUD, *promptness, quickness*

PRONTO, *soon*

PRONUNCIACIÓN, *pronunciation*

PRONUNCIADO (A), *pronounced, strong, sharp*

PROPAGACIÓN, *propagation, diffusion*

PROPANO, *propane*

PROPELENTE, *propellant*

PROPENSIÓN, *propensity, tendency, inclination; predisposition* (MED)

PROPENSO (A), *prone, susceptible*

PROPICIO (A), *propitious, favorable*

PROPIEDAD, *ownership, possession; property*

PROPIETARIO (A), *owner*

PROPORCIÓN, *proportion; ratio* (MAT)

PROPORCIONADO (A), *shapely, well proportioned*

PROPORCIONAL, *proportional*

PROPOSICIÓN, *proposal, proposition*

PROPÓSITO, *intention, purpose*

PRORRATA, *quota, share, pro rata*

PROSA, *prose*

PROSAICO (A), *prosaic, mundane*

PROSECUCIÓN, *continuation; prosecution* (DER)

PROSPECCIÓN, *exploration, prospecting*

PROSPECTO, *leaflet, prospectus; directions for use*

PROSPERIDAD, *prosperity*

PRÓSPERO (A), *prosperous, thriving*

PRÓSTATA, *prostate*

PROSTÍBULO, *brothel*

PROSTITUCIÓN, *prostitution*

PROSTITUTO (A), *prostitute*

PROTAGONISTA, *protagonist, main figure*

PROTECCIÓN, *protection*

PROTECCIONISMO, *protectionism*

PROTECTOR (A), *protective*

PROTEÍNA, *protein*

PRÓTESIS, *prosthesis*

PROTESTA, *protest, objection* (DER)

PROTOCOLO, *protocol*

PROTOTIPO, *prototype*

PROTUBERANCIA, *protuberance, bulge*

PROVERBIO, *proverb*

PROVIDENCIAL, *providential*

PROVINCIA, *province*

PROVOCACIÓN, *provocation*

PROVOCATIVO (A), *provocative*

PRÓXIMAMENTE, *soon, shortly*

PROXIMIDAD, *closeness, proximity*

PRÓXIMO (A), *near, close*

PROYECTIL, *projectile, missile* (MIL)

PROYECTO, *project, plan*

PROYECTOR, *projector* (CINE)

PRUDENCIA, *caution, care*

PRUDENCIAL, *sensible, moderate, prudential*

PRUDENTE, *sensible, prudent*

PÚBER, *adolescent*

PUBERTAD, *puberty*

PUBLICACIÓN, *publication*

PUBLICIDAD, *advertising, publicity*

PUBLICISTA, *publicist*

PÚBLICO (A), *public*

PUDÍN, *pudding*

PUEBLO, *the people/nation; countryside; small town*

PUERIL, *childish, puerile*

PUERTA, *door, gate*

PUERTO, *port*

PÚGIL, *boxer*

PULCRITUD, *neatness, tidiness, pulchritude*

PULCRO (A), *neat, tidy*

PULMONÍA, *pneumonia*

PULÓVER, *pullover, tank top*

PULPA, *pulp*

PÚLPITO, *pulpit*

PULSO, *pulse* (MED)

PUNIBLE, *punishable*

PUNICIÓN, *punishment*

PUNITIVO (A), *punitive, retributive*

PUNKI, *punk*

PUNTA, *point, end, tip, side; headland*

PUNTO, *point (strong, weak, boiling, etc.), dot, spot*

PUNTUACIÓN, *punctuation; grade; score* (DEP)

PUNTUAL, *punctual; specific, precise; detailed*

PUNTUALIDAD, *punctuality*

PUPILA, *pupil*

PUPILO (A), *boarder, ward,* (DER)

PURÉ, *thick soup; mashed potatoes*

PURGA, *purgative* (MED); *purge, eliminate*

PURGANTE (adj), *purgative, purifying, cathartic*

PURGATORIO (A), *purgatory*

PURIFICACIÓN, *purification*

PURISTA, *purist*

PURO (A), *pure, authentic, unalloyed, true, perfect*

PURPÚREO (adj), *purple*

PÚRPURA (n), *purple*

PÚSTULA, *pustule, pimple*

PUTATIVO (A), *putative, supposed, reputed*

PUTREFACCIÓN, *putrefaction, decay*

PUTREFACTO (A) ó PÚTRIDO (A), *rotten, putrid, putrefied*

Easily Recognizable Verbs

PACIFICAR, *to pacify, calm, appease*

PALPITAR, *to beat, throb, palpitate*

PARAFRASEAR, *to paraphrase*

PARALIZAR, *to paralyze, stop*

PARCELAR, *to parcel out, divide*

PARLAMENTAR, *to negotiate*

PARODIAR, *to parody, take off on sb*

PARTICIPAR, *to participate, take part in*

PARTICULARIZAR, *to distinguish, characterize*

PARTIR, *to divide, split, cut*

PASAR, *to pass, go past, get by*

PASTEURIZAR, *to pasteurize*

PATENTAR, *to patent*

PENALIZAR, *to penalize*

PENETRAR, *to enter, get into, penetrate*

PENSAR, *to think, reflection, think up*

PERCIBIR, *to perceive, notice*

PERDONAR, *to forgive*

PERFECCIONAR, *to perfect, improve*

PERFORAR, *to perforate, pierce*

PERFUMAR, *to perfume, scent*

PERJUDICAR, *to damage, harm, prejudice*

PERJURAR, *to swear blindly, to commit perjury*

PERMANECER, *to stay, remain*

PERMITIR, *to allow, permit*

PERMUTAR, *to permute, exchange, swap*

PERPETRAR, *to perpetrate, commit, perform*

PERPETUAR, *to perpetuate, continue, extend*

PERSEVERAR, *to persevere, persist*

PERSISTIR, *to persist*

PERSONALIZAR, *to personalize, get personal*

PERSONIFICAR, *to personify, embody*

PERSUADIR, *to persuade*

PERTURBAR, *to disrupt, disturb, perturb*

PERVERTIR, *to corrupt, pervert, distort*

PETICIONAR, *to petition*

PETRIFICAR, *to petrify, be petrified*

PILLAR, *to catch, get, land*

PINTAR, *to paint*

PIRATEAR, *to hijack, pirate, bootleg*

PIVOTAR, *to pivot, revolve around*

PLANIFICAR, *to plan*

PLANTAR, *to plant, sow*

PLASTIFICAR, *to laminate*

PLURALIZAR, *to generalize, pluralize*

POLARIZAR, *to concentrate, polarize*

POLEMIZAR, *to argue*

PONTIFICAR, *to pontificate*

POPULARIZAR, *to popularize*

PORTAR, *to carry, bear; behave, conduct*

POSIBILITAR, *to make possible, feasible*

POSPONER, *to relegate, postpone*

POSTULAR, *to postulate*

PRACTICAR, *to practice; exercise, carry out, perform*

PRECEDER, *to go before, to precede*

PRECIPITAR, *to throw down, hasten, precipitate*

PRECISAR, *to specify, be necessary; need, require*

PREDECIR, *to predict, forecast*

PREDESTINAR, *to predestine*

PREDETERMINAR, *to predetermine*

PREDICAR, *to preach*

PREDISPONER, *to predispose, prejudice*

PREDOMINAR, *to predominate, prevail over*

PREEXISTIR, *to pre-exist*

PREFERIR, *to prefer*

PREJUZGAR, *to prejudge*

PREMEDITAR, *to premeditate on*

PREOCUPAR, *to be preoccupied, worried, bothered*

PREPARAR, *to prepare, make, get ready*

PRESAGIAR, *to presage, forebode*

PRESCRIBIR, *to prescribe; expire, run out*

PRESENCIAR, *to be present at, attend, witness*

PRESENTAR, *to present, propose, submit*

PRESENTIR, *to feel, be aware of*

PRESERVAR, *to protect, preserve, maintain*

PRESIDIAR, *to rule, dominate, preside, chair*

PRESTIGIAR, *to honor, give prestige to*

PRESUMIR, *to presume, assume*

PRESUPONER, *to presuppose, assume*

PRETENDER, *to aspire to, expect, mean, try to*

PRETEXTAR, *to use as an excuse or pretext*

PREVALECER, *to prevail against*

PREVARICAR, *to prevent justice*

PREVENIR, *to prevent*

PRIVATIZAR, *to privatize*

PROBAR, *to prove*

PROCLAMAR, *to proclaim, declare*

PRODUCIR, *to produce* (CINE); *make, generate*

PROFANAR, *to desecrate, profane*

PROGRAMAR, *to plan, to program* (INFORM)

PROHIBIR, *to prohibit, ban*

PROLIFERAR, *to proliferate*

PROLONGAR, *to prolong, extend*

PROMOCIONAR, *to promote*

PROMULGAR, *to enact, announce*

PRONOSTICAR, *to predict, forecast*

PRONUNCIAR, *to pronounce, deliver, make an opinion*

PROPAGAR, *to spread, disseminate*

PROPONER, *to propose, put forward*

PROPULSAR, *to propel, promote, drive*

PROSCRIBIR, *to ban, banish, prohibit*

PROSPERAR, *to prosper, thrive*

PROTESTAR, *to protest, complain*

PROVOCAR, *to provoke, incite*

PUBLICAR, *to publish, issue*

PUGNAR, *to fight, struggle*

PUNTUAR, *to mark, punctuate*

PURIFICAR, *to purify, cleanse*

STUDY NOTES:

Q

Interchangeable Words

QUANTUM

QUARK

QUÁSAR

QUIMONO ó KIMONO

QUÓRUM

Easily Recognizable Nouns, Adjectives and Adverbs

QUEPIS ó KEPIS, *kepi*

QUIETO (A), *still, motionless; quiet! be still!*

QUIETUD, *stillness*

QUININA, *quinine*

QUINTAESENCIA, *quintessence*

QUINTETO, *quintet*

QUÍNTUPLE ó QUÍNTUPLO (A), *quintuple*

Easily Recognizable Verbs

QUITAR, *to take down, take off, take out*

STUDY NOTES:

R

Interchangeable Words

RACIAL

RACIC

RADAR

RADIAL, *also a medical term*

RADICAL, *also a mathematical and chemical term*

RADIO; *radius* (MAT)

RADÓN

RAFTING, *as a sport*

RAGTIME

RAGÚ ó RAGOUT

RAID, *as an incursion or police raid*

RAÍL, *handrail, railroad rail*

RALLY

RANKING (s), *as in competition*

RAP, *rap music*

RATIO

RAVIOLI

RAYÓN

REACTOR, *fission or nuclear reactor*

REAL, true; *royal*

RECITAL (MUS), *concert*

RÉCORD ó RECORD

RECTAL

RECTANGULAR

RECTOR (A) (adj), *guiding, principal; rector* (n) (RELIG)

REFERÉNDUM

REFLECTOR, *spotlight, search light, reflector*

RÉFLEX

REGALÍA, *privilege(s); royal trappings*

RÉGIMEN, *as system, regulations; regime*

REGIÓN

REGIONAL

REGULAR

RELAX, *relaxation*

RELIGIÓN

REMAKE (s)

REMUNERABLE

RENAL

REPLAY

RÉPLICA; *reply, answer; aftershock; replica* (ARTE)

REPULSIÓN

RÉQUIEM

RESIDUAL

RETICULAR

RETINA

RETRO

REUNIÓN; *meeting*

REVERSIBLE

REVERSIÓN

REVISIÓN (DER); *inspection, examination*

REVIVAL

REVOCABLE

REVÓLVER

RIFLE

RIGOR, *strictness, accuracy*

RING, *boxing ring*

RISIBLE

RITUAL

RIVAL

ROAST BEEF ó ROSBIF

ROBOT

ROCK ó ROCK AND ROLL, *rock group*

ROCOCÓ

RODEO (DEP)*; also means a detour; roundabout (adj)*

ROMANCE, *romance language*

ROTONDA, *in a building, also a traffic circle, circus*

ROUND (s), *as in boxing, golf*

ROYALTY

RUGBY

RUMBA

RUMOR; *murmur*

RURAL

Easily Recognizable Nouns, Adjectives and Adverbs

RABÍ ó RABBI ó RABINO, *rabbi*

RACIÓN, *portion, ration* (MIL)

RACISMO, *racism*

RACISTA, *racist*

RADIACIÓN, *radiation*

RADIACTIVIDAD, *radioactivity*

RADIACTIVO (A), *radioactive*

RADIADOR, *radiator*

RADIANTE, *radiant, brilliant, luminous, shining*

RADICALISMO, *radicalism*

RADICALIZACIÓN, *radicalization*

RADIOCASETE, *radio cassette*

RADIOCONTROL, *remote control*

RADIODIFUSIÓN, *broadcasting*

RADIOGRAFÍA, *radiography*

RADIÓLOGO (A), *radiologist*

RADIOTAXI, *radio cab, taxi*

RAMIFICACIÓN, *ramification*

RAMPA, *ramp*

RAMPANTE, *rampant*

RANCHERO (A), *rancher, settler*

RANCHO, *mess* (MIL); *ranch, small farm*

RANCIO (A), *rancid; old, mellow*

RANGO, *rank, standing, status*

RAPACIDAD, *rapacity, greed; ravenous, covetous*

RÁPIDAMENTE, *quickly*

RAPIDEZ, *speed, rapidity*

RÁPIDO (A), *fast, rapid, quick, express; quickly*

RAPSODIA, *rhapsody*

RARAMENTE (adv), *rarely, seldom, infrequently*

RARO (A), *odd, strange, rare*

RATA, *rat; miser*

RATIFICACIÓN, *ratification*

RAYO, *ray, beam, shaft of light*

RAZÓN, *to be right; reason*

RAZONAMIENTO, *reasoning, reflection*

RAZONABLE, *reasonable*

RAZONAMIENTO, *reasoning, reflection*

REACCIÓN, *reaction*

REACTIVACIÓN, *revival*

REACTIVO (A), *reactive* (QUIM) *stimulant*

READMISIÓN, *readmission; reemployment*

REAFIRMACIÓN, *reaffirmation*

REAGRUPACIÓN, *regrouping*

REAJUSTE, *readjustment*

REALIDAD, *reality, truth*

REALISMO, *realism*

REALISTA, *realistic (adj), realist (n)*

REALIZABLE, *attainable, practical, feasible*

REALIZACIÓN, *implementation, fulfillment*

REALIZADOR (A), *producer* (CINE)

REALMENTE, *actually, really, in fact*

REANIMACIÓN, *resuscitation* (MED); *recovery*

REAPARICIÓN, *reappearance, comeback* (CINE)

REAPERTURA, *reopening*

REARME, *rearmament*

REBATIBLE, *refutable*

REBELIÓN, *rebellion, revolt*

RECALCITRANTE, *recalcitrant*

RECALIFICACIÓN, *reassessment*

RECAPITALIZACIÓN, *recapitalization, refinance*

RECAPITULACIÓN, *recapitulation, summation*

RECARGABLE, *rechargeable, refillable*

RECEPCIÓN, *reception*

RECEPCIONISTA, *receptionist*

RECEPTÁCULO, *receptacle*

RECEPTIVIDAD, *receptivity, receptiveness*

RECEPTIVO (A), *receptive*

RECESIÓN, *recession* (ECON)

RECESIVO (A), *recessive* (MED)

RECESO, *recess*

RECIBIMIENTO, *welcome, reception*

RECIBO, *receipt, bill*

RECICLABLE, *recyclable*

RECICLADO (A), *recycled, reused; reclaimed*

RECIDIVA, *relapse, decline, regress, fade*

RECIÉN, *newly, just*

RECIENTE, *recent, fresh, new, current*

RECIENTEMENTE, *recently, lately*

RECIPROCIDAD, *reciprocity*

RECÍPROCO (A), *mutual, reciprocal, common, joint*

RECLINABLE, *reclining*

RECLUSIÓN, *imprisonment, confinement; seclusion*

RECLUSO (A), *imprisoned, prisoner*

RECOMENDABLE, *recommendable, advisable*

RECOMENDACIÓN, *recommendation*

RECOMENDADO (A), *registered, recommended*

RECOMPENSA, *reward, recompense*

RECONCILIACIÓN, *reconciliation*

RECÓNDITO (A), *recondite, hidden, arcane, esoteric*

RECONOCIBLE, *recognizable*

RECONOCIDO, *recognized*

RECONQUISTA, *recapture*

RECONSTRUCCIÓN, *reconstruction*

RECONVERSIÓN, *restructuring, reorganization*

RECORDMAN, *record holder*

RECREACIÓN, *recreation, amusement*

RECREATIVO (A), *recreational, arcade*

RECRIMINACIÓN, *reproach, recrimination*

RECTA, *straight line, straight* (DEP)

RECTÁNGULO, *rectangle*

RECTIFICACIÓN, *rectification, correction*

RECTITUD, *rectitude, uprightness*

RECTO (A), *straight, upright, honest or upright person; also can mean rectum* (ANAT)

RECUPERACIÓN, *economic recovery, data* (INFORM); *recapture* (MIL); *reclamation, redemption*

RECURRENTE, *recurrent, frequent, periodic*

REDACCIÓN, *writing, editing*

REDACTOR (A), *writer, editor, drafter*

REDENCIÓN, *redemption, repayment*

REDENTOR (A), *redeemer (n), redeeming (adj)*

REDISTRIBUCIÓN, *redistribution*

REDUCCIÓN, *reduction* (QUIM) (ECON); *cut*

REDUCIDO (A), *small, limited*

REDUCTO, *stronghold, redoubt*

REDUNDANCIA, *redundancy, superfluous*

REDUNDANTE, *redundant*

REELECCIÓN, *re-election*

REENCARNACIÓN, *reincarnation*

REESTRUCTURACIÓN, *restructuring, reorganizing*

REFECTORIO, *refectory*

REFERENCIA, *reference; account, report*

REFERENTE, *concerning, relating to, about*

REFERÍ, *umpire, referee*

REFINADO (A), *refined*

REFINAMIENTO, *refinement*

REFINERÍA, *refinery*

REFLECTANTE, *reflective*

REFLEXIÓN, *reflection, thought*

REFLEXIVO (A), *reflective, thoughtful*

REFORMA, *reform; alterations*

REFORMACIÓN, *reformation*

REFORMATORIO, *reformatory*

REFRACCIÓN, *refraction*

REFRACTARIO (A), *refractory, heat-resistant material*

REFRÁN, *proverb, saying, refrain*

REFRIGERACIÓN, *refrigeration, cooling*

REFRIGERADO (A), *cooled, air conditioned, refrigerated*

REFRIGERADOR (A), *refrigerator, cool room, coolant, cooling unit or system*

REFUGIO, refuge*, shelter*

REFULGENTE, *brilliant, refulgent*

REFUTACIÓN, *refutation, rebut, deny, expose*

REGATA, *regatta*

REGENERACIÓN, *regeneration*

REGENTA, *wife of the regent*

REGENTE, *regent*

REGIMIENTO, *regiment* (MIL); *crowd*

REGIONALISMO, *regionalism*

REGISTRADORA, *cash register*

REGISTRO, *registry office; search; registration*

REGRESIÓN, *regression, fall, decrease*

REGRESIVO (A), *regressive, backward*

REGRESO, *return*

REGULACIÓN, *adjustment* (MAT) (MECAN)

REGULADOR (A), *regulator, throttle, control button*

REGULARIDAD, *regularity; regularly*

REGULARIZACIÓN, *regularization*

REGULARMENTE, *usually, normally, generally*

REHABILITACIÓN, *rehabilitation*

REINCORPORACIÓN, *reincorporation; return, reinstatement*

REIMPRESIÓN, *reprint*

REITERACIÓN, *reiteration, repetition*

REITERADO (A), *repeated*

REITERADAMENTE, *repeatedly*

RELACIÓN, *relationship, connection*

RELACIONADO, *related*

RELAJACIÓN, *relaxation*

RELAJADO (A), *relaxed*

RELAJANTE, *relaxing; sedative* (MED)

RELATIVIDAD, *relativity*

RELATIVO (A), *relative to, regarding*

RELATO, *story, tale, account, report*

RELEVANCIA, *relevance, importance*

RELEVANTE, *outstanding, important, relevant*

RELIEVE, *relief* (GEOL) (ARTE)

RELIGIOSO (A), *religious, (adj); member of a religious order; monk, nun*

REMEDIO, *solution, remedy; choice, alternative*

REMISIBLE, *forgivable*

REMISIÓN, *consignment, reference, shipment; slackening; remission* (RELIG)

REMISO (A), *reluctant*

REMODELACIÓN, *redesigning, reshuffling, remodeling*

REMOTO (A), *remote, distant, faraway*

REMUNERACIÓN, *remuneration*

RENCOR, *rancor, bitterness, resentment*

RENCOROSO (A), *resentful, bitter (person)*

RENEGADO (A), *renegade, rebel; apostate* (RELIG)

RENOMBRADO (A), *renowned, famous*

RENOMBRE, *renown, fame*

RENOVABLE, *renewable*

RENOVACIÓN, *renewal, renovation*

RENOVADO, *renewed, refurbished, revamped, redone*

RENTA, *profit, income*

RENTABLE, *profitable*

RENTABILIDAD, *profitability*

RENUNCIA, *giving up, resignation, renunciation*

REORGANIZACIÓN, *reorganization*

REORIENTACIÓN, *reorientation, redeployment*

REPARACIÓN, *reparation, repair, compensation*

REPARTICIÓN, *sharing out, distribution*

REPATRIACIÓN, *repatriation*

REPELENTE, *repellent, repulsive; insect repellent*

REPERCUSIÓN, *repercussion*

REPERTORIO, *repertoire* (MUS), *selection; index, catalog*

REPETICIÓN, *repetition, reiteration*

REPETIDO (A), *repeated*

REPETITIVO (A), *repetitive, redundant; tedious, wordy*

REPLETO (A), *full of, crammed with, replete*

REPORTE, *report*

REPOSADO (A), *relaxed, calm, quiet*

REPOSO, *repose*

REPOSTERÍA, *cakes and pastries shop*

REPRESENTACIÓN, *representation*

REPRESENTANTE (n), *representative*

REPRESENTATIVO (A), *representative*

REPRESIÓN, *repression, suppression*

REPRESIVO (A), *repressive, restraining, subduing*

REPRIMENDA, *reprimand, rebuke, reproach, admonish*

REPROBABLE, *reprehensible*

REPROBACIÓN, *censure, rejection, condemnation*

REPROCHE, *reproach, censure, disapproval*

REPRODUCCIÓN, *reproduction, duplication, replica*

REPTIL, *reptile (n), reptilian (adj)*

REPUDIO, *disown, rejection, repudiation*

REPUGNANCIA, *disgust, repugnance, loathing*

REPUGNANTE, *disgusting, repugnant, revolting*

REPULSA, *rejection, condemnation, rebuff*

REPULSIVO (A), *repulsive, disgusting*

REPUTACIÓN, *reputation*

RESCISIÓN, *repeal, annulment, cancellation*

RESENTIDO (A), *resentful, bitter*

RESENTIMIENTO, *resentment, bitterness*

RESERVA, *reservation; booking; reserve* (MIL); *objection; supply, stock*

RESERVADAMENTE, *in confidence*

RESERVADO (A), *reserved, discreet, confidential*

RESIDENCIA, *stay, residence, second home*

RESIDENCIAL, *residential*

RESIDENTE, *resident*

RESIDUO, *residue, waste; remainder* (MAT)

RESIGNACIÓN, *resignation*

RESIGNADO (adj), *resigned*

RESINA, *resin*

RESINOSO, *resinous*

RESISTENCIA, *resistance, opposition, defiance*

RESISTENTE, *tough, strong, resistant*

RESOLUCIÓN, *resolution, determination, purpose, resolve, dedication; commitment, pledge, promise*

RESOLUTO (A), *resolute, determined, persistent, tenacious, obstinate*

RESONANCIA, *resonance, echo*

RESPECTIVAMENTE (adv), *respectively*

RESPECTIVO (A), *respective*

RESPECTO, *in this respect, with respect to*

RESPETABLE, *respectable, considerable*

RESPETO, *respect for*

RESPETUOSO (A), *respectful, courteous, polite, cordial, gracious; civil, accommodating*

RESPIRACIÓN, *breathing, respiration*

RESPIRATORIO (A), *respiratory*

RESPLANDOR, *brightness, glow, gleam*

RESPONDÓN (A), *insolent, mouthy, cheeky*

RESPONDONA, *insolent person*

RESPONSABILIDAD, *responsibility*

RESPONSABLE, *responsible for sthg*

RESTA (MAT), *subtraction*

RESTAURACIÓN, *restoration*

RESTAURADOR (A), *restorer; restaurant owner*

RESTAURANTE, *restaurant*

RESTITUCIÓN, *return, replacement, restitution*

RESTO, *rest; remainder* (MAT)

RESTRICCIÓN, *restriction, limitation, restraint, curtailment; limit; poise, constraint*

RESTRICTIVO (A), *restrictive*

RESTRINGIDO, *restricted, limited, prohibited*

RESULTA, *result*

RESULTADO, *result, outcome, score*

RESULTANTE, *resultant; resulting*

RESUMEN, *summary, synopsis, abstract, digest*

RESURGIMIENTO, *resurgence, return, revival*

RESURRECCIÓN, *resurrection*

RETALIACIÓN, *retaliation, avenge; counter, reciprocate; settle, get even, strike back*

RETARDO, *delay*

RETENCIÓN, *retention, deduction*

RETICENCIA, *unwillingness, reluctance, reserved*

RETICENTE, *unwilling, reluctant; shy, timid, reticent*

RETIRO, *pension; withdrawal; retirement*

RETIRO, *retreat* (RELIG)

RETORNABLE, *returnable*

RETÓRICA, *rhetoric*

RETÓRICO (A), *rhetorical*

RETRACCIÓN, *retraction*

RETRÁCTIL, *retractable*

RETRETA, *retreat* (MIL); *open air concert*

RETRIBUCIÓN, *pay, payment, reward*

RETROACTIVO (A), *retroactive*

RETROSPECTIVO (A), *retrospective*

REUMÁTICO (A), *rheumatic*

REUMATISMO, *rheumatism*

REUNIFICACIÓN, *reunification*

REUTILIZABLE, *reusable*

REVALUACIÓN, *revaluation*

REVELACIÓN, *revelation, admission, disclosure*

REVELADO, *developing*

REVELADOR (A), *revealing (adj), developer (n)*

REVERBERACIÓN, *reverberation*

REVERENDO, *reverend* (RELIG)

REVERSIBILIDAD, *reversibility*

REVERSO, *reverse side, other side, reverse*

REVOCACIÓN, *revocation*

REVOLUCIÓN, *revolution*

RICAMENTE, *richly*

RICO (A), *rich*

RIDICULEZ, *silly thing, nonsense, trifle*

RIDÍCULO (A), *ridiculous, laughable, derisory*

RIGIDEZ, *rigidity, stiffness*

RÍGIDO (A), *rigid, stiff, inflexible*

RIGUROSO (A), *strict, rigorous*

RISA, *laugh*

RISOTADA, *guffaw, loud laugh*

RÍTMICO (A), *rhythmic, rhythmical*

RITO, *rite* (RELIG)

RIVALIDAD, *rivalry, competition*

ROBUSTO (A), *robust, tough, strong, sturdy*

ROCA, *rock*

ROCOSO (A), *rocky, stony*

ROL (s), *roll (of paper), muster; role*

ROLLO, *roll, as a cylinder*

RON, *rum*

ROSA, *rose; pink*

ROSADO (A), *pink, rosy; rosé*

ROSARIO, *rosary* (RELIG)

ROTACIÓN, *rotation, change, swap, exchange, switch, alternate; gyrate, whirl, pivot*

ROTATIVO, *newspaper; rotary press*

ROTATIVO (A) (adj), *rotary, revolving*

RUBÍ (s), *ruby*

RUBIO (A), *fair, blonde*

RUDIMENTARIO (A), *rudimentary*

RUDIMENTOS, *rudiments*

RUFIÁN, *villain, scoundrel, pimp*

RUIN, *wicked, despicable; mean, shabby*

RUINA, *ruin; destruction, collapse*

RUINDAD, *meanness, lowness*

RUINOSO (A), *dilapidated; disastrous, ruinous*

RULETA, *roulette*

RUMIANTE (adj), *ruminant*

RUMOROSO (A), *murmuring, dabbling*

RUPTURA, *rupture*

RÚSTICO (A), *rustic, country, rough, coarse*

RUTA, *route, road*

RUTINA, *routine* (INFORM); *daily routine, habit*

RUTINARIO (A) (adj), *routine, unimaginative*

Easily Recognizable Verbs

RACIONALIZAR, *to rationalize*

RACIONAR, *to ration*

RADIAR, *to radiate; broadcast; radiate* (MED)

RASPAR, *to scrape, scratch, scratch out*

RATIFICAR, *to ratify, confirm; support*

RAZONAR, *to reason out, reason, argue*

REACCIONAR, *to react* (QUIM)

REACONDICIONAR, *to recondition; reorganize, restructure*

REACTIVAR, *to reactivate*

READAPTAR, *to readapt, retrain*

READMITIR, *to readmit*

REAFIRMAR, *to reaffirm, confirm, reassert*

REAGRUPAR, *to regroup*

REAJUSTAR, *to rearrange, make changes*

REALIZAR, *to make, carry out, go on; to do, fulfill*

REANIMAR, *to cheer up, reactivate, liven up, animate*

REAVIVAR, *to revive*

REBUSCAR, *to search carefully*

RECAPITULAR, *to recapitulate, summarize*

RECIBIR, *to receive, get*

RECICLAR, *to recycle*

RECITAR, *to recite*

RECLAMAR, *to claim, demand*

RECOMENDAR, *to advise, recommend*

RECOMPENSAR, *to reward, compensate*

RECONCILIAR, *to reconcile*

RECONFORTAR, *to comfort; cheer, encourage*

RECONQUISTAR, *to reconquer, recapture, recover*

RECONSIDERAR, *to reconsider*

RECONSTITUIR, *to reconstitute*

RECONSTRUIR, *to reconstruct*

RECOPILAR, *to compile, summarize, codify*

RECRIMINAR, *to reproach*

RECTIFICAR, *to correct, improve, rectify*

RECUPERAR, *to recover, regain, regroup, recoup*

RECUSAR, *to reject, refuse*

REDIMIR, *to redeem; ransom*

REDISTRIBUIR, *to redistribute*

REDOBLAR, *to redouble*

REDUCIR, *to reduce, bring down, cut, lower*

REEDUCAR, *to reeducate*

REEMPLAZAR, *to replace, substitute*

REENCARNAR, *to reincarnate*

REESTRUCTURAR, *to restructure, reorganize*

REEVALUAR, *to reappraise*

REFINAR, *to perfect, refine*

REFLEXIONAR, *to reflect, think*

REFORESTAR, *to reforest*

REFORMATEAR, *to reformat* (INFORM)

REFORMAR, *to reform, change one's ways; renovate*

REFRACTAR, *to refract*

REFRESCAR, *to cool, cool down; refresh the memory*

REFRIGERAR, *to refrigerate, air condition, chill*

REFUTAR, *to refute*

REGENERAR, *to regenerate*

REGISTRAR, *to search, record, note*

REGLAMENTAR, *to regulate*

REGULAR, *to adjust, regulate, control*

REGULARIZAR, *to regularize, standardize*

REGURGITAR, *to regurgitate*

REHABILITAR, *to rehabilitate, reinstate, restore*

REINCORPORAR, *to reincorporate, reinstate*

REINSTALAR, *to reinstall, reinstate*

REINTRODUCIR, *to reintroduce*

REINVENTAR, *to reinvent*

REITERAR, *to reiterate, repeat*

RELACIONAR, *to relate, connect*

RELATAR, *to relate, retell*

RELEGAR, *to relegate*

REMEDIAR, *to remedy, put right, solve*

REMEMORAR, *to remember, recall*

REMENDAR, *to mend, darn*

REMITIR, *to remit, send*

REMODELAR, *to remodel*

REMONTAR, *to remonstrate, negotiate; mend, repair*

REMOVER, *to remove, dig up, move around, stir*

REMUNERAR, *to remunerate*

RENEGAR, *to deny strongly, renounce, disown*

RENEGOCIAR, *to renegotiate*

RENOVAR, *to renew, renovate, upgrade*

RENUNCIAR, *to renounce, abandon*

REORGANIZAR, *to reorganize, reshuffle*

REORIENTAR, *to change*

REPARAR, *to repair, mend, fix*

REPARTIR, *to share out, partition, divide*

REPATRIAR, *to repatriate*

REPENSAR, *to rethink, reconsider*

REPORTEAR, *to report, report on*

REPOSAR, *to repose, rest*

REPELER, *to repel, repulse; drive back*

REPETIR, *to repeat*

REPRESENTAR, *to represent, look like*

REPROBAR, *to reprove, condemn*

REPRODUCIR, *to reproduce, copy, imitate*

REPUDIAR, *to repudiate, disown*

REQUERIR, *to require, demand*

RESCINDIR, *to rescind, cancel*

RESERVAR, *to reserve, book*

RESIDIR, *to reside*

RESISTIR, *to resist, withstand, bear*

RESOLVER, *to resolve, settle, decide*

RESONAR, *to resound, echo*

RESPECTAR, *to respect, regard*

RESPIRAR, *to breathe, exude*

RESPONDER, *to answer, respond to*

RESTAURAR, *to restore*

RESTITUIR, *to return, restore*

RESULTAR, *to become, turn out to be, the result of*

RESUMIR, *to summarize*

RETARDAR, *to delay, hold up, slow down*

RETIRAR, *to retire, withdraw*

RETENER, *to hold back, retain, detain*

RETORNAR, *to return*

RETRACTAR, *to retract*

REUTILIZAR, *to reuse*

REVALIDAR, *to confirm, ratify*

REVALORIZAR, *to assess*

REVALUAR, *to revalue*

REVELAR, *to reveal, show*

REVERBERAR, *to reverberate*

REVIVIR, *to revive*

REVOCAR, *to revoke*

REVOLVER, *to turn around, stir, mix*

RIDICULIZAR, *to ridicule, deride*

ROTAR, *to rotate*

STUDY NOTES:

S

Interchangeable Words

SABLE

SACERDOTAL

SACRAMENTAL

SACRISTÁN

SAFARI

SAGA

SALAMI ó SALAME

SALIVA

SALMÓN

SALÓN, *living room, hall*

SALSA, *sauce*

SAMBA

SAMOVAR

SAMURÁI

SÁNDWICH

SANGRÍA

SARCOMA

SARI

SATÁN ó SATANÁS

SATIN ó SATÉN

SAUNA

SCOTCH, *whisky; scotch tape*

SCOUT (s)

SCRIPT (s)

SECTOR (GEOM)

SECTORIAL

SECULAR; *ancient*

SEDÁN

SELECTOR

SELF-SERVICE, *self-service restaurant*

SEMEN; *seed*

SEMICIRCULAR

SEMICONDUCTOR

SEMIFINAL

SEMINAL

SENATORIAL

SENIOR ó SÉNIOR

SENSOR

SENSUAL, *sensuous*

SENTIMENTAL

SEPARABLE *(from)*

SEPIA, *the color*

SERIAL

SERMÓN, *lecture*

SET, *tennis* (DEP)

SETTER, *dog*

SEX-APPEAL

SEX-SHOP

SEXUAL, (vida sexual = sex life)

SEXY ó SEXI

SHERIFF

SHERRY

SHIATSU

SHOCK ó CHOC

SHOW, *theater; fuss, bother*

SIDECAR

SIESTA

SILICOSIS

SILO

SIMILAR (to)

SIMPLE, *easy; straightforward*

SINGLES, *tennis* (DEP); *also single* (MUS)

SINGULAR, *peculiar, odd, unique, outstanding*

SITU (IN SITU), *on the spot*

SKATE BOARD

SKETCH (CINE) (TEATRO)

SKI (DEP)

SKINHEAD

SLOGAN ó ESLOGAN

SMASH (s), (DEP)

SMOG

SNOB

SNORKELING

SNOWBOARD ó SNOWBOARDING

SOCIABLE

SOCIAL

SODA, *soda water, club soda*

SOFÁ (SOFÁ CAMA), *sofa bed, settee, sofa*

SOFTWARE (INFORM)

SOLAR *(also an undeveloped plot of land)*

SOLÁRIUM

SOLO (A), *alone*

SÓLO, *just, only*

SOLUBLE

SOMMELIER ó SUMILLER

SONAR, *also the verb to ring; soñar is the verb to dream*

SONATA

SOPRANO

SOTO VOCE

SOUFFLÉ ó SUFLÉ

SOUL (MUS)

SOUVENIR (s)

SOVIET

SPAGHETTI ó ESPAGUETI

SPANIEL, *the dog*

SPARRING, *sparring partner*

SPOT, *advertising, commercial spot*

SPRAY ó ESPRAY, *aerosol*

SPRINT ó ESPRINT (DEP)

SPRINTER ó ESPRINTER (DEP)

SQUASH, *the game*

SQUATTER

STAFF

STÁNDARD ó STANDARD

STANDING, *social status, standing* as *a rank*

STARTER, *automotive starter*

STATUS

STATUS QUO

STEP, *aerobics*

STICK (s), *hockey stick*

STOCK, *supply, inventory*

STOP, *a stop/halt sign*

STRESS

STRIPTEASE

SUAVE

SUBCLASS

SUBDIVISIÓN

SUBLIME

SUBLIMINAL

SUBNORMAL (MED)

SUBSECTOR, *subsection*

SUBTROPICAL

SUBVERSIÓN

SUITE (MUS); *a hotel suite*

SULTÁN

SUMO, *wrestling; great, supreme*

SÚPER, *as great, super, supermarket; premium gas*

SUPERFICIAL

SUPERIOR (adj); *mother superior* (RELIG)

SUPERNOVA

SUPERVISIÓN

SUPERVISOR

SURF ó SURFING

SUSCEPTIBLE

SUSHI

SUSPENSE

SUSPENSIÓN; *an automobile suspension*

SWING (MUS)

SWITCH, *electrical; ignition switch*

Easily Recognizable Nouns, Adjectives and Adverbs

SABOTAJE, *sabotage*

SABOTEADOR (A), *saboteur*

SACA (m), *sack, bag*

SACARINA, *saccharine or saccharin*

SACO (f), *sack, bag*

SACRAMENTO, *sacrament*

SACRIFICIO, *sacrifice*

SACRILEGIO, *sacrilege*

SACRÍLEGO (A), *sacrilegious*

SACRISTÍA, *sacristy, vestry*

SACRO (A), *holy, sacred* (MUS) (ARTE)

SACROSANTO (A), *sacrosanct, inviolable*

SÁDICO (A), *sadistic (adj), cruel, perverse, monstrous, ruthless, brutal, deviant; sadist (n), pervert, deviate*

SADISMO, *sadism, perversity, debauchery, dissipation, brutality, cruelty*

SADOMASOQUISMO, *sadomasochism*

SADOMASOQUISTA, *sadomasochistic*

SAGACIDAD, *astuteness, shrewdness, cleverness*

SAGAZ, *shrewd, astute, clever*

SAL, *salt*

SALAME, *salami; idiot*

SALARIO, *wages, wage, salary, pay*

SALAZ, *salacious, prurient, lustful, lecherous*

SALIDA, *way out, exit*

SALIENTE, *salient, important, conspicuous*

SALINIDAD, *salinity*

SALINO (A), *saline*

SALMONELA, *salmonella*

SALSA, *sauce; salsa* (MUS)

SALUBRE, *healthy, salubrious, wholesome, pleasant*

SALUD, *health* (MED)

SALUDABLE, *healthy*

SALVA, *salvo* (MIL); *round of/storm of applause*

SALVACIÓN, *salvation* (RELIG); *rescue*

SANCIÓN, *sanction* (ECON), *punishment, penalty*

SANDALIA, *sandal*

SÁNSCRITO (A), *Sanskrit*

SANTIFICACIÓN, *sanctification*

SARCASMO, *sarcasm*

SARCÁSTICO (A), *sarcastic, derisive, mocking; scornful, ridiculing, taunting*

SARCÓFAGO, *sarcophagus*

SARDINA, *sardine*

SARDÓNICO (A), *sardonic, cynical, ironic*

SARGENTO, *sergeant*

SATÁNICO (A), *satanic, diabolical*

SATANISMO, *Satanism*

SATÉLITE, *satellite*

SATINADO (A), *glossy, shiny*

SÁTIRA, *satire, mockery, caricature; lampoon, parody, mimic, pillory*

SATÍRICO (A) (adj), *satirical*

SATISFACCIÓN, *satisfaction, gratification; comfort*

SATISFACTORIO (adj), *satisfactory, acceptable*

SATISFECHO (A), *satisfied, contented*

SATURACIÓN, *saturation; soaked, drenched*

SAXO, *sax*

SAXOFÓN, *saxophone*

SAXOFONISTA, *saxophonist*

SEBÁCEO (A), *sebaceous*

SECCIÓN, *section* (MAT); *cross-section*

SECESIÓN, *secession, defection, separation*

SECOYA ó SECUOYA, *sequoia*

SECRECIÓN, *secretion*

SECRETARÍA, *secretary's office, secretary ship*

SECRETARIO (A), *secretary*

SECRETO (A), *secret, confidential*

SECTA, *sect, denomination, cult, persuasion*

SECUENCIA, *sequence, progression, chronology, series*

SECUENCIAL, *sequential*

SECUNDARIO (A), *secondary, minor, supporting role*

SEDANTE, *sedative; soothing* (MUS)

SEDENTARIO (A), *sedentary*

SEDICIÓN, *sedition, disloyalty*

SEDICIOSO (A), *seditious, dissidence, rabble-rousing*

SEDIMENTACIÓN, *sedimentation*

SEDIMENTARIO (A), *sedimentary*

SEDIMENTO, *sediment, deposit*

SEDUCCIÓN, *seductiveness, attraction, charm*

SEDUCTOR (A), *attractive, charming, seductive*

SEGMENTACIÓN, *division, segmentation*

SEGMENTO, *segment* (GEOM), *piece, sector, group*

SEGREGACIÓN, *segregation*

SEGUIDO (A), *consecutive; continuous*

SEGURIDAD, *safety, security*

SEGURO (A), *safe, secure, protected*

SEÍSMO, *earthquake, tremor*

SELECCIÓN, *selection, preference, option*

SELECTIVIDAD, *selectivity*

SELECTIVO (A), *selective*

SELECTO (A), *exclusive, restricted; private*

SEMANAL, *weekly*

SEMANARIO (A), *weekly (adj), as a weekly publication*

SEMBLANTE, *look, countenance, expression, aspect*

SEMENTAL, a *stud horse, stallion*

SEMESTRAL (adj), *biannual, semiannual*

SEMESTRE (n), *a period of six months, semester*

SEMIAUTOMÁTICO (A), *semiautomatic*

SEMICÍRCULO, *semicircle*

SEMIFINALISTA, *semifinalist*

SEMINARIO, *seminary,* (RELIG); *seminar, lecture*

SEMPITERNO, *eternal*

SENADO, *senate*

SENADOR (A), *senator*

SENIL, *senile, declining, failing*

SENILIDAD, *senility, old age, dotage*

SENSACIÓN, *sensation, sense, impression, awareness*

SENSACIONAL, *sensational, spectacular, great, marvelous, fabulous, fantastic*

SENSACIONALISMO, *sensationalism*

SENSACIONALISTA, *sensationalist*

SENSATEZ, *wisdom, common sense, good sense*

SENSATO (A), *sensible, reasonable, logical, rational*

SENSIBILIDAD, *feeling, sensitivity*

SENSIBLE, *sensitive, impressionable*

SENSITIVO (A), *sense, sentient*

SENSORIAL (adj), *sensory*

SENSUALIDAD, *sensuality, eroticism, sexuality*

SENTENCIA, *sentence* (DER)

SENTIMENTALISMO, *sentimentality*

SENTIMIENTO, *feeling, to get carried away*

SEPARACIÓN, *separation, division*

SEPARADO (A), *separate, separately*

SEPARATISMO, *separatism*

SÉPTICO (A), *septic, putrid; putrefying*

SEPTIEMBRE, *September*

SEPULCRAL, *sepulchral*

SEPULCRO, *tomb, grave, sepulcher*

SEPULTURA, *burial, grave*

SERENAMENTE, *serenely, calmly, quietly*

SERENATA, *serenade*

SERENIDAD, *tranquility, serenity, calmness*

SERENO (A), *calm, serene; settled, fine; clear*

SERIEDAD, *seriousness, responsibility, reliability*

SERIO (A), *serious, grave*

SERPENTÍN, *coil*

SERPENTINA, *serpentine; also a paper streamer*

SERPIENTE, *snake, serpent*

SERVIBLE, *serviceable*

SERVICIAL, *attentive, helpful, obliging*

SERVICIO, *service; employment; maintenance*

SERVIDOR (A), *servant; computer server*

SERVIL, *servile, menial, obsequious*

SERVILISMO, *subservience, servility*

SÉSAMO, *sesame*

SESIÓN, *meeting, session*

SEVERIDAD, *severity, roughness, strictness*

SEVERO (A), *severe, harsh, rough*

SEXISTA, *sexist*

SEXO, *sex*

SEXTETO, *sextet*

SEXUALIDAD, *sexuality, erotic, carnal*

SHAKESPERIANO (A), *Shakespearian*

SHARE, *TV audience share*

SHOPPING, *shopping center or mall*

SHORT, *shorts*

SIBILANTE, *sibilant*

SIDERAL, *sidereal*

SIEMPRE, *always*

SIENA, *the color sienna*

SÍFILIS, *syphilis*

SIFILÍTICO (A), *syphilitic* (MED)

SIGNATARIO (A), *signatory*

SIGNATURA, *catalogue number, press mark*

SIGNIFICACIÓN, *significance, relevance*

SIGNIFICADO (A), *meaning, content, gist, sense, drift*

SIGNIFICATIVO (A), *significant, meaningful*

SIGNO, *sign*

SÍLABA, *syllable*

SILENCIO, *silence*

SILENCIOSO (A), *silent, quiet, mute, still, calm, placid, serene, tranquil; speechless*

SILICATO, *silicate*

SÍLICE, *silica*

SILICIO, *silicon*

SILICONA, *silicone*

SILOGISMO, *syllogism*

SILUETA, *figure, outline, silhouette*

SIMBIOSIS, *symbiosis, mutually advantageous union*

SIMBÓLICO (A), *symbolic, token*

SIMBOLISMO, *symbolism, represents, denotes*

SÍMBOLO, *symbol*

SIMETRÍA, *symmetry*

SIMÉTRICO (A), *symmetrical*

SÍMIL, *simile* (LITER)

SIMILITUD, *similarity, resemblance*

SIMIO (A), *simian, ape*

SIMPATÍA, *friendliness, affection, sympathy*

SIMPÁTICO (A), *nice, likeable, friendly*

SIMPLEMENTE, *simply, just*

SIMPLEZA, *trifle, silliness; gullibility*

SIMPLICIDAD, *simplicity*

SIMPLIFICACIÓN, *simplification*

SIMPLISTA, *simplistic*

SIMPLÓN (A), *simple, simple minded person*

SIMPOSIO, *symposium*

SIMULACIÓN, *simulation, pretense, imitation*

SIMULACRO, *simulated (as mock trial, fire drill); sham*

SIMULADO (A), *feigned, simulated*

SIMULTÁNEO (A), *simultaneous*

SINAGOGA, *synagogue*

SINCERIDAD, *sincerity, frankness, honesty, openness*

SINCERO (A), *sincere*

SINCOPADO (A), *syncopated*

SINCRÓNICO (A), *simultaneous*

SINCRONIZACIÓN, *synchronization, coincides*

SINDICACIÓN, *unionization, syndication*

SINDICAL, *trade union (adj)*

SINDICATO, *trade union (n)*

SÍNDROME, *syndrome*

SINERGIA, *synergy*

SINFÍN, *vast number, countless*

SINFONÍA, *symphony*

SINFÓNICO (A), *symphonic*

SINGULARIDAD, *peculiarity, singularity*

SINIESTRO (A) (adj), *sinister, evil; forbidding, gloomy*

SINIESTRO (n), *disaster, accident, crash*

SINNÚMERO, *countless, no end of*

SINÓNIMO (A), *synonymous (adj); synonym (n)*

SINOPSIS, *synopsis, diagram*

SINÓPTICO (A), *synoptic; diagram, chart*

SINTAXIS, *syntax*

SÍNTESIS, *synthesis, summary; integration, mixture*

SINTÉTICO (A), *synthetic, artificial; false, fake*

SÍNTOMA, *symptom*

SINTOMÁTICO (A), *symptomatic, characteristic, suggestive, indicative, representative*

SÍPER ó ZÍPER, *zipper*

SIRENA, *siren; mermaid*

SIROCO, *sirocco*

SÍSMICO (A), *seismic*

SISMÓGRAFO, *seismograph*

SISTEMA, *system, group, structure, way, plan*

SISTEMÁTICO (A), *systematic, organized, planned*

SISTÉMICO (A), *systemic*

SITUACIÓN, *situation, position, location, spot, site, locale; setting, condition, status*

SITUADO (A), *situated, placed*

SOBORNO, *bribery*

SOBRANTE, *remaining (adj), surplus (n); spare*

SOBREABUNDANCIA, *excess, surplus, extra*

SOBREABUNDANTE, *excessive, immoderate, exorbitant, extreme, inordinate, unreasonable; surfeit*

SOBRECOSTO, *extra cost*

SOBREDOSIS, *overdose*

SOBREHUMANO (A), *superhuman*

SOBREMANERA (adv), *exceedingly*

SOBRENATURAL, *supernatural*

SOBRENOMBRE, *nickname; epithet*

SOBREPESO, *excess weight*

SOBREPRODUCCIÓN, *over production*

SOBREPUESTO (A), *superimposed*

SOBRESALIENTE, *outstanding*

SOBRESALTO, *start, fright, alarm, panic, scare*

SOBRETASA, *surcharge*

SOBRETIEMPO, *overtime*

SOBRETODO, *overcoat*

SOBRIEDAD, *restraint, moderation, sobriety*

SOBRIO (A), *restrained, moderate, simple, sober*

SOCARRÓN (A), *sarcastic, snide, slyly, sneering*

SOCARRONERÍA, *sarcasm, snide humor*

SOCIABILIDAD, *sociability*

SOCIEDAD, *society*

SOCIOLOGÍA, *sociology*

SOCIÓLOGO (A), *sociologist*

SOCRÁTICO (A), *Socratic*

SODIO, *sodium*

SODOMÍA, *sodomy*

SODOMITA, *sodomite*

SOFISMA, *sophism*

SOFISTA, *sophist*

SOFISTICACIÓN, *sophistication*

SOFISTICADO (A), *sophisticated, cultured, experienced*

SOFOCADO, *out of breath*

SOFOCANTE, *suffocating, stifling*

SOLAMENTE, *only (adv); expressly*

SOLDADO, *soldier*

SOLEDAD, *loneliness, solitude, desolation, isolation*

SOLEMNE, *formal, solemn, serious, dignified*

SOLEMNIDAD, *pomp, solemnity*

SOLICITANTE, *applicant*

SOLÍCITO (A), *solicitous, obliging; eager, anxious, caring, considerate, thoughtful, attentive*

SOLICITUD, *request, application*

SOLIDARIDAD, *solidarity; alone, secluded, single*

SOLIDARIO (A), *shared, caring*

SÓLIDO, *solid shape* (GEOM)

SÓLIDO (A), *solid, firm, stable, substantial, sturdy*

SOLILOQUIO, *soliloquy*

SOLISTA, *soloist*

SOLITARIO (A), *solitary, lonely, deserted, unattended*

SOLSTICIO, *solstice*

SOLUCIÓN, *solution, mixture, blend; answer*

SOLVENCIA, *solvency, reliability*

SOLVENTE, *solvent, reliable, free of debt, sound*

SOMÁTICO (A), *somatic*

SOMBRA, *shadow, shade; screen, cover; tint*

SOMBREADO, *artistic shading, darkening*

SOMBRERO, *hat*

SOMBRILLA, *parasol, sunshade*

SOMBRÍO (A), *gloomy, dark, somber, shaded, murky*

SOMNOLENCIA, *sleepiness, drowsiness*

SOMNOLIENTO (A), *sleepy, drowsy*

SONAMBULISMO, *sleepwalking*

SONÁMBULO (A), *sleepwalker*

SONETO, *sonnet*

SÓNICO (A), *sonic, sound*

SONIDO (m), *sound*

SOPA, *soup*

SOPOR, *drowsiness, torpor, sluggishness, lethargy*

SOPORÍFERO (A) ó SOPORÍFICO (A), *soporific (adj), sleeping pill (n)*

SOPORTABLE, *bearable*

SOPORTAL, *porch*

SOPORTE, *support, bracket, base, stand*

SORBETE, *sherbet*

SÓRDIDO (A), *dirty, sordid, squalid*

SORIASIS, *psoriasis*

SOSO (A), *bland, tasteless, insipid, dull, unsalted*

SOSPECHA, *suspicion*

SOSTÉN, *support, prop; bra; sustenance*

SOSTENIBILIDAD, *sustainability*

SOSTENIBLE, *sustainable*

SOSTENIDO (A), *sustained; sharp* (MUS)

SOYA, *soy*

SPORT, *sports coat/jacket*

SUAVEMENTE, *gently, softly, smoothly*

SUAVIDAD, *softness, smoothness*

SUBALTERNO (A), *auxiliary, subordinate, secondary*

SUBATÓMICO (A), *subatomic*

SUBCOMITÉ, *subcommittee*

SUBCONSCIENTE, *subconscious*

SUBCONTRATA, *subcontract*

SUBCONTRATISTA, *subcontractor*

SUBCULTURA, *subculture*

SUBCUTÁNEO (A), *subcutaneous*

SUBDIRECTOR (A), *deputy director*

SUBEMPLEO, *underemployment*

SUBESPECIE, *subspecies*

SUBESTACIÓN, *substation*

SUBGRUPO, *subgroup*

SUBJETIVIDAD, *subjectivity*

SUBJETIVISMO, *subjectivism*

SUBJETIVO (A), *subjective, prejudiced, biased*

SUBJUNTIVO (A), *subjunctive mood; imagined, wished*

SUBLIMACIÓN, *exaltation, sublimation*

SUBMARINO (A) (adj), *underwater; submarine*

SUBMUNDO, *underworld*

SUBORDEN, *suborder*

SUBORDINACIÓN, *subordination, obedience*

SUBORDINADO (A), *subordinate, secondary*

SUBPRODUCTO, *by-product, derivative, subsidiary*

SUBROGACIÓN, *subrogation, substitution, replacement*

SUBSCRIPCIÓN ó SUSCRIPCIÓN, *subscription*

SUBSIDIARIO (A), *subsidiary, ancillary, accessory*

SUBSIDIO, *allowance, benefit, subsidy*

SUBSIGUIENTE, *subsequent*

SUBSISTEMA, *subsystem*

SUBSISTENCIA, *subsistence*

SUBSISTENTE, *surviving*

SUBSTANCIA ó SUSTANCIA, *substance*

SUBSTANCIOSO ó SUSTANCIOSO, *substantial*

SUBSTITUCIÓN ó SUSTITUCIÓN, *replacement, substitution, alternate*

SUBSTITUIBLE, *replaceable*

SUBSTITUTIVO (A) ó SUSTITUTIVO (A) (adj), *substitute*

SUBSTRACCIÓN ó SUSTRACCIÓN, *theft; subtraction* (MAT)

SUBTERFUGIO, *subterfuge, artifice, trick, scheme*

SUBTERRÁNEO (A), *subterranean, underground; concealed*

SUBTEXTO, *subtext, underlying theme*

SUBTÍTULO, *subtitle, caption, secondary title*

SUBURBANO (A), *suburban*

SUBVERSIVO (A), *subversive, seditious, treasonous*

SUCCIÓN, *suction*

SUCESIÓN, *succession*

SUCESIVAMENTE, *successively*

SUCESIVO (A), *successive, consecutive, following*

SUCESOR (A), *successor*

SUCESORIO (A) (adj), *succession*

SUCINTO (A), *succinct, concise, pithy, short, brief*

SUÉTER, *sweater*

SUFICIENCIA, *competence*

SUFICIENTE, *enough, adequate*

SUFLÉ, *soufflé*

SUFRIMIENTO, *suffering, toughness, anguish*

SUGESTIÓN, *suggestion, hypnotic*

SUGESTIONABLE, *suggestible, impressionable*

SUGESTIVO (A), *stimulating, exciting, arousing, stirring*

SUICIDA, *suicidal*

SUICIDIO, *suicide*

SUMA, *addition, total; adding, adding up*

SUMAMENTE, *extremely, highly*

SUMARIAL, *summary, synopsis, abstract, digest*

SUMARIO (A), *brief, concise*

SUMERGIBLE, *submersible*

SUMISIÓN, *submission, surrender*

SUMISO (A), *submissive, deferential, servile*

SUPERABUNDANCIA, *excess, superabundance*

SUPERABUNDANTE, *excessive, superabundant*

SUPERACIÓN, *improvement; overcoming*

SUPERESTRUCTURA, *superstructure*

SUPERFICIALIDAD, *superficially, externally, cursory*

SUPERFINO (A), *superfine*

SUPERFLUO (A), *superfluous, unnecessary, excessive*

SUPERHOMBRE, *superman*

SUPERINTENDENTE, *superintendent*

SUPERIORIDAD, *superiority, supremacy, dominance*

SUPERLATIVO (A) (adj), *exceptional, superlative*

SUPERLATIVO, *superlative* (GRAM)

SUPERMERCADO, *supermarket*

SUPERPOSICIÓN, *superimposing, inflicting, burdening*

SUPERPOTENCIA, *superpower*

SUPERPRODUCCIÓN, *overproduction* (ECON); *blockbuster* (CINE)

SUPERPUESTO (A), *superimposed*

SUPERSÓNICO (A), *supersonic*

SUPERSTICIÓN, *superstition*

SUPERSTICIOSO (A), *superstitious*

SUPINO (A), *supine*

SUPLEMENTARIO (A), *supplementary, extra*

SUPLEMENTO, *supplement*

SUPLENCIA, *substitution, replacement*

SUPLENTE, *substitute, deputy*

SÚPLICA, *request, supplication*

SUPOSICIÓN, *supposition, belief, assumption*

SUPOSITORIO, *suppository*

SUPREMACÍA, *supremacy*

SUPREMO (A), *supreme, highest*

SUPRESIÓN, *abolition, suppression, elimination*

SUPUESTO (n), *assumption, supposition, hypothesis*

SUPUESTO (A), *alleged, assumed, supposed*

SUPURACIÓN, *suppuration, decomposition, rot*

SURREALISMO, *surrealism*

SURREALISTA, *surrealist*

SUSCEPTIBILIDAD, *susceptibility, vulnerability*

SUSCRIPTOR (A), *subscriber*

SUSPENSO (n), *suspense; anxiety, agitation, tension*

SUSPENSO (A), *perplexed*

SUSPICACIA, *suspicion, mistrust*

SUSPICAZ, *suspicious, doubtful, skeptical, distrustful*

SUSTANCIA, *substance*

SUSTANCIAL, *essential, vital, significant*

SUSTENTACIÓN, *support, maintenance, upkeep*

SUSTENTO, *sustenance, support, provision*

SUTIL, *subtle, keen, sharp; delicate, fine*

SUTILEZA, *subtlety, guile, cunning; delicacy*

SUTURA, *suture*

Easily Recognizable Verbs

SABOTEAR, *to sabotage*

SACRIFICAR, *to sacrifice*

SALIVAR, *to salivate, spit*

SALPIMENTAR, *to season, add salt and pepper*

SALTEAR, *to sauté*

SALUDAR, *to greet*

SALVAGUARDAR, *to safeguard*

SALVAR, to *save*

SANCIONAR, *to sanction, penalize*

SANTIFICAR, *to sanctify, consecrate*

SATANIZAR, *to demonize*

SATIRIZAR, *to satirize*

SATISFACER, *to satisfy, please, fulfill*

SATURAR, *to saturate, flood, soak, drench*

SAZONAR, *to season, flavor*

SECCIONAR, *to section, cut off*

SECUESTRAR, *to kidnap, confiscate, seize*

SECULARIZAR, *to secularize*

SECUNDAR, *to second, join, support*

SEDAR, *to sedate*

SEDUCIR, *to attract, charm, seduce*

SEGMENTAR, *to cut or divide into pieces, segment*

SEGREGAR, *to segregate; secrete* (ANAT)

SEGUIR, *to follow, follow up; chase, pursue*

SELECCIONAR, *to select, pick, choose*

SENTENCIAR, *to sentence, condemn; give an opinion*

SEPARAR, *to separate, split up, detach, sever*

SEPULTAR, *to bury*

SERPENTEAR, *to wind, meander; creep*

SERVIR, *to serve, help, assist*

SIGNIFICAR, *to mean, express, signify*

SILENCIAR, *to hush up, keep quiet, silence*

SIMBOLIZAR, *to symbolize*

SIMPLIFICAR, *to simplify, clarify, untangle*

SIMULAR, *to simulate; feign, sham*

SINCOPAR, *to syncopate*

SINCRONIZAR, *to synchronize*

SINGULARIZAR, *to distinguish, single out, stand out*

SINTETIZAR, *to synthesize* (QUIM); *to summarize*

SISTEMATIZAR, *to systematize*

SITUAR, *to place, put; post* (MIL)

SOBORNAR, *to bribe, suborn, corrupt*

SOBREACTUAR, *to overact*

SOBREALIMENTAR, *to overfeed*

SOBRECONTRATAR, *to overbook*

SOBREESTIMAR, *to overestimate*

SOBREEXCITAR, *to overexcite*

SOBREEXPLOTAR, *to overexploit, drain*

SOBREIMPRESIONAR, *to superimpose*

SOBREPASAR, *to exceed, overshoot, beat*

SOBRESALIR, *to project, overhang, jut out; stand out*

SOBREVALORAR, *to overvalue, overrate*

SOBREVIVIR, *to survive, outlive*

SOCIALIZAR, *to socialize*

SODOMIZAR, *to sodomize*

SOFOCAR, *to suffocate, stifle, put out, crush, stop*

SOLDAR, *to solder, weld, join*

SOLICITAR, *to solicit, ask for, seek, canvass*

SOLIDIFICAR, *to solidify, harden*

SOLUCIONAR, *to solve, resolve, settle*

SOLVENTAR, *to settle, resolve, pay*

SONDAR, *to probe; sound, take soundings*

SOPORTAR, *to support, stand, endure, resist*

SOSTENER, *to support, hold up; defend*

SUBCONTRATAR, *to outsource, subcontract*

SUBDIVIDIR, *to subdivide*

SUBESTIMAR, *to underestimate, underrate*

SUBLIMAR, *to sublimate, divert, alter*

SUBORDINAR, *to subordinate*

SUBROGAR, *to subrogate, substitute, replace*

SUBSCRIBIR, *to subscribe, to sign, endorse*

SUBSIDIAR, *to subsidize*

SUBSISTIR, *to live, exist, survive, subsist*

SUBTITULAR, *to subtitle*

SUBVENCIONAR, *to subsidize*

SUBVERTIR, *to subvert*

SUCCIONAR, *to suck up, soak up, absorb*

SUCEDER, *to happen; succeed sb, replace*

SUCUMBIR, *to succumb (to), die, fall*

SUFRIR, *to suffer, bear, put up with*

SUGERIR, *to suggest*

SUICIDARSE, *to commit suicide*

SUMERGIR, *to submerge, immerse, dip, sink*

SUPERVISAR, *to supervise*

SUPLANTAR, *to supplant, take the place of*

SUPLICAR, *to plead for sthg, implore, beg*

SUPLIR, *to replace, compensate, fulfill*

SUPRIMIR, *to abolish, suppress, remove*

SUPURAR, *to suppurate, fester* (MED)

SUSCRIBIR, *to subscribe, to sign, endorse*

SUSPENDER, *to hang up, hang from sthg, suspend*

SUSTENTAR, *to hold up, support, sustain*

SUSTITUIR, *to replace, substitute*

SUTURAR, *to stitch, suture*

STUDY NOTES:

T

Interchangeable Words

TABASCO

TAE-KWON-DO

TALISMÁN

TALMUD

TAMPÓN; *an ink pad*

TÁNDEM

TANGIBLE, *concrete*

TANGO

TAPIOCA

TARÁNTULA

TAROT

TARTÁN

TAXI

TEFLÓN

TELEFAX ó FAX

TELEMÁRKETING

TELEVISIÓN, *be on, work in*

TÉLEX

TEMPERAMENTAL

TEMPO

TEMPORAL (adj), *relative to time; temporary, provisional*

TENDÓN

TENDONITIS ó TENDINITIS

TENOR (MUS)

TENSIÓN

TEQUILA

TERMINAL, *ending* (MED); *a station*

TERRIBLE

TERRIER, *the dog*

TERRITORIAL

TERROR

TEST

TEXTILES

TEXTUAL; *exact*

TIARA

TIBIA

TIC, *nervous tic*

TICKET, *ticket, receipt*

TIMBAL (MUS)

TITÁN

TOGA

TOLERABLE

TÓMBOLA

TONAL

TOP-MODEL, *supermodel*

TOPLESS ó TOP-LESS

TORNADO

TORPEDO

TORPOR

TORSIÓN, *twist, twisting*

TORSO

TOTAL

TÓTEM

TOUR (s)

TRACTOR

TRÁILER; *caravan, semi-trailer*

TRANCE, *trance; a period of time, a situation*

TRANSCONTINENTAL

TRANSFUSIÓN, *transfusion*

TRANSPORTABLE

TRANSISTOR

TRANSVERSAL (GEOM)

TRAUMA

TRIAL (DEP)

TRIANGULAR (adj); *the verb to triangulate*

TRIBAL

TRIBUNAL, *court, bench*

TRÍCEPS

TRICOLOR, *French flag*

TRIDIMENSIONAL

TRILATERAL

TRIMOTOR

TRÍO

TRIPLE

TRIVIAL

TROPICAL

TROUPE

TRUST (s), *a trust, cartel*

TSUNAMI

TUBA

TUBERCULOSIS

TUBULAR, *also a bicycle tire*

TUMOR (MED)

TUNDRA

TURBO, *turbocharger*

TUTOR

TUTTI FRUTTI

TUTÚ

TV, *television*

TWEED

TWIST, *the dance*

Easily Recognizable Nouns, Adjectives and Adverbs

TABACO, *tobacco products and plant*

TABERNA, *tavern, bar*

TABERNÁCULO, *tabernacle*

TABLETA, *tablet* (MED)

TABÚ, *taboo*

TABULADOR, *tab, tabulator*

TÁCITO (A), *tacit, unwritten, unspoken*

TACITURNO (A), *taciturn, silent, reticent; sullen, moody*

TÁCTICA, *tactics, tactic, gambit, strategy, approach*

TÁCTICO (A), *tactical (adj); tactician (n)*

TÁCTIL, *tactile; tangible*

TACTO, *sense of touch; tact, touch*

TALCO, *talcum powder; talc* (QUIM)

TALENTO, *talent*

TALENTOSO (A), *talented, gifted*

TAMARINDO, *tamarind*

TAMBIÉN, *also, too, as well*

TANGENCIAL, *tangential, divergent; peripheral, irrelevant, unrelated*

TANGENTE, *tangent*

TARDE (adv), *late*

TARDÍO (A), *late, belated; slow*

TARDO (A), *slow, sluggish*

TARIFA, *charge, fare, flat rate, tariff*

TARTA, *cake, tart, pie*

TÁRTARO, *tartar*

TAUTOLOGÍA, *tautology, redundancy, duplication*

TAXATIVO (A), *limited, restricted, sharp, emphatic*

TAXIDERMIA, *taxidermy*

TAXISTA, *taxi driver*

TÉCNICA, *technique, craftsmanship, approach*

TÉCNICO (A), *technical (adj); technician (n)*

TECNOLOGÍA, *technology*

TECTÓNICO (A), *tectonic*

TEDIO, *boredom, tedium, monotony, ennui*

TEDIOSO (A), *tedious*

TELECOMUNICACIÓN, *telecommunication*

TELEDIARIO, *television news*

TELÉFONO, *telephone, phone*

TELEGRAFÍA, *telegraphy*

TELÉGRAFO, *telegraph*

TELEGRAMA, *telegram*

TELEMANÍA, *TV addiction*

TELEPATÍA, *telepathy*

TELEPÁTICO (A), *telepathic, clairvoyant, psychic*

TELETIPO, *teletype*

TELESCÓPICO (A), *telescopic*

TELESCOPIO, *telescope*

TELEVISADO (A), *televised*

TELEVISOR, *television set*

TEMÁTICA, (n) *subject matter, topic, issue, point*

TEMÁTICO (A) (adj), *thematic; theme park*

TEMBLOR, *tremor, shiver*

TEMBLOROSO (A), *shaky*

TEMERARIO (A), *rash, reckless, bold, hasty*

TEMERIDAD, *recklessness, folly, boldness*

TEMEROSO (A), *frightened*

TEMIBLE, *fearsome, frightful*

TEMOR, *fear, dread, terror, fright, alarm*

TEMPERADO (A), *temperate, moderate, mild*

TEMPERAMENTO, *temperament, nature, disposition*

TEMPERATURA, *temperature*

TEMPESTAD, *tempest, storm*

TEMPESTUOSO (A), *stormy*

TEMPLO, *temple*

TEMPORARIO (A), *seasonal*

TENACIDAD, *tenacity, retentive; persistent, resolute*

TENDENCIA, *tendency, trend*

TENDENCIOSO (A), *tendentious, biased*

TENENCIA, *tenancy, occupancy, possession*

TENIS, *tennis*

TENISTA, *tennis player*

TENSO, *taut, stiff, rigid; tense, nervous*

TENSOR (A), *strut, guy wire*

TENTACIÓN, *temptation, draw, lure, inducement*

TENTÁCULO, *tentacle*

TENTADOR (A), *tempting (adj); tempter, temptress (n)*

TENTATIVA, *attempt*

TENUE, *fine, tenuous, thin; weak, meager, frail*

TEOLOGÍA, *theology*

TEOLÓGICO (A), *theological*

TEÓLOGO (A), *theologian*

TEOREMA, *theorem*

TEORÍA, *theory*

TEÓRICAMENTE, *theoretically, in theory*

TEÓRICO (A), *theoretical*

TERAPEUTA, *therapist*

TERAPÉUTICO (A), *therapeutic*

TERAPIA, *therapy*

TERMAL, *thermal*

TÉRMICO (A), *heat*; *thematic*

TERMINACIÓN, *completion, ending, termination*

TERMINADO, *finished, accomplished, closed, stopped*

TERMINANTE, *categorical, conclusive, final, outright*

TERMINANTEMENTE, *categorically, conclusively*

TÉRMINO, *end, conclusion*

TERMINOLOGÍA, *terminology, nomenclature, wording*

TERMITA ó TERMITE, *termite*

TERMÓMETRO, *thermometer*

TERMONUCLEAR, *thermonuclear*

TERMOSTATO, *thermostat*

TERRACOTA, *terracotta*

TERRAZA, *terrace, balcony, flat roof*

TERRAZO, *terrazzo*

TERREMOTO, *earthquake*

TERRENAL, *earthly, worldly*

TERRENO, *land, terrain* (GEOL); *earthly*

TERRITORIO, *territory; region, district* (POL)

TERRORÍFICO (A) *(adj), terrible, terrifying, frightening*

TERRORISMO, *terrorism*

TERRORISTA, *terrorist*

TESIS, *thesis, theory*

TESÓN, *tenacity, perseverance, persistence*

TESTADO (A), *testate*

TESTADOR (A), *testator, testatrix*

TESTAMENTARIA, *documentation (of a will), estate*

TESTAMENTARIO (A), *testamentary (adj); executor, executrix (n)*

TESTAMENTO, *legacy, will, testament*

TESTARUDO (A), *stubborn, pigheaded*

TESTÍCULO, *testicle* (ANAT)

TESTIMONIAL, *token, nominal*

TESTIMONIO, *account, testimony; spoken evidence*

TESTOSTERONA, *testosterone*

TÉTANOS ó TÉTANO, *tetanus* (MED)

TEXTIL, *textile*

TEXTO, *text*

TEXTUALMENTE, *textually, exactly*

TEXTURA, *texture*

TIEMPO, *time*

TIERRA, *earth, the Earth*

TIFÓN, *typhoon; waterspout*

TIFUS, *typhus*

TIGRE, *tiger*

TIMIDEZ, *shyness, timidity*

TÍMIDO (A), *shy, timid*

TÍMPANO, *eardrum, tympanum* (MED); *drum* (MUS)

TINTA, *ink*

TINTE, *dye, dyestuff, stain*

TÍPICO (A), *typical*

TIPO, *type, kind, sort; guy, dame*

TIPOGRAFÍA, *printing, typography*

TIPOGRÁFICO (A), *typographical*

TIPÓGRAFO (A), *printer*

TIRANÍA, *tyranny*

TIRÁNICO (A), *a tyrannical, possessive government*

TIRANO (A) (adj), *a tyrannical, despotic person*

TIRANO (n), *tyrant, despot*

TITÁNICO, *titanic*

TITANIO, *titanium*

TÍTULO, *title*

TOBOGÁN, *shute, slide; toboggan*

TODO (A), *all*

TODOTERRENO, *all terrain vehicle*

TOILETTE, *wash room, toilet*

TOLERADO (A), *tolerated*

TOLERANCIA, *tolerance, patience, leniency*

TOLERANTE, *tolerant, fair, considerate*

TOMATE, *tomato*

TOMATERA, *tomato plant*

TOMO, *tome, book, volume*

TONALIDAD, *tonality, intonation; tone,* (MUS)

TONEL, *barrel, cask*

TÓNICO (A), *revitalizing, tonic, stimulating*

TONIFICACIÓN, *invigoration*

TONIFICADOR (A) (adj), *invigorating*

TONO, *tone, pitch*

TONSURA, *tonsure*

TONTO (A), *silly, stupid*

TONTERÍA, *rubbish, nonsense, garbage*

TOPOGRAFÍA, *topography*

TOPOGRÁFICO (A), *topographical*

TOPÓGRAFO (A), *topographer*

TORÁCICO (A), *thoracic*

TÓRAX, *thorax*

TORMENTA, *storm* (METEO); *turmoil*

TORMENTO, *torment, torture, anguish, agony*

TORMENTOSO (A), *stormy; troubled*

TORNEO, *tournament, competition*

TORNILLO, *screw, bolt*

TORNIQUETE, *tourniquet* (MED); *turnstile*

TORO, *bull*

TORRE, *tower, high-rise*

TORRENCIAL, *torrential*

TORRENTE, *torrent, flood*

TORRENTOSO, *rushing, fast-flowing*

TÓRRIDO (A), *torrid*

TORTA, *thump, punch, sock; tart, flan*

TORTILLA, *omelette or omelet*

TORTITA, *pancake*

TORTUGA, *tortoise*

TORTUOSO (A), *tortuous, winding; devious*

TORTURA, *torture*

TORTURADOR (A), *torturer*

TOSTADA, *piece of toast*

TOSTADO (A), *toasted, browned, tanned*

TOSTADORA, *toaster*

TOSTÓN, *bore, nuisance, tedious speech; crouton*

TOTALIDAD, *whole, totality*

TOTALITARIO (A), *totalitarian*

TOTALITARISMO, *totalitarianism*

TOTALMENTE, *totally, completely*

TOUROPERADOR (A), *tour operator*

TOXICIDAD, *toxicity*

TÓXICO (A) (adj), *toxic, poisonous*

TÓXICO (n), *poison, toxic substance*

TOXICOLOGÍA, *toxicology*

TOXICOMANÍA, *drug addiction*

TOXICÓMANO (A), *drug addict*

TOXINA, *toxin*

TRACCIÓN, *traction, drive; pulling*

TRADICIÓN, *tradition*

TRADICIONAL, *traditional*

TRÁDING (adj), *trading*

TRÁFICO, *traffic; trade*

TRAGEDIA, *tragedy*

TRÁGICO (A), *tragic*

TRAGICOMEDIA, *tragicomedy*

TRAICIONERO (A), *perfidious, unreliable; treacherous*

TRAIDOR (A) (adj), *traitorous, deceitful; traitor*

TRAMPOLÍN, *trampoline, springboard*

TRANQUILAMENTE, *peacefully, leisurely*

TRANQUILIDAD, *peaceful, calm, tranquility*

TRANQUILIZADOR (A), *calming, soothing, reassuring*

TRANQUILIZANTE, *tranquilizer* (MED)

TRANQUILO (A) (adj), *peaceful, calm; quiet* (MUS)

TRANSACCIÓN, *transaction; deal*

TRANSATLÁNTICO (A), *transatlantic*

TRANSCRIPCIÓN, *transcription, transcript*

TRANSFERENCIA, *transfer* (FIN)

TRANSFIGURACIÓN, *transfiguration*

TRANSFORMACIÓN, *transformation, change*

TRANSFORMISTA, *quick-change artist; transvestite*

TRANSGRESIÓN, *transgression, offense, misdeed*

TRANSGRESOR (A), *transgressor*

TRANSICIÓN, *transition, changeover; alteration*

TRANSIGENCIA, *willingness to compromise, tolerance*

TRANSIGENTE, *compromising, tolerant, forgiving*

TRANSITIVO (A), *transitive*

TRÁNSITO, *traffic, transit* (COM)

TRANSITORIO (A), *transitory, temporary, provisional*

TRANSLITERACIÓN, *transliteration*

TRANSLÚCIDO (A), *translucent*

TRANSMIGRACIÓN, *migration, transmigration*

TRANSMISIBLE, *transmissible, contagious* (MED)

TRANSMISIÓN, *transmission* (AUTO); *broadcast*

TRANSMUTACIÓN, *transmutation*

TRANSPARENCIA, *transparency, openness*

TRANSPARENTE (adj), *transparent, diaphanous, filmy*

TRANSPLANTE ó TRASPLANTE, *transplant* (MED); *transfer*

TRANSPORTE, *transport, transportation*

TRANSPOSICIÓN, *transposition*

TRÁQUEA, *trachea* (MED)

TRASCENDENTE ó TRASCENDENTIAL, *transcendent, significant, vital*

TRASCENDENCIA, *significance, importance; implications, consequences*

TRASTO, *trash; piece of junk*

TRATABLE, *easy going, friendly, sociable*

TRAUMÁTICO (A), *traumatic, shocking, upsetting, disturbing, painful, agonizing, harrowing, harmful*

TRAVESÍA, *crossing, voyage*

TREMENDO (A), *tremendous, overpowering*

TRÉMULO, *tremulous, shaky; quavering*

TREN, *train*

TREPANACIÓN, *trepanation*

TREPIDANTE, *frantic; fear, anxiety; intolerable*

TRIADA, *triad*

TRIBU, *tribe*

TRIBULACIÓN, *tribulation, hardship*

TRIBUTACIÓN, *tax, taxation, payment*

TRIBUTARIO (A), *tax; tributary* (GEOL)

TRIBUTO, *tax, price, tribute*

TRICICLO, *tricycle*

TRIDENTE, *trident*

TRIDIMENSIONAL, *three-dimensional*

TRIENAL, *triennial*

TRIGONOMETRÍA, *trigonometry*

TRILLÓN, *trillion*

TRILOGÍA, *trilogy*

TRIMESTRAL, *trimester, quarterly*

TRIMESTRE, *quarter, term*

TRINIDAD, *the Trinity* (RELIG)

TRIPARTITO, *tripartite*

TRIPLICADO, *triplicate*

TRÍPODE, *tripod*

TRIVIALIDAD, *triviality, triteness*

TRIVIALIZACIÓN, *trivializing, minimizing*

TROFEO, *trophy*

TROGLODITA, *troglodyte, rough, brutish; oaf, lout*

TROMBO, *thrombus*

TROMBÓN, *trombone*

TROMBOSIS, *thrombosis*

TROMPA, *horn* (MUS)

TROMPETA, *trumpet*

TRÓPICO, *tropic*

TROPO, *trope*

TROTE, *trot; scamper, scoot*

TRUFA, *truffle*

TRUSÍMO, *truism*

TRUNCADO (A), *truncated, shortened; incomplete*

TUBE, *pipe, flute*

TUBO, *tube*

TULIPÁN, *tulip*

TUMULTO, *riot, disturbance, uproar, turmoil*

TUMULTUOSO (A), *tumultuous, disorderly*

TÚNEL, *tunnel*

TÚNICA, *tunic, robe*

TUPÉ, *toupee or toupee, hairpiece*

TURBACIÓN, *upset, disturbance, alarm, worry*

TURBADO, *disturbed, alarmed, worried*

TURBADOR (adj), *disturbing, alarming, embarrassing*

TURBANTE, *turban*

TURBINA, *turbine*

TURBIO (A), *turbid, cloudy, muddy*

TURBULENCIA, *turbulence, tumultuous, commotion*

TURBULENTO (A), *turbulent, rebellious, stormy, troubled*

TURGENCIA, *turgidity*

TURGENTE, *turgid, swollen, inflated; pompous*

TURISMO, *tourism*

TURISTA, *tourist*

TURÍSTICO (A) (adj), *tourist*

TURNO, *turn, shift; change; revolve, spin*

TUTORÍA, *guardianship*

Easily Recognizable Verbs

TABULAR, *to tabulate*

TATUAR, *to tattoo*

TELEFONEAR, *to telephone*

TELEGRAFIAR, *to telegraph*

TELEVISAR, *to televise*

TEMBLAR, *to tremble (with), shiver, (with)*

TEMER, *to fear*

TENSAR, *to tauten, draw*

TEORIZAR, *to theorize*

TERMINAR, *to finish*

TESTAR, *to make a will*

TESTIFICAR, *to witness, attest to*

TESTIMONIAR, *to testify; demonstrate, show*

TINTAR, *to dye*

TIPIFICAR, *to classify, standardize, typify*

TIRANIZAR, *to tyrannize, domineer*

TOLERAR, *to tolerate*

TONIFICAR, *to invigorate*

TORTURAR, *to torture*

TOSTAR, *to toast, roast, brown*

TRAFICAR, *to traffic, deal*

TRANQUILIZAR, *to calm (down), reassure*

TRANSCENDER (DE), *to transcend, go beyond*

TRANSCRIBIR, *to transcribe, duplicate, record*

TRANSFERIR, *to transfer, convey, hand over*

TRANSFORMAR, *to transform, convert, modify*

TRANSGREDIR, *to transgress*

TRANSMITIR, *to transmit, send, transfer*

TRANSMUTAR, *to transmute, change*

TRANSPARENTAR, *to reveal, allow, show; betray*

TRANSPORTAR, *to transport, move, transfer, send*

TRASPASAR, *to pierce, penetrate*

TRASPLANTAR, *to transplant, shift, uproot*

TRAUMATIZAR, *to traumatize, shock*

TREPIDAR, *to shake, vibrate; hesitate, waver*

TRIBUTAR, *to pay, have respect (for); pay taxes*

TRIPLICAR, *to triple, treble*

TRITURAR, *to triturate, grind, crush*

TRIVIALIZAR, *to trivialize, minimize, play down*

TROTAR, *to trot, travel about*

TRUNCAR, *to truncate, shorten, cut short*

TURNAR, *to take turns*

TUTELAR, *to protect, guard, supervise*

STUDY NOTES:

U

Interchangeable Words

UKELELE

ULTERIOR

ULTIMÁTUM

ULTRA, *extreme*

UMBILICAL

UNDERGROUND

UNILATERAL

UNIÓN, *joint, merger*

UNISEX

UNIVERSAL

UREA

USUAL

UTOPÍA

Easily Recognizable Nouns, Adjectives and Adverbs

ÚLCERA, *ulcer, sore* (MED)

ULCERACIÓN, *ulceration*

ULTERIORMENTE, *subsequently*

ULTIMACIÓN, *conclusion, completion*

ÚLTIMAMENTE, *recently, of late, lately*

ÚLTIMO (A), *last*

ULTRAFINO, *ultrafine*

ULTRAMAR, *overseas, abroad*

ULTRAMODERNO (A), *ultramodern*

ULTRAMARINOS, *groceries*

ULTRARRÁPIDO (A), *high speed, extra fast*

ULTRASÓNICO (A), *ultrasonic*

ULTRASONIDO, *ultrasound*

ULTRAVIOLETA, *ultraviolet*

UMBRAL, *threshold, verge*

UMBRÍO (A), *shady*

UNÁNIME, *unanimous*

UNANIMIDAD, *unanimity*

UNCIÓN, *unction*

UNICIDAD, *uniqueness*

ÚNICO (A), *only, unique, single*

UNICORNIO, *unicorn*

UNIDAD, *unit* (MAT) (MIL) (MED)

UNIDIMENSIONAL, *one-dimensional*

UNIDO (A), *united, close; close-knit*

UNIDIRECCIONAL, *unidirectional, one way*

UNIFAMILIAR (adj), *single-family*

UNIFICACIÓN, *unification, standardization*

UNIFICADOR (A), *unifying*

UNIFORMADO (A), *uniformed*

UNIFORME, *uniform, even, smooth, level; dress*

UNIFORMIDAD, *uniformity, regularity; evenness, smoothness*

UNIPERSONAL (adj), *single, individual*

UNÍSONO, *unison* (MUS)

UNÍSONO (A) (adj), *in unison, unanimous*

UNIVERSALIDAD, *universality*

UNIVERSIDAD, *university, institute*

UNIVERSITARIO (A) (adj), *university*

UNIVERSO, *universe* (ASTROM)

UNÍVOCO (A), *univocal*

URANIO, *uranium*

URBANIDAD, *politeness, courtesy, urbanity*

URBANIZACIÓN, *urbanization*

URBANO (A), *urban, city; policeman*

URBE, *large city, metropolis*

URGENCIA, *urgency, emergency* (MED*), urgent need*

URGENTE, *urgent, express, pressing, rush*

URGENTEMENTE (adv), *urgently*

URINARIO, *urinary (adj); urinal (n)*

UROLOGÍA, *urology*

URÓLOGO (A), *urologist*

USADO (A), *second hand, used*

USO, *use*

USURA, *usury*

USURARIO (A), *usurious*

USURERO (A), *usurer*

USURPACIÓN, *usurpation*

USURPADOR (A), *usurping (adj), usurper (n)*

UTENSILIO, *tool, implement, utensil*

UTILERÍA, *equipment, props*

UTILIDAD, *usefulness, utility*

UTILITARIO (A), *utility car, run-around car*

UTILIZABLE, *useable, available, ready for use*

UTILIZACIÓN, *use, utilization*

UTÓPICO (A), *utopian*

Easily Recognizable Verbs

ULTIMAR, *to finalize, finish, complete*

ULULAR, *to ululate, howl*

UNIFICAR, *to unite, join, unify*

UNIFORMAR, *to make uniform, standardize*

UNIFORMIZAR, *to blend*

UNIVERSALIZAR, *to make universal*

URBANIZAR, *to urbanize, become civilized, develop*

USAR, *to use; wear*

USURPAR, *to usurp, encroach, seize*

UTILIZAR, *to use, make use of, utilize*

STUDY NOTES:

V

Interchangeable Words

VAGINA (ANAT)

VAGINAL (ANAT)

VAGINITIS (ANAT)

VAPOR

VARIABLE

VASCULAR

VAUDEVILLE ó VODEVIL

VECTOR

VENAL

VENERABLE

VERANDA, *veranda*

VERBAL

VERSIÓN*; translation*

VERSUS

VÉRTEBRA

VERTEBRAL

VERTICAL

VÉRTIGO

VETO

VÍA

VIABLE

VICEVERSA ó VICE VERSA

VICHYSOISSE

VICUÑA

VIDEO, *system, recorder*

VIDEOCASSETTE ó VIDEOCASETE, *video cassette*

VIDEOCLIP

VIDEOTERMINAL

VIGOR

VILLA; *also a small town, chalet*

VIOLA

VIOLÍN

VIP (s), *(very important person/ persons)*

VIRGINAL

VIRTUAL

VIRTUOSO (A) (MUS); *also means virtuous (adj)*

VIRUS

VISA

VISCERA (s)

VISCERAL

VISIBLE

VISIÓN

VISOR, *viewfinder* (FOTO); *bombsight* (MIL)

VISUAL

VITAL

VITRO ó IN VITRO

VOCAL

VODKA

VOLUBLE

VOYEUR

VULGAR, *common*

VULVA

VULNERABLE

VACACIONES, *vacation, holiday (s)*

VACANTE, *vacant, empty (adj); vacancy (n)*

VACILACIÓN, *hesitation, indecision, vacillation*

VACILANTE, *hesitant, indecisive, faltering*

VACIO (A), *vacant, empty*

VACUIDAD, *shallowness, vacuity*

VACUO (A), *shallow, vacuous*

VAGABUNDO (A), *wandering, roving; stray*

VAGAMENTE, *vaguely, indistinctly*

VAGANCIA, *laziness, idleness; vagrancy* (DER)

VAGO (A), *lazy, idle, vague, slack*

VAGÓN, *carriage, car, wagon*

VAGONETA, *pickup truck*

VAGUEDAD, *vagueness, uncertain, imprecise*

VAINILLA, *vanilla*

VALEDERO (A), *in force until, valid until*

VALENCIA, *valence* (QUIM)

VALEROSO (A) (adj), *brave, courageous*

VÁLIDO (A), *valid*

VALIOSO (A), *valuable, precious, costly; cherished*

VALLE, *valley*

VALOR, *value, worth; desirability, utility*

VALORACIÓN, *valuation, assessment*

VALVA, *valve*, (BOT) (ZOOL)

VÁLVULA, *valve* (MECAN)

VAMPIRO, *vampire*

VAMPIRIZA ó VAMPIRESA, *vamp, femme fatale*

VANAGLORIA, *vainglory, extreme vanity*

VANDALISMO, *vandalism, damage, injury, loss*

VÁNDALO (A), *loutish; vandal, hooligan*

VANGUARDIA, *vanguard, forefront, spearhead*

VANGUARDISTA (adj), *avant-garde, revolutionary*

VANIDAD, *vanity, conceit; arrogance, pride*

VANIDOSO (A), *vain, conceited*

VANO (A), *vain, empty, groundless*

VAPORIZADOR, *vaporizer*

VAPOROSO (A), *diaphanous, sheer, light*

VARIABILIDAD, *changeability, variability*

VARIACIÓN, *variation* (MUS), *change* (METEO)

VARIADO (A), *varied, assorted, mixed*

VARIANTE, *version, variety, variant*

VARICOSO (A), *varicose*

VARIEDAD, *variety*

VARIO (A) ó VARIOS, *several, various; motley*

VARIOPINTO (A), *diverse, miscellaneous, colorful, varied, mixed; motley, sundry, assorted*

VARONIL, *virile, manly, mannish*

VASALLO (A), *vassal, subject; humble, dependent*

VASECTOMÍA, *vasectomy*

VASELINA, *petroleum jelly*

VASO, *glass*

VASTO (A), *vast, wide, huge*

VÁTER ó WATER, *toilet, restroom, lavatory*

VECINAL, *local, vicinity, locale; proximity*

VECINDAD, *neighborhood, vicinity, area, district*

VECINDARIO, *community*

VECINO (A), *neighboring, nearby, locality, precinct*

VEGETACIÓN, *vegetation*

VEGETAL (adj), *vegetable; plant*

VEGETARIANO (A), *vegetarian*

VEGETATIVO (A), *vegetative*

VEHEMENCIA, *vehemence, fervor, eagerness*

VEHEMENTE, *vehement, forceful, ardent*

VEHÍCULO, *vehicle; carrier* (MED)

VELOCIDAD, *speed, velocity*

VELOCÍMETRO, *speedometer*

VELOCISTA, *sprinter*

VENDIBLE (adj), *salable, marketable*

VENENO, *poison, venom, toxin; malice, spite*

VENENOSO (A), *poisonous, venomous; malicious*

VENERACIÓN, *veneration, worship*

VENÉREO (A), *venereal* (MED)

VENGADOR (A), *avenging (adj), avenger (n)*

VENGANZA, *vengeance, revenge*

VENGATIVO (A), *vengeful, vindictive*

VENTILACIÓN, *ventilation*

VENTILADOR, *ventilator, fan, air vent*

VENTOSO (A), *windy, blustery, gusty, blowing; flatulent*

VENTRÍCULO, *ventricle*

VENTRÍLOCUO (A), *ventriloquist*

VERACIDAD, *truthfulness, veracity*

VERAZ, *truthful*

VERBO, *verb*

VERBORREA, *verbal diarrhea, verbosity*

VERBOSO (A) (adj), *verbose, wordy*

VERDAD, *the truth; real*

VERDADERAMENTE, *really*

VEREDICTO, *verdict* (DER)

VERÍDICO (A) (adj), *true, truthful, real, credible*

VERIFICACIÓN (n), *verification, confirmation*

VERMUT, *vermouth*

VERNÁCULO (A), *vernacular, jargon, dialect*

VERSÁTIL, *versatile; fickle*

VERSATILIDAD, *versatility; fickleness*

VERSO, *verse, poem*

VERTEBRADO (A), *vertebrate*

VESÍCULA, *gall bladder, vesicle*

VESTÍBULO, *entrance hall, lobby, foyer, vestibule*

VESTIDO (A), *dressed*

VESTIDOR, *dressing/changing room; locker room*

VESTIGIO, *vestige, sign, trace; suggestion, hint*

VESTIMENTA, *clothing, wardrobe*

VETERANÍA, *seniority, long service*

VETERANO (A), *veteran* (MIL); *experienced, old hand*

VETERINARIO (A), *veterinary (adj), veterinary doctor (n)*

VIABILIDAD, *viability, feasibility, possibility*

VIADUCTO, *viaduct*

VÍBORA, *viper*

VIBRACIÓN, *vibration*

VIBRADOR (A), *vibrating (adj), vibrator (n)*

VIBRANTE, *vibrating, vibrant, resonant*

VICIADO (A), *foul, stale; corrupt, contaminated*

VICIO, *vice, bad habit; fault, shortcoming*

VICIOSO (A), *dissolute, depraved*

VICISITUD, *vicissitude; uncertainty, shift, change*

VÍCTIMA, *victim, casualty*

VICTORIA, *victory; win* (DEP)

VIDENTE, *clairvoyant, seer*

VIDEOCÁMARA, *camcorder, video camera*

VIDEOCONFERENCIA, *video conference*

VIDEOJUEGO, *video game*

VIDEOTECA, *video library*

VIENTO, *wind* ; *course* (NAUT)

VIGENCIA, *validity, applicability; authenticity*

VIGENTE, *in force, in use, current*

VIGÍA, *watch tower, lookout*

VIGILANCIA, *vigilance, care*

VIGILANTE, *vigilant (adj), guard, watchman (n)*

VIGOROSO (A), *vigorous, energetic; strenuous*

VILLANÍA, *vile act; obscenity*

VILLANO (A), *villainous, base; surf*

VINAGRE, *vinegar; disagreeable person*

VINAGRETA, *vinaigrette*

VINDICACIÓN, *vindication, vengeance; claim*

VINO, *wine*

VIOLACIÓN, *rape; violation, infringement*

VIOLADOR (A), *rapist, violator, offender*

VIOLENCIA, *violence, vehemence, ferocity*

VIOLENTO (A), *violent, intense, force, power*

VIOLETA, *violet*

VIOLINISTA, *violinist*

VIPERINO (A), *venomous, viperous; treacherous*

VIRGEN (adj), *virgin, blank, unused, pure*

VIRGINIDAD, *virginity*

VIRGO, *Virgo* (ASTROL)

VÍRICO (A), *viral, virus*

VIRIL, *virile, manly, macho*

VIRILIDAD, *virility, manliness, machismo*

VIRTUD, *virtue*

VIRTUOSISMO, *virtuosity*

VIRULENCIA, *virulence* (MED)

VIRULENTO (A), *virulent* (MED)

VIS A VIS, *face to face*

VISCOSA, *viscose* (QUIM)

VISCOSIDAD, *viscosity, slime, thickness*

VISCOSO (A), *viscous, slimy, thick*

VISIBILIDAD, *visibility*

VISIONARIO (A), *visionary*

VISITA, *visit, call*

VISITANTE, *visitor (n); visiting (adj)*

VISTA, *sight, eyesight, vision, view*

VISTAZO, *look, glance*

VISUALIZACIÓN, *visualization*

VITALIDAD, *vitality; vital*

VITAMINA, *vitamin*

VÍTREO (A), *vitreous* (GEOL), *glassy*

VITUPERABLE, *reprehensible, despicable*

VITUPERIO, *condemnation, harsh criticism, censure*

VIVACIDAD, *liveliness, vigor, vivacity*

VIVAMENTE, *vividly, deeply, intensely*

VIVARACHO (A), *lively, vivacious, bright*

VIVAZ (adj), *vivid, lively, alert, sharp; perennial*

VIVENCIA, *experience*

VIVEZA, *swiftness, liveliness*

VÍVIDO (A), *vivid, graphic*

VIVIDOR (A), *parasite, scrounger, hustler*

VIVIENDA, *housing, dwelling, residence*

VIVIENTE, *living beings, creatures*

VIVÍPARO (A), *viviparous*

VIVISECCIÓN, *vivisection*

VOCABLO, *word, term*

VOCABULARIO, *vocabulary*

VOCACIÓN, *vocation, calling, trade, profession*

VOCACIONAL, *vocational*

VOCALISTA, *vocalist, singer*

VOCATIVO, *vocative*

VOCERÍO (n), *shouting, clamor*

VOLÁTIL, *volatile, unpredictable*

VOLATILIDAD, *volatility*

VOLCÁN, *volcano*

VOLCÁNICO (A), *volcanic*

VOLEA, *volley* (DER)

VOLEIBOL, *volleyball*

VOLEIPLAYA, *beach volleyball*

VOLITIVO (A), *discretion, preference*

VOLUBILIDAD, *instability, fickleness*

VOLTIO, *volt*

VOLUMEN, *volume* (MAT), *size*

VOLUMINOSO (A), *bulky, voluminous*

VOLUNTAD, *willpower, will, volition*

VOLUNTARIO (A), *voluntary, arbitrary; volunteer*

VOLUNTARIOSO (A), *willing, persistent, dedicated*

VOLUPTUOSIDAD, *voluptuousness, fullness, sensuous*

VOLUPTUOSO (A), *voluptuous*

VOLUTA, *spiral, column; scroll*

VOMITIVO (A), *emetic* (MED); *disgusting, repulsive*

VÓMITO, *vomiting, vomit*

VORACIDAD, *voracity*

VORAZ, *voracious, raging, ravenous; fierce*

VÓRTICE, *whirlpool, vortex*

VOTACIÓN, *ballot; voting*

VOTANTE, *voter (n), voting (adj)*

VOTO, *vote*

VOZARRÓN, *loud/booming voice*

VUDÚ, *voodoo*

VULCANOLOGÍA, *vulcanology*

VULGARIDAD, *vulgarity, coarseness*

VULGARISMO, *vulgarism* (GRAM)

VULGARIZACIÓN, *popularization*

VULGARMENTE, *commonly, popularly*

VULNERABILIDAD, *vulnerability*

VULNERACIÓN, *violation, infringement*

Easily Recognizable Verbs

VACILAR, *to hesitate, be indecisive, sway; stagger*

VAGAR, *to wander, roam*

VALIDAR, *to validate, ratify, sanction*

VALORAR, *to value, evaluate, assess, appreciate*

VAPORIZAR, *to vaporize, spray*

VARIAR, *to alter, change, vary*

VEGETAR, *to vegetate, grow*

VENGAR, *to avenge, take revenge*

VENTILAR, *to air, clear, ventilate*

VERBALIZAR, *to verbalize, express*

VERIFICAR, *to verify, check, authenticate*

VIBRAR, *to vibrate, shake*

VICIAR, *to corrupt, pervert; nullify*

VIGILAR, *to watch over, watch*

VIGORIZAR, *to invigorate*

VILIPENDIAR, *to vilify, revile; despise*

VINDICAR, *to avenge, revenge, vindicate*

VIOLAR, *to violate, rape; break, infringe*

VISIONAR, *to view, see; preview*

VISITAR, *to visit, call on* (MED)

VISUALIZAR, *to visualize, make out; display*

VITALIZAR, *to revitalize, strengthen*

VITRIFICAR, *to vitrify*

VITUPERAR, *to criticize harshly, condemn, censure*

VIVIFICAR, *to revitalize*

VIVIR, *to experience, live, be alive*

VOCALIZAR, *to vocalize, utter, enunciate*

VOCIFERAR, *to shout, proclaim, yell*

VOLCAR, *to knock over, tip up, empty out, overturn*

VOMITAR, *to vomit, bring up*

VOTAR, *to vote for, vote on*

VULCANIZAR, *to vulcanize*

STUDY NOTES:

W

Interchangeable Words

WALKIE-TALKIE

WALKMAN

WATERPOLO, *water polo*

WATT ó WAT, *electric wattage, watt*

WEB ó WWW, *(world wide web)*

WEBCAM

WEBMASTER ó WEB MÁSTER

WESTERN (CINE)

WHISKEY ó WHISKY

WINDSURFING ó WINDSURF

WING, (POL), *right wing, left wing*

Easily Recognizable Nouns, Adjectives and Adverbs

WÁTER, *toilet*

WÉLTER, *welterweight fighter*

WISQUERÍA ó WHISKERÍA, *bar*

STUDY NOTES:

X

Easily Recognizable Nouns, Adjectives and Adverbs

XENOFOBIA, *xenophobia*

XENÓFOBO (A), *xenophobic*

XEROCOPIA, *photocopy*

STUDY NOTES:

Y

Interchangeable Words

YAK

YEN (FIN)

YETI

YIDDISH ó JIDDISCH

YOGA

YOYO ó YO-YO

YUPPIE ó YUPPY

Easily Recognizable Nouns, Adjectives and Adverbs

YANQUI, *Yankee*

YANQUILANDIA, *the USA*

YARDA, *yard*

YATE, *yacht*

YOGUI, *yogi*

YOGUR*, yogurt*

YUDO, *judo*

YUGULAR, *jugular vein*

YUTE, *jute*

YUXTAPOSICIÓN, *juxtaposition*

STUDY NOTES:

Z

Interchangeable Words

ZEN

ZIGZAG

ZINC ó CINC

ZODIACAL ó ZODÍACO

ZOMBI ó ZOMBIE

ZOO

ZOOM (FOTO), *zoom lens*

Easily Recognizable Nouns, Adjectives and Adverbs

ZAPPING, *channel-hopping*

ZAR, *tsar, czar*

ZARINA, *czarina, tsarina*

ZEPELÍN, *zeppelin*

ZETA, *zed*

ZIGOTO, *zygote*

ZÍPER ó SÍPER

ZONA, *zone*

ZOOFILIA, *bestiality*

ZOOLOGÍA, *zoology*

ZOÓLOGO (A), *zoologist*

ZORRA (n), *vixen, prostitute*

ZORRO (adj), *foxy, crafty person; also a fox*

Easily Recognizable Verbs

ZIGZAGUEAR, *to zigzag*

STUDY NOTES:

APPENDIX

Appearing below is a listing of the most useful Spanish "ación" nouns as they appear in the foregoing guide. As a convenience for users of this guide these nouns have been converted into the preterite tense, singular. Please note that there is some overlapping between these nouns and verbs. For example:

ACEPTACIÓN	ACEPTAR	TO ACCEPT
ACUSACIÓN	ACUSAR	TO ACCUSE
AFECTACIÓN	AFECTAR	TO AFFECT
AFIRMACIÓN	AFIRMAR	TO AFFIRM
ALTERACIÓN	ALTERAR	TO ALTER

Spanish "ación" nouns are converted into past tense (preterite) verbs by dropping the "ación" ending and adding "é" to form the first person singular or "ó" for the third person singular. Please note that changes are required in the first person singular preterite for verb stems ending in C, Z and G: C ▶ QU, Z ▶ C and G ▶ GU. The preterite tense refers to specific past actions that occurred: at a fixed point in time (I ate at 6:00 this morning); a specific number of times (I ate ten eggs; I called four times); during an enclosed amount of time (I waited for ten days; I lived here for three years; I saw her last month).

In each of these examples time is specific, either by the clock, the calendar or the number of times. When a quantity is not specified it is implied (I went to her party; We ate at his home; The event was cancelled).

A

NOUNS	FIRST PERSON	THIRD PERSON	TRANSLATION
ACUMULACIÓN	ACUMULÉ I accumulated	ACUMULÓ He, she, it, you, accumulated	ACCUMULATED
ACENTUACIÓN	ACENTUÉ	ACENTUÓ	ACCENTUATED
ACEPTACIÓN	ACEPTÉ	ACEPTÓ	ACCEPTED
ACLARACIÓN	ACLARÉ	ACLARÓ	CLARIFIED
ACREDITACIÓN	ACREDITÉ	ACREDITÓ	ACCREDITED
ACTUACIÓN	ACTUÉ	ACTUÓ	PERFORMED, ACTED
ACTUALIZACIÓN	ACTUALICÉ	ACTUALIZÓ	UPDATED
ACUÑACIÓN	ACUÑÉ	ACUÑÓ	MINTED, COINED
ACUSACIÓN	ACUSÉ	ACUSÓ	ACCUSED
ADAPTACIÓN	ADAPTÉ	ADAPTÓ	ADAPTED
ADIVINACIÓN	ADIVINÉ	ADIVINÓ	FORECASTED, PREDICTED
ADJUDICACIÓN	ADJUDIQUÉ	ADJUDICÓ	AWARDED
ADMINISTRACIÓN	ADMINISTRÉ	ADMINISTRÓ	ADMINISTRATED
ADMIRACIÓN	ADMIRÉ	ADMIRÓ	ADMIRED
ADORACIÓN	ADORÉ	ADORÓ	ADORED
ADULTERACIÓN	ADULTERÉ	ADULTERÓ	ADULTERATED
AFECTACIÓN	AFECTÉ	AFECTÓ	AFFECTED
AFILIACIÓN	AFILIÉ	AFILIÓ	AFFILIATED
AFIRMACIÓN	AFIRMÉ	AFIRMÓ	AFFIRMED
AGITACIÓN	AGITÉ	AGITÓ	AGITATED

AGRUPACIÓN	AGRUPÉ	AGRUPÓ	GROUPED
ALEGACIÓN	ALEGUÉ	ALEGÓ	DECLARED
ALIMENTACIÓN	ALIMENTÉ	ALIMENTÓ	FED
ALIENACIÓN	ALIENÉ	ALIENÓ	ALIENATED
ALTERACIÓN	ALTERÉ	ALTERÓ	ALTERED
ALUCINACIÓN	ALUCINÉ	ALUCINÓ	HALLUCINATED
AMORTIZACIÓN	AMORTICÉ	AMORTIZÓ	REDEEMED
AMPLIACIÓN	AMPLIÉ	AMPLIÓ	EXTENDED, ENLARGED
AMPLIFICACIÓN	AMPLIFIQUÉ	AMPLIFICÓ	AMPLIFIED
AMPUTACIÓN	AMPUTÉ	AMPUTÓ	AMPUTATED
ANIMACIÓN	ANIMÉ	ANIMÓ	ANIMATED
ANOTACIÓN	ANOTÉ	ANOTÓ	NOTED, ANNOTATED
ANTICIPACIÓN	ANTICIPÉ	ANTICIPÓ	ANTICIPATED
APORTACIÓN	APORTÉ	APORTÓ	CONTRIBUTED
APRECIACIÓN	APRECIÉ	APRECIÓ	APPRECIATED
APROBACIÓN	APROBÉ	APROBÓ	APPROVED, PASSED
APROPIACIÓN	APROPIÉ	APROPIÓ	APPROPIATED
APROXIMACIÓN	APROXIMÉ	APROXIMÓ	APPROXIMATED
ARGUMENTACIÓN	ARGUMENTÉ	ARGUMENTÓ	ARGUED, REASONED
ARTICULACIÓN	ARTICULÉ	ARTICULÓ	ARTICULATED
ASIGNACIÓN	ASIGNÉ	ASIGNÓ	ASSIGNED, ALLOCATED
ASIMILACIÓN	ASIMILÉ	ASIMILÓ	ASSIMULATED
ASOCIACIÓN	ASOCIÉ	ASOCIÓ	ASSOCIATED
ASPIRACIÓN	ASPIRÉ	ASPIRÓ	ASPIRED
ATOMIZACIÓN	ATOMICÉ	ATOMIZÓ	SPRAYED
AUTORIZACIÓN	AUTORICÉ	AUTORIZÓ	AUTHORIZED
AUTORREGULACIÓN	AUTORREGULÉ	AUTORREGULÓ	SELF-REGULATED

B

BEATIFICACIÓN	BEATIFIQUÉ	BEATIFICÓ	BEATIFIED
BIFURCACIÓN	BIFURQUÉ	BIFURCÓ	FORKED
BONIFICACIÓN	BONIFIQUÉ	BONIFICÓ	DISCOUNTED

C

CALCIFICACIÓN	CALCIFIQUÉ	CALCIFICÓ	CALCIFIED
CALCULACIÓN	CALCULÉ	CALCULÓ	CALCULATED
CALIFICACIÓN	CALIFIQUÉ	CALIFICÓ	GRADED, RATED
CANALIZACIÓN	CANALICÉ	CANALIZÓ	CHANNELED
CANCELACIÓN	CANCELÉ	CANCELÓ	CANCELLED
CANONIZACIÓN	CANONICÉ	CANONIZÓ	CANONIZED
CAPITALIZACIÓN	CAPITALICÉ	CAPITALIZÓ	CAPITALIZED
CAPITULACIÓN	CAPITULÉ	CAPITULÓ	CAPITULATED, SURRENDERED
CARACTERIZACIÓN	CARACTERICÉ	CARACTERIZÓ	CHARACTERIZED, DISTINGUISHED
CASACIÓN	CASÉ	CASÓ	ANNULED
CELEBRACIÓN	CELEBRÉ	CELEBRÓ	CELEBRATED
CENTRALIZACIÓN	CENTRALICÉ	CENTRALIZÓ	CENTRALIZED
CERTIFICACIÓN	CERTIFIQUÉ	CERTIFICÓ	CERTIFIED
CESACIÓN	CESÉ	CESÓ	CEASED, SUSPENDED
CIRCULACIÓN	CIRCULÉ	CIRCULÓ	CIRCULATED
CLARIFICACIÓN	CLARIFIQUÉ	CLARIFICÓ	CLARIFIED
CLASIFICACIÓN	CLASIFIQUÉ	CLASIFICÓ	CLASSIFIED

COAGULACIÓN	COAGULÉ	COAGULÓ	COAGULATED
CODIFICACIÓN	CODIFIQUÉ	CODIFICÓ	CODIFIED
COLABORACIÓN	COLABORÉ	COLABORÓ	COLLABORATED
COLECTIVIZACIÓN	COLECTIVICÉ	COLECTIVIZÓ	COLLECTIVIZED
COLONIZACIÓN	COLONICÉ	COLONIZÓ	COLONIZED
COMPARACIÓN	COMPARÉ	COMPARÓ	COMPARED
COMPENSACIÓN	COMPENSÉ	COMPENSÓ	COMPENSATED
COMPILACIÓN	COMPILÉ	COMPILÓ	COMPILED
COMPROBACIÓN	COMPROBÉ	COMPROBÓ	CHECKED, VERIFIED
CONCENTRACIÓN	CONCENTRÉ	CONCENTRÓ	CONCENTRATED
CONCILIACIÓN	CONCILIÉ	CONCILIÓ	CONCILIATED
CONDENSACIÓN	CONDENSÉ	CONDENSÓ	CONDENSED
CONDIMENTACIÓN	CONDIMENTÉ	CONDIMENTÓ	SEASONED
CONDONACIÓN	CONDONÉ	CONDONÓ	REPRIEVED, REMITTED
CONFEDERACIÓN	CONFEDERÉ	CONFEDERÓ	CONFEDERATED
CONFIRMACIÓN	CONFIRMÉ	CONFIRMÓ	CONFIRMED
CONFISCACIÓN	CONFISQUÉ	CONFISCÓ	CONFISCATED
CONFLAGRACIÓN	CONFLAGRÉ	CONFLAGRÓ	FLARED-UP, BROKE OUT
CONGRATULACIÓN	CONGRATULÉ	CONGRATULÓ	CONGRATULATED
CONGREGACIÓN	CONGREGUÉ	CONGREGÓ	CONGREGATED, ASSEMBLED
CONJUGACIÓN	CONJUGUÉ	CONJUGÓ	CONJUGATED
CONMEMORACIÓN	CONMEMORÉ	CONMEMORÓ	COMMEMORATED
CONMUTACIÓN	CONMUTÉ	CONMUTÓ	COMMUTED
CONNOTACIÓN	CONNOTÉ	CONNOTÓ	CONNOTATED
CONSERVACIÓN	CONSERVÉ	CONSERVÓ	CONSERVED
CONSIDERACIÓN	CONSIDERÉ	CONSIDERÓ	CONSIDERED
CONSOLACIÓN	CONSOLÉ	CONSOLÓ	CONSOLED
CONSOLIDACIÓN	CONSOLIDÉ	CONSOLIDÓ	CONSOLIDATED

CONSTATACIÓN	CONSTATÉ	CONSTATÓ	CONFIRMED, VERIFIED
CONSTERNACIÓN	CONSTERNÉ	CONSTERNÓ	DISMAYED
CONSUMACIÓN	CONSUMÉ	CONSUMÓ	COMMITTED
CONTAMINACIÓN	CONTAMINÉ	CONTAMINÓ	CONTAMINATED
CONTEMPLACIÓN	CONTEMPLÉ	CONTEMPLÓ	CONTEMPLATED
CONTESTACIÓN	CONTESTÉ	CONTESTÓ	ANSWERED, REPLIED
CONTINUACIÓN	CONTINUÉ	CONTINUÓ	CONTINUED
CONTRATACIÓN	CONTRATÉ	CONTRATÓ	CONTRACTED (FOR), HIRED
CONVERSACIÓN	CONVERSÉ	CONVERSÓ	CONVERSED
COOPERACIÓN	COOPERÉ	COOPERÓ	COOPERATED
COORDINACIÓN	COORDINÉ	COORDINÓ	COORDINATED
CREMACIÓN	CREMÉ	CREMÓ	CREMATED
CULMINACIÓN	CULMINÉ	CULMINÓ	CULMINATED
CULTIVACIÓN	CULTIVÉ	CULTIVÓ	CULTIVATED

D

DECELERACIÓN	DECELERÉ	DECELERÓ	DECELERATED
DECLARACIÓN	DECLARÉ	DECLARÓ	DECLARED
DECORACIÓN	DECORÉ	DECORÓ	DECORATED
DEDICACIÓN	DEDIQUÉ	DEDICÓ	DEDICATION
DEGRADACIÓN	DEGRADÉ	DEGRADÓ	DETERIORATED
DEGUSTACIÓN	DEGUSTÉ	DEGUSTÓ	TASTED, SAMPLED
DELEGACIÓN	DELEGUÉ	DELEGÓ	DELEGATED
DELIBERACIÓN	DELIBERÉ	DELIBERÓ	DELIBERATED
DELINEACIÓN	DELINEÉ	DELINEÓ	DELINEATED

DEMOSTRACIÓN	DEMOSTRÉ	DEMOSTRÓ	DEMONSTRATED
DENEGACIÓN	DENEGUÉ	DENEGÓ	REFUSED, DENIED
DENOMINACIÓN	DENOMINÉ	DENOMINÓ	NAMED, DENOMINATED
DENUNCIACIÓN	DENUNCIÉ	DENUNCIÓ	DENOUNCED
DEPORTACIÓN	DEPORTÉ	DEPORTÓ	DEPORTED
DEPRAVACIÓN	DEPRAVÉ	DEPRAVÓ	DEPRAVED
DEPRECIACIÓN	DEPRECIÉ	DEPRECIÓ	DEPRECIATED
DEPURACIÓN	DEPURÉ	DEPURÓ	TREATED, PURIFIED
DEROGACIÓN	DEROGUÉ	DEROGÓ	REVOKED, REPEALED
DESAPROBACIÓN	DESAPROBÉ	DESAPROBÓ	DISAPPROVED
DESCALIFICACIÓN	DESCALIFIQUÉ	DESCALIFICÓ	DISQUALIFIED
DESCOORDINACIÓN	DESCOORDINÉ	DESCOORDINÓ	UNCOORDINATED
DESESPERACIÓN	DESESPERÉ	DESESPERÓ	DESPAIRED
DESHIDRATACIÓN	DESHIDRATÉ	DESHIDRATÓ	DEHYDRATED
DESINFORMACIÓN	DESINFORMÉ	DESINFORMÓ	MISLED
DESOCUPACIÓN	DESOCUPÉ	DESOCUPÓ	UNEMPLOYED
DESORGANIZACIÓN	DESORGANICÉ	DESORGANIZÓ	DISORGANIZED
DESPOBLACIÓN	DESPOBLÉ	DESPOBLÓ	DEPOPULATED
DESPREOCUPACIÓN	DESPREOCUPÉ	DESPREOCUPÓ	UNCONCERNED
DESTILACIÓN	DESTILÉ	DESTILÓ	DISTILLED
DESVIACIÓN	DESVIÉ	DESVIÓ	DEVIATED, DEFLECTED
DETERIORACIÓN	DETERIORÉ	DETERIORÓ	DETERIORATED
DETERMINACIÓN	DETERMINÉ	DETERMINÓ	DETERMINED
DETESTACIÓN	DETESTÉ	DETESTÓ	DETESTED
DETONACIÓN	DETONÉ	DETONÓ	DETONATED, EXPLODED
DISCRIMINACIÓN	DISCRIMINÉ	DISCRIMINÓ	DISCRIMINATED
DOMINACIÓN	DOMINÉ	DOMINÓ	DOMINATED
DONACIÓN	DONÉ	DONÓ	DONATED

E

ELABORACIÓN	ELABORÉ	ELABORÓ	PRODUCED
EMBARCACIÓN	EMBARQUÉ	EMBARCÓ	EMBARKED
EMIGRACIÓN	EMIGRÉ	EMIGRÓ	EMIGRATED
ENSOÑACIÓN	ENSOÑÉ	ENSOÑÓ	DREMPT, FANTASIZED
ENUMERACIÓN	ENUMERÉ	ENUMERÓ	ENUMERATED
ENUNCIACIÓN	ENUNCIÉ	ENUNCIÓ	ENUNCIATED
EQUIVOCACIÓN	EQUIVOQUÉ	EQUIVOCÓ	MISTAKEN
ERRADICACIÓN	ERRADIQUÉ	ERRADICÓ	ERRADICATED
ESPECIFICACIÓN	ESPECIFIQUÉ	ESPECIFICÓ	SPECIFIED
ESTERILIZACIÓN	ESTERILICÉ	ESTERILIZÓ	STERILIZED
ESTIMULACIÓN	ESTIMULÉ	ESTIMULÓ	STIMULATED
ESTIPULACIÓN	ESTIPULÉ	ESTIPULÓ	STIPULATED
ESTRANGULACIÓN	ESTRANGULÉ	ESTRANGULÓ	STRANGLED
EVACUACIÓN	EVACUÉ	EVACUÓ	EVACUATED
EVALUACIÓN	EVALUÉ	EVALUÓ	EVALUATED
EVAPORACIÓN	EVAPORÉ	EVAPORÓ	EVAPORATED
EXAGERACIÓN	EXAGERÉ	EXAGERÓ	EXAGGERATED
EXALTACIÓN	EXALTÉ	EXALTÓ	EXALTED
EXASPERACIÓN	EXASPERÉ	EXASPERÓ	EXASPERATED
EXCAVACIÓN	EXCAVÉ	EXCAVÓ	EXCAVATED
EXCITACIÓN	EXCITÉ	EXCITÓ	EXCITED
EXCLAMACIÓN	EXCLAMÉ	EXCLAMÓ	EXCLAIMED
EXFOLIACIÓN	EXFOLIÉ	EXFOLIÓ	EXFOLIATED
EXHALACIÓN	EXHALÉ	EXHALÓ	EXHALED
EXHUMACIÓN	EXHUMÉ	EXHUMÓ	EXHUMED

EXONERACIÓN	EXONERÉ	EXONERÓ	EXONERATED
EXPECTACIÓN	EXPECTÉ	EXPECTÓ	EXPECTED
EXPERIMENTACIÓN	EXPERIMENTÉ	EXPERIMENTÓ	EXPERIMENTED
EXPIRACIÓN	EXPIRÉ	EXPIRÓ	EXPIRED
EXPLICACIÓN	EXPLIQUÉ	EXPLICÓ	EXPLAINED
EXPLORACIÓN	EXPLORÉ	EXPLORÓ	EXPLORED
EXPLOTACIÓN	EXPLOTÉ	EXPLOTÓ	EXPLOITED
EXPORTACIÓN	EXPORTÉ	EXPORTÓ	EXPORTED
EXPROPIACIÓN	EXPROPIÉ	EXPROPIÓ	EXPROPRIATED
EXTERMINACIÓN	EXTERMINE	EXTERMINÓ	EXTERMINATED
EXTIRPACIÓN	EXTIRPÉ	EXTIRPÓ	ERADICATED
EXTRAPOLACIÓN	EXTRAPOLÉ	EXTRAPOLÓ	EXTRAPOLATED

F

FABRICACIÓN	FABRIQUÉ	FABRICÓ	MANUFACTURED
FACTURACIÓN	FACTURÉ	FACTURÓ	INVOICED
FALSIFICACIÓN	FALSIFIQUÉ	FALSIFICÓ	FORGED
FASCINACIÓN	FASCINÉ	FASCINÓ	FASCINATED
FERMENTACIÓN	FERMENTÉ	FERMENTÓ	FERMENTED
FILTRACIÓN	FILTRÉ	FILTRÓ	FILTERED
FINALIZACIÓN	FINALICÉ	FINALIZÓ	CONCLUDED, ENDED
FINANCIACIÓN	FINANCIÉ	FINANCIÓ	FUNDED, FINANCED
FLOTACIÓN	FLOTÉ	FLOTÓ	FLOATED
FLUCTUACIÓN	FLUCTUÉ	FLUCTUÓ	FLUCTUATED
FORMACIÓN	FORMÉ	FORMÓ	FORMED
FORMULACIÓN	FORMULÉ	FORMULÓ	FORMULATED

FRUSTRACIÓN	FRUSTRÉ	FRUSTRÓ	FRUSTRATED

G

GOBERNACIÓN	GOBERNÉ	GOBERNÓ	GOVERNED
GRADUACIÓN	GRADUÉ	GRADUÓ	GRADUATED

I

IDENTIFICACIÓN	IDENTIFIQUÉ	IDENTIFICÓ	IDENTIFIED
ILUMINACIÓN	ILUMINÉ	ILUMINÓ	ILLUMINATED
IMAGINACIÓN	IMAGINÉ	IMAGINÓ	IMAGINED
IMITACIÓN	IMITÉ	IMITÓ	IMITATED
IMPLANTACIÓN	IMPLANTÉ	IMPLANTÓ	IMPLANTED
IMPLICACIÓN	IMPLIQUÉ	IMPLICÓ	IMPLICATED
IMPLORACIÓN	IMPLORÉ	IMPLORÓ	IMPLORED
IMPROVISACIÓN	IMPROVISÉ	IMPROVISÓ	IMPROVISED
IMPUTACIÓN	IMPUTÉ	IMPUTÉ	ACCUSED
INAUGURACIÓN	INAUGURÉ	INAUGURÓ	INAUGURATED
INAUGURACIÓN	INAUGURÉ	INAUGURÓ	OPENED
INCITACIÓN	INCITÉ	INCITÓ	INCITED
INCLINACIÓN	INCLINÉ	INCLINÓ	INCLINED
INCREPACIÓN	INCREPÉ	INCREPÓ	REBUKED, REPRIMANDED
INCRIMINACIÓN	INCRIMINÉ	INCRIMINÓ	INCRIMINATED
INCRUSTACIÓN	INCRUSTÉ	INCRUSTÓ	INLAID
INCULPACIÓN	INCULPÉ	INCULPÓ	ACCUSED, CHARGED
INDEMNIZACIÓN	INDEMNICÉ	INDEMNIZÓ	INDEMNIFIED

INFLACIÓN	INFLÉ	INFLÓ	INFLATED
INFORMACIÓN	INFORMÉ	INFORMÓ	INFORMED
INICIACIÓN	INICIÉ	INICIÓ	INITIATED
INMOLACIÓN	INMOLÉ	INMOLÓ	SACRIFICED, IMMOLATED
INOCULACIÓN	INOCULÉ	INOCULÓ	INOCULATED
INSINUACIÓN	INSINUÉ	INSINUÓ	INSINUATED
INSPIRACIÓN	INSPIRÉ	INSPIRÓ	INSPIRED
INSTALACIÓN	INSTALÉ	INSTALÓ	INSTALLED
INSTAURACIÓN	INSTAURÉ	INSTAURÓ	ESTABLISHED
INSTIGACIÓN	INSTIGUÉ	INSTIGÓ	INSTIGATED
INTERPRETACIÓN	INTERPRETÉ	INTERPRETÓ	INTERPRETED
INTERROGACIÓN	INTERROGUÉ	INTERROGÓ	INTERROGATED
INTIMACIÓN	INTIMÉ	INTIMÓ	NOTIFIED
INTIMIDACIÓN	INTIMIDÉ	INTIMIDÓ	INTIMIDATED
INTOXICACIÓN	INTOXIQUÉ	INTOXICÓ	POISONED
INVESTIGACIÓN	INVESTIGUÉ	INVESTIGÓ	INVESTIGATED
INVITACIÓN	INVITÉ	INVITÓ	INVITED
IRRITACIÓN	IRRITÉ	IRRITÓ	IRRITATED

J

JUBILACIÓN	JUBILÉ	JUBILÓ	RETIRED

L

LACERACIÓN	LACERÉ	LACERÓ	LACERATED
LAMENTACIÓN	LAMENTÉ	LAMENTÓ	LAMENTED
LEGALIZACIÓN	LEGALICÉ	LEGALIZÓ	LEGALIZED
LICITACIÓN	LICITÉ	LICITÓ	TENDERED
LIMITACIÓN	LIMITÉ	LIMITÓ	LIMITED

M

MANIFESTACIÓN	MANIFESTÉ	MANIFESTÓ	MANIFESTED, DISPLAYED
MANIPULACIÓN	MANIPULÉ	MANIPULÓ	MANIPULATED
MAQUINACIÓN	MAQUINÉ	MAQUINÓ	PLOTTED
MARGINACIÓN	MARGINÉ	MARGINÓ	ALIENATED
MASIFICACIÓN	MASIFIQUÉ	MASIFICÓ	OVERCROWDED
MATRICULACIÓN	MATRICULÉ	MATRICULÓ	MATRICULATED
MECANIZACIÓN	MAQUINÉ	MAQUINÓ	MECHANIZED
MEDITACIÓN	MEDITÉ	MEDITÓ	MEDITATED
MEMORIZACIÓN	MEMORICÉ	MEMORIZÓ	MEMORIZED
MIGRACIÓN	MIGRÉ	MIGRÓ	MIGRATED
MODERACIÓN	MODERÉ	MODERÓ	MODERATED
MODERNIZACIÓN	MODERNICÉ	MODERNIZÓ	MODERNIZED
MODIFICACIÓN	MODIFIQUÉ	MODIFICÓ	MODIFIED
MODULACIÓN	MODULÉ	MODULÓ	MODULATED
MORTIFICACIÓN	MORTIFIQUÉ	MORTIFICÓ	TORTURED, MORTIFIED
MOVILIZACIÓN	MOVILICÉ	MOVILIZÓ	MOBILIZED
MULTIPLICACIÓN	MULTIPLIQUÉ	MULTIPLICÓ	MULTIPLIED
MUTACIÓN	MUTÉ	MUTÓ	CHANGED, MUTATED

N

NACIONALIZACIÓN	NACIONALICÉ	NACIONALIZÓ	NATIONALIZED
NATACIÓN	NADÉ	NADÓ	SWAM
NAVEGACIÓN	NAVEGUÉ	NAVEGÓ	NAVIGATED
NEGACIÓN	NEGUÉ	NEGÓ	DENIED
NIVELACIÓN	NIVELÉ	NIVELÓ	LEVELED
NOMINACIÓN	NOMINÉ	NOMINÓ	NOMINATED
NORMALIZACIÓN	NORMALICÉ	NORMALIZÓ	NORMALIZED
NOTACIÓN	NOTÉ	NOTÓ	NOTED
NOTIFICACIÓN	NOTIFIQUÉ	NOTIFICÓ	NOTIFIED
NUMERACIÓN	NUMERÉ	NUMERÓ	NUMBERED

O

OBSERVACIÓN	OBSERVÉ	OBSERVÓ	OBSERVED
OCUPACIÓN	OCUPÉ	OCUPÓ	OCCUPIED
OPERACIÓN	OPERÉ	OPERÓ	OPERATED
ORDENACIÓN	ORDENÉ	ORDENÓ	ORDERED, ARRANGED
ORGANIZACIÓN	ORGANICÉ	ORGANICÓ	ORGANIZED
ORIENTACIÓN	ORIENTÉ	ORIENTÓ	ORIENTED
ORNAMENTACIÓN	ORNAMENTÉ	ORNAMENTÓ	ADORNED

P

PACIFICACIÓN	PACIFIQUÉ	PACIFICÓ	PACIFIED
PARALIZACIÓN	PARALICÉ	PARALIZÓ	STOPPED, PARALYZED
PARTICIPACIÓN	PARTICIPÉ	PARTICIPÓ	PARTICIPATED
PENALIZACIÓN	PENALICÉ	PENALIZÓ	PENALIZED
PENETRACIÓN	PENETRÉ	PENETRÓ	PENETRATED
PERFORACIÓN	PERFORÉ	PERFORÓ	PERFORATED
POLARIZACIÓN	POLARICÉ	POLARIZÓ	POLARIZED
PRECIPITACIÓN	PRECIPITÉ	PRECIPITÓ	PRECIPITATED
PREDOMINACIÓN	PREDOMINÉ	PREDOMINÓ	PREDOMINATED
PREMEDITACIÓN	PREMEDITÉ	PREMEDITÓ	PREMEDITATED
PREOCUPACIÓN	PREOCUPÉ	PREOCUPÓ	WORRIED, PREOCCUPIED
PREPARACIÓN	PREPARÉ	PREPARÓ	PREPARED
PRESENTACIÓN	PRESENTÉ	PRESENTÓ	PRESENTED
PRESERVACIÓN	PRESERVÉ	PRESERVÓ	PRESERVED
PRIVATIZACIÓN	PRIVATICÉ	PRIVATIZÓ	PRIVATIZED
PROCLAMACIÓN	PROCLAMÉ	PROCLAMÓ	PROCLAIMED
PROFANACIÓN	PROFANÉ	PROFANÓ	PROFANED
PROTESTACIÓN	PROTESTÉ	PROTESTÓ	PROTESTED
PROVOCACIÓN	PROVOQUÉ	PROVOCÓ	PROVOKED

R

REACTIVACIÓN	REACTIVÉ	REACTIVÓ	REACTIVATED
REALIZACIÓN	REALICÉ	REALIZÓ	REALIZED

RECAPITALIZACIÓN	RECAPITALICÉ	RECAPITALIZÓ	RECAPITALIZED
RECITACIÓN	RECITÉ	RECITÓ	RECITED
RECLAMACIÓN	RECLAMÉ	RECLAMÓ	RECLAIMED
RECOMENDACIÓN	RECOMENDÉ	RECOMENDÓ	RECOMMENDED
RECREACIÓN	RECREÉ	RECREÓ	RECREATED
RECTIFICACIÓN	RECTIFIQUÉ	RECTIFICÓ	RECTIFIED
RECUPERACIÓN	RECUPERÉ	RECUPERÓ	RECUPERATED
REFORMACIÓN	REFORMÉ	REFORMÓ	REFORMED
REGENERACIÓN	REGENERÉ	REGENERÓ	REGENERATED
REGISTRACIÓN	REGISTRÉ	REGISTRÓ	REGISTERED
REHABILITACIÓN	REHABILITÉ	REHABILITÓ	REHABILITATED
REMODELACIÓN	REMODELÉ	REMODELÓ	REMODELED, REDESIGNED
REMUNERACIÓN	REMUNERÉ	REMUNERÓ	REMUNERATED
RENOVACIÓN	RENOVÉ	RENOVÓ	RENOVATED
REORGANIZACIÓN	REORGANICÉ	REORGANIZÓ	REORGANIZED
REPARACIÓN	REPARÉ	REPARÓ	REPAIRED
REPRESENTACIÓN	REPRESENTÉ	REPRESENTÓ	REPRESENTED
RESTAURACIÓN	RESTAURÉ	RESTAURÓ	RESTORED
REESTRUCTURACIÓN	REESTRUCTURÉ	REESTRUCTURÓ	RESTRUCTURED
RETRACTACIÓN	RETRACTÉ	RETRACTÓ	RETRACTED
REVERBERACIÓN	REVERBERÉ	REVERBERÓ	REVERBERATED
REVOCACIÓN	REVOQUÉ	REVOCÓ	REVOKED
ROTACIÓN	ROTÉ	ROTÓ	ROTATED

S

SALVACIÓN	SALVÉ	SALVÓ	SAVED

SANTIFICACIÓN	SANTIFIQUÉ	SANTIFICÓ	SANCTIFIED, CONSECRATED
SATURACIÓN	SATURÉ	SATURÓ	SATURATED
SEGMENTACIÓN	SEGMENTÉ	SEGMENTÓ	DIVIDED
SEGREGACIÓN	SEGREGUÉ	SEGREGÓ	SEGREGATED
SEPARACIÓN	SEPARÉ	SEPARÓ	SEPARATED
SIMPLIFICACIÓN	SIMPLIFIQUÉ	SIMPLIFICÓ	SIMPLIFIED
SIMULACIÓN	SIMULÉ	SIMULÓ	SIMULATED
SINCRONIZACIÓN	SINCRONICÉ	SINCRONIZÓ	SYNCHRONIZED
SITUACIÓN	SITUÉ	SITUÓ	SITUATED
SOLIDIFICACIÓN	SOLIDIFIQUÉ	SOLIDIFICÓ	SOLIDIFIED
SUBORDINACIÓN	SUBORDINÉ	SUBORDINÓ	SUBORDINATED
SUBROGACIÓN	SUBROGUÉ	SUBROGÓ	SUBROGATED
SUPLANTACIÓN	SUPLANTÉ	SUPLANTÓ	REPLACED

T

TERMINACIÓN	TERMINÉ	TERMINÓ	COMPLETED, ENDED
TOLERACIÓN	TOLERÉ	TOLERÓ	TOLERATED
TRANSFORMACIÓN	TRANSFORMÉ	TRANSFORMÓ	TRANSFORMED
TRANSMUTACIÓN	TRANSMUTÉ	TRANSMUTÓ	TRANSMUTED
TRANSPORTACIÓN	TRANSPORTÉ	TRANSPORTÓ	TRANSPORTED
TRIBULACIÓN	TRIBULÉ	TRIBULÓ	TAXED
TURBACIÓN	TURBÉ	TURBÓ	UPSET, DISTURBED

U

UNIFICACIÓN	UNIFIQUÉ	UNIFICÓ	UNIFIED
URBANIZACIÓN	URBANICÉ	URBANIZÓ	URBANIZED
USURPACIÓN	USURPÉ	USURPÓ	USURPED
UTILIZACIÓN	UTILICÉ	UTILIZÓ	UTILIZED, APPLIED

V

VACILACIÓN	VACILÉ	VACILÓ	VACILLATED, HESITATED
VALORACIÓN	VALORÉ	VALORÓ	VALUED
VARIACIÓN	VARIÉ	VARIÓ	VARIED
VEGETACIÓN	VEGETÉ	VEGETÓ	VEGETATED
VENERACIÓN	VENERÉ	VENERÓ	VENERATED
VENTILACIÓN	VENTILÉ	VENTILÓ	VENTILATED
VERIFICACIÓN	VERIFIQUÉ	VERIFICÓ	INSPECTED, CHECKED
VERSIFICACIÓN	VERSIFIQUÉ	VERSIFICÓ	VERSIFIED
VIBRACIÓN	VIBRÉ	VIBRÓ	VIBRATED
VISUALIZACIÓN	VISUALICÉ	VISUALIZÓ	VISUALIZED
VULGARIZACIÓN	VULGARICÉ	VULGARIZÓ	POPULARIZED

STUDY NOTES: